THE NATIONAL PRESS CLUB'S

Best Contemporary Speakers

VOLUME 1

A selection of the best speeches, with illustrations, given at the National Press Club in 1994

PRODUCED BY: Federal News Service

KENDALL/HUNT PUBLISHING COMPANY
4050 Westmark Drive   Dubuque, Iowa 52002

Interior Design and Typesetting:
Trimensions, Inc., Baltimore, MD

Printed in the United States of America
10 9 8 7 6 5 4 3 2 1

*This book is dedicated to the men and women
who have worked diligently to inform,
change, enlighten and educate the public.*

Thank you for your contribution to society.

CONTENTS

NOTE TO THE READER

The reader will notice that this book is a collection of many wonderful and intriguing speeches which appear in no particular order. Every speech has been recorded verbatim, exactly as it was originally spoken to the international media in the ballroom of the National Press Club.

The editors hope that you will listen, learn and thoroughly enjoy the essence of the speakers' words and the thoughts they shared.

HISTORICAL SIGNIFICANCE OF THE NATIONAL PRESS CLUB

Perched atop the National Press Building within sight of the White House and just down Pennsylvania Avenue from the Capitol, the National Press Club has become a prime meeting place in Washington for newsmakers and news gatherers.

Now with more than 4,500 members and growing, the National Press Club is the largest press club in the United States, if not the world. It has gained an international reputation as the podium of choice for leaders seeking to sway public opinion.

Through its doors have come presidents of the United States, as well as kings and queens, prime ministers and premiers, senators and congressmen, cabinet officials and ambassadors, scholars, entertainers, business leaders and athletes.

All of them come because they know they will find both national and international reporters from wire services, newspapers, television, radio, news magazines, newsletters and now, even computer networks.

It all started because in 1908 the bars in Washington closed at midnight. That did not necessarily correspond with the hours of the reporters who worked at the local newspapers and national bureaus for out-of-town papers which were clustered close to what then was known as "newspaper row." These offices had been drawn to the block bordered by E, F and 14th Streets to be close to the telegraph office and to the Willard Hotel, a prime watering hole for congressmen and administration officials.

On March 12, 1908, 32 newspapermen with an idea and $300, plus promises of support from 200 of their colleagues, framed a constitution for the National Press Club.

The club founders laid down a credo which promised "to promote social enjoyment among the members, to cultivate literary taste, to encourage friendly intercourse among newspapermen and those with whom they are thrown in contact in the pursuit of their vocation, to aid members in distress."

In the 87 years since then, the club's purpose has expanded to include helping members with their professional development, aiding them in gathering news and promoting freedom of information and journalism ethics.

As the club rapidly expanded, it quickly outgrew its first three homes. In the 1920s, the club's board decided to build a high-rise office building to house the scattered news bureaus and serve as the underpinning for the club. After President Calvin Coolidge laid the cornerstone, the National Press Building was completed in 1927.

Ever since New Year's Day 1910, when President William Howard Taft climbed the stairs to the second floor clubhouse to pay his respects, U.S. presidents have been welcomed guests and automatic members. In stark contrast to today's adversarial relationship between press and politician, President Woodrow Wilson once said he enjoyed visiting the club because it was one place where he could relax. Warren Harding, a newspaper publisher before turning politician, voted in club elections and occasionally visited the club to plays cards with the boys.

And boys they were. Women were not allowed to be members until 1971. In 1919, the year women's suffrage became part of the Constitution, women reporters founded their own club, the

Women's National Press Club, and it developed parallel programs. After women were permitted to join the NPC, the Women's National Press Club admitted men and changed its name to the Washington Press Club. The two clubs merged in 1985.

Regular weekly luncheons for speakers began in 1932 with an appearance by President-elect Franklin D. Roosevelt. But long before that, the club had featured visits or addresses by, among hundreds of others, Sarah Bernhardt, Orville Wright, Charles Lindbergh, William Jennings Bryan, Andrew Carnegie, Victor Herbert, Adm. Robert E. Peary, and Charlie Chaplin.

An average of 70 luncheons are held each year. Along the way the National Press Club has played host to such world leaders as Nikita Khruschev, Winston Churchill, Madame Chiang Kai Shek, Golda Meir, Indira Ghandi, Charles DeGaulle, Boris Yeltsin, Yasser Arafat and Nelson Mandela.

Both Ronald Reagan and Jimmy Carter announced their campaigns for the presidency at the club, and Bill Clinton made one of his first national appearances when he spoke here as governor of Arkansas in 1987.

Actress Lauren Bacall once draped her lithesome body across our upright piano while then-Vice President Harry Truman entertained the troops during World War II at one of the club's Saturday afternoon USO canteens. The picture of that event is one of the most famous in photojournalism. The room that still holds the piano the vice president played is called the Truman Lounge in his honor.

Over the years the club has developed a wide variety of professional and social programs. Apart from the luncheon series, newsmakers also appear at less formal morning sessions, and congressmen and senators now meet regularly with club members over breakfast. A series of forums to discuss major issues of the day are organized by club members, and professional development activities are regularly offered. The club has taken a leading role in promoting freedom of information by offering its annual national and international Freedom of the Press Awards.

The club's library has evolved into a journalism resource center with access to a wide variety of data bases, newspaper archives and the Internet global computer network. A staff of professional librarians helps members with research and offers classes in computer-assisted reporting.

Membership in the club is open to journalists, who maintain controlling voting power, and to former journalists, government information officers and to those considered by journalists to be regular news sources.

Speaking at the National Press Club to mark his retirement, CBS commentator Eric Sevareid summed up what the National Press Club means to its members when he called it the "sanctum sanctorum of American journalists."

"It's the Westminster Hall, it's Delphi, it's Mecca," said Sevareid, "the Wailing Wall for everybody in this country having anything to do with the news business; the only hallowed place I know of that's absolutely bursting with irreverence."

Gilbert F. Klein, Jr.
1994 National Press Club President

NATIONAL PRESS CLUB 1994

OFFICERS

GILBERT F. KLEIN, PRESIDENT
Media General

MONROE KARMIN, VICE PRESIDENT
Bloomberg Business News

WENDY KOCH, SECRETARY
Small Newspaper Group

CLAYTON BOYCE, TREASURER
Knight-Ridder/Tribune New Service

HARRY STOFFER, FINANCIAL SECRETARY
Pittsburgh Post-Gazette

GOVERNORS

SONJA HILLGREN, CHAIRWOMAN
Farm Journal

ALAN ADAMS, VICE CHAIRMAN
Research Recommendations

GILBERT LEWTHWAITE
Baltimore Sun

LARRY LIPMAN
Cox Newspapers

MICK ROOD
King Publishing Group

RICHARD SAMMON
Congressional Quarterly

KATHY KIELY
Houston Post

MICHAL MAINWARING
Freelance Journalist

DAVID K. MARTIN
Federal Emergency Management Agency

SPEAKERS COMMITTEE

CHRISTY WISE, CHAIRWOMAN
Freelance Journalist

ROSEMARY GOUDREAU, VICE CHAIRWOMAN
Knight-Ridder Newspapers

VINEETA ANAND
Pensions & Investments

DAVID ANDERSON
U.S. Department of Housing & Urban Development

RACHEL BAIL
Voice of America

JEFFREY BARKER
Arizona Republic

DAN CARNEY
Houston Post

ELEANOR CLIFT
Newsweek

MARSHALL COHEN
Freelance Photographer

STAN CROCK
Business Week

MARY CROWLEY
Phillips Publishers

KEN DALECKI
Kiplinger Washington Editors

FREDRICA DUNN
Federal Aviation Administration

CHERYL FIELDS
Chronicle of Higher Education

JOHN FOGARTY
Kiplinger California Letter

VERA GLASER
Freelance Journalist

GREG GORDON
Minneapolis Star-Tribune

BARBARA HARRIS
Congressional Youth Leadership Conference

JANET HELLER
Freelance Journalist

WILLIAM D. HICKMAN
E. Bruce Harrison Co.

GERALD JACKSON
Retired

ED LEWIS
Nissan North America, Inc.

JOAN LOWRY
Scripps Howard News Service

DORIS MARGOLIS
Editorial Associates

SANDRA MCELWAINE
Freelance Journalist

HALE MONTGOMERY
Capstone Communications & Washington Editor, GPS World

IKE PAPPAS
Ike Pappas Network Productions

JACK REYNOLDS
Jack Reynolds Communications

PEGGY ROBERSON
Hearst Newspapers

DICK RYAN
Detroit News

GORDON SMITH
The Gordon L. Smith Co.

SUSAN SPAULDING
The Daily Oklahoman

JULIA SPICER
GTE

SOLVEIG SPIELMANN
Washington International Business Reports

REGINALD STUART
Knight-Ridder Newspapers

FEDERAL NEWS SERVICE'S
CONTRIBUTION TO THE MEDIA

Knowledge is the amount of information one possesses.
Wisdom is the use of that information.

Abraham Lincoln

For more than a decade, American life has been greatly influenced by Federal News Service, the only transcript wire service in the world. The FNS corporate mission is to produce and distribute accurate and timely verbatim transcripts of news events as they occur, thus providing a source of unblemished historical information. FNS is unique because it provides the actual words of the speaker, not news stories. FNS believes in giving America the facts and allowing individuals to draw their own conclusions. Whenever a prominent official testifies or foreign dignitary speaks, FNS produces a word-for-word written record that is immediately made available to the public. By providing an easily accessible service for collecting and distributing information, FNS contributes to a better understanding of the vital issues of our times: both for today's leaders as well as the general public.

In ten short years, FNS has grown from its original three-person operation with coverage of White House, Department of State and Department of Defense daily briefings to today's greatly expanded coverage of presidential speeches and press conferences, congressional hearings, Supreme Court decisions, primary and general election events during presidential campaigns, United Nations press releases and remarks by cabinet and senior-level officials, including the U.S. Trade Representative and the chairman of the Federal Reserve Board. In addition, FNS covers a wide range of television news programs and conferences sponsored by such internationally recognized groups as the Brookings Institution, the Atlantic Council, the Heritage Foundation, the Carnegie Endowment for International Peace and the Washington Institute for Near East Policy.

This critical information not only assists the U.S. government's foreign and domestic decision-making agencies, but also is used by corporations and financial institutions to plan investments and make strategic decisions. Law firms, lobbyists, trade associations and educators rely daily on FNS to track the news.

Cortes Randell, founder and president of FNS, has guided the company to become the largest provider of government transcripts in the world by ensuring high quality, low cost service to all customers. As a result, the subscriber base renews at almost one hundred percent each year. Today, FNS transmits to over 114 countries and has bureaus in Moscow, Tokyo and Brussels. To cater to the rapidly expanding Spanish-speaking market, FNS also provides a Spanish-language newswire in addition to our other services.

As part of our commitment to customer service, Federal News Service prides itself on being at the forefront of the latest developments in telecommunications technology. We actively assist our clients in choosing the information system most conducive to their needs, whether it be satellite, cyberspace, CD-ROM, personal computer or printer. In addition, all of FNS's products are available on LEGI-SLATE, DIALOG (File 660), LEXIS/NEXIS (FEDNEW), Dow Jones, Data Times, Desktop Data, Newsnet and on the Internet at www.fednews.com. You may contact FNS directly at

202-347-1400 to receive additional information on other services and options available. Local libraries may also carry a FNS CD-ROM disc with more than four years of transcripts.

People often ask how Federal News Service covers the Capital so thoroughly. Each morning, the final touches are made to the FNS daily schedule and reporters are assigned to cover specific events, not with pen and paper, but with audio tape recorders. The reporters then pass tapes back and forth between the location of the event and FNS's home base. Once the tapes arrive, a digital audio computer system splits the recorded remarks into three-minute sections that are sent to the headphones of highly skilled transcribers. Once a transcriber types a three-minute segment, it is sent to a mainframe computer that collates and combines the segments into a completed transcript.

Cortes Randell, founder and president of FNS.

Next the transcript is edited for errors and sent by satellite to an indexing center where individual analysts proof the document a second time and code it, using more than 1,500 topics FNS clients have selected. (This indexing allows a client to receive only the information they are interested in within minutes of the event.) Finally, the indexed transcripts are then sent by satellite to newswires, media, most branches of government, lobbyists, trade associations, law firms, corporations, etc.

Federal News Service would like to recognize those persons who are responsible for making "The National Press Club's Best Contemporary Speakers: Volume I" possible: Christina Randell, Director of Marketing and Product Development, who shepherded the project to completion; Bob Redd, Doug Engelbrecht, Alice Tate, Joy Rabb, Kevin Lambert, Joe Petrisko, Carol Anderson, James Townsend, Nancy Shia, Scott Hoffman, Tedd Pitts, Matt Groce, Carrie Mitchell, Laurie Creasey, Maggie Pooley, Beth Corwin, Maggie Rogers, Jill Matteson, Cate Hagman, Bob Hoenstine, Richard Northrop and Jane Margaret Dow who did the final edit on the book. Thank you for your hard work.

A special thanks is also due to our friends at the National Press Club and Archive who not only allowed FNS to produce this book, but who also assisted us during our years of growth. Together the NPC and FNS now provide the media and interested individuals with transcripts, audio and video tapes of NPC luncheon speakers.

Federal News Service is pleased to provide these enlightening and inspirational speeches in "The National Press Club's Best Contemporary Speakers: Volume I."

The Editors

FOREWORD

꽃잎

*L*ast May, at the height of the crisis over North Korea's nuclear weapon capability, South Korean elder statesman Kim Dae-Jung asked to speak at the National Press Club. He proposed three courses of action to ease tensions: the U.S. government should invite North Korean leader Kim Il Sung to visit; President Clinton should appoint former President Jimmy Carter as a special envoy to North Korea; and the press club should invite Kim Il Sung to speak.

I didn't know about the first two, but the third I could do. I responded that historians have said the club had played a role in the Korean War. When then-Secretary of State Dean Acheson spoke here in 1950, he failed to mention the Korean peninsula as part of the American defense perimeter. The North Koreans took that as a sign that the United States would not fight to stop their invasion of the South. If the club could play a small role in resolving the 44-year-old conflict, then we would be pleased to invite Kim Il Sung.

Within 24 hours, this news boomeranged through Seoul and back to Washington. Was it true, Korean reporters wanted to know. Would the press club invite Kim Il Sung? Please, beseeched the South Korean ambassador. Don't do it. It will play into Kim Il Sung's propaganda machine.

But the club has no position on the great questions of international politics. Our job is to provide a stage for the players on the world scene so that journalists can gather information. If Kim Il Sung were to leave North Korea, obtain a visa to visit Washington and speak at the club, it would be a momentous breakthrough in international relations. We issued the invitation.

As it turned out, Kim Il Sung did not accept. Little did we know he was close to death. But Jimmy Carter was appointed President Clinton's special envoy to North Korea. That led to an agreement that calmed what had been the most tense international crisis of the Clinton administration. How important was the role the National Press Club played? That must wait for future historians. But Kim Dae-Jung later summed it up this way, "Had Kim Il Sung died before President Carter's visit, the entire free world would have been in great confusion and anxiety about the future course of United States-North Korean disputes. In that sense, the National Press Club made a great contribution toward a potentially peaceful resolution of the disputes."

That's what the National Press Club has become: a place where news is produced, where ideas can be expounded, and where appeals can be made. When South African President Nelson Mandela made his triumphal visit to Washington, he chose to speak at the club. When Jean-Bertrand Aristide needed a forum to calm fears about what he would do when he returned to Haiti, he came to our podium. When President Clinton felt besieged and maligned in the days leading up to the congressional elections, he sent his chief of staff, Leon Panetta, to present the administration's case to the club. And when Mario Cuomo sought to rally Democrats out of the ashes of that election, he asked to appear.

The press club is a place where an entertainer like Garrison Keillor can make us laugh while giving us a boot in the pants, and it provides a rostrum for such diverse personalities as Poet Laureate Rita Dove and media mogul Ted Turner.

Why do they come to the National Press Club? Because in the six decades since Franklin Roosevelt appeared here to begin our regular luncheon series, the club has gained a reputation as the world's foremost forum. Newsmakers know they can get an hour to present their arguments not only to our audience of Washington correspondents, but also to a national audience on C-SPAN, National Public Radio and the Internet global computer network. Journalists come because they know of the club's record for producing news and because they know they can get their questions answered.

Perhaps the question most asked of the NPC president is, 'how do you select your speakers?' Much of the work is done by the club's Speakers Committee, which in 1994 was ably chaired by freelance writer and author Christy Wise. In sometimes raucous meetings, the committee debates who are the most significant creative forces in the world today among the heads of state, Cabinet secretaries, legislators, governors, CEOs, political operatives, academics, authors, entertainers and artists. But most important, the committee seeks out people who are making news. The committee's list goes to the club's president for final approval before invitations are sent.

Club lunches have been available on audio and video cassettes for years. And recently we have been able to provide almost instantaneous transcripts through the Federal News Service. But still these events seemed to be lost to history.

Therefore for the first time, the club is compiling a book of what we consider to be the most significant speeches of the year. From the 78 speakers of 1994, we selected the top 13. It wasn't easy. It was like choosing among your children because so many speakers gave such outstanding presentations. We picked some because they were so widely known; others because their appearance was a focal point of the year's national or international events; a few because their message seemed to be timeless; and a couple because they were just plain fun.

Gilbert F. Klein, Jr.
1994 National Press Club President

NATIONAL PRESS CLUB

LUNCHEON
October 7, 1994

$\mathscr{S}$ PEAKER

NELSON MANDELA
President of the Republic of South Africa

MODERATED BY: Gil Klein

Head Table Guests

✦❧✦

Margaret Warner
MacNeil/Lehrer Newshour

Peter Fabricius
South Africa's Argus Newspapers

Abdul Salam Massarueh
*Washington Bureau Chief of Arab-American Media Service and President of the
Foreign Correspondents Association*

Max Schindler
Television Director for NBC News

Ambassador Harry Schwarz
South African Ambassador to the United States

Reginald Stewart
Assistant News Editor of Knight-Ridder Newspapers

Zinzi Mandela-Hlongwane
Daughter of President Mandela

Christy Wise
Freelance Journalist and Chairwoman of the National Press Club Speakers Committee

His Excellency Alfred Nzo
Foreign Minister of the Republic of South Africa

David Anderson
*U.S. Department of Housing and Urban Development and the member of the
National Press Club Speakers Committee who arranged today's luncheon*

Honorable Princeton Lyman
American Ambassador to South Africa

David Broder
Columnist with the Washington Post

Adriaan Rossouw
Washington Bureau Chief of National Press of South Africa

Jeff Ballou
Conus Communications and President of the Washington Association of Black Journalists

GIL KLEIN

MODERATOR

*g*ood afternoon. Welcome to the National Press Club. My name is Gil Klein. I'm the club's president and a national correspondent with Media General Newspapers, writing for the Richmond Times-Dispatch, the Tampa Tribune and the Winston-Salem Journal.

I'd like to welcome my fellow club members in the audience today, as well as those of you who are watching us on C-SPAN or listening to us on National Public Radio or the Internet global computer network.

Today we are indeed honored to have with us Nelson Mandela, the President of the Republic of South Africa. We at the National Press Club have followed the struggles of South Africa closely. To our podium have come Oliver Tambo, Chief Buthelezi and President F.W. de Klerk. The conflict has been a focal point of our generation of journalists, but in all of history there have been few struggles with such satisfying outcomes. South Africa has been able to transform itself into a truly democratic country without being torn by ethnic fighting and division that is destroying so many other countries in the post Cold War world.

Much of the credit for that must go to our speaker today. Released from 27 years of imprisonment, he did not sound a call to arms and rally his forces in bloody revolution. He has served as a statesman and conciliator who preached forgiveness to bring together all of his nation's competing interests. Now his goal is to help bring democracy, peace and prosperity to all of Africa and to celebrate, as he said yesterday to a joint session of Congress, the oneness of the human race.

Every generation produces but a few giants, those people whose accomplishments define their times and last in the history books. Ladies and gentlemen, we are privileged to have one of those people here with us today. Please join me in a warm press club welcome for Nelson Mandela, the president of the Republic of South Africa. *(Applause.)*

NELSON MANDELA

Chairperson, ladies and gentlemen, I told a story when I was having lunch at the White House and I think in view of the generous comments which have been made by the chairperson, I should repeat that story so as to put his remarks in context.

Because one day I was visited by a young lady of four from next door. I was sitting in the lounge and she just broke in; she didn't knock. She did not greet. And then she said to me, "How old are you?" *(Laughter.)*

I said, "Well, I can't remember, but I was born long, long ago."

She said, "A year ago?" *(Laughter.)*

I said, "No, longer than that."

"Two years?"

I said, "Much longer than that."

"But how long?"

I said, "Well, I have told you that I can't remember, but it was a long time."

Then she suddenly switched subjects and said, "Why did you go to jail?"

I said, "No, I didn't go to jail because I liked; some people sent me there."

"Who?"

"People who don't like me."

"How long did you remain there?"

I said, "Well, again, I can't remember, but it was a very, very long time." *(Laughter.)*

And she repeated, "one, two years," and my answer was the same. And then she asked again, "But how long?"

So I said, "Well, I've already told you I can't remember, but it was a long time."

And she said, "You are a stupid old man." *(Laughter.)*

And having said so, she continued to chat with me—we were there for about an hour—as if she had paid me a compliment. *(Laughter.)*

So, ladies and gentlemen, if I don't rise to your expectations, please be more diplomatic than that young lady. *(Laughter.)*

I must also say that I have looked forward to addressing this club. The press is one of the foundations of liberty, of freedom. And any country which is committed to democratic values will ensure that there is freedom of the press and that journalists are able to write freely and without fear and that the conduct of public officials in particular should always be under the searchlight.

We have just graduated from being members of the liberation movement, in which we have sacrificed a great deal. If you met some of the leaders of the liberation movement, you will feel the gravity of the crime that has been committed by the apartheid government in our country. Some of these men went into prison with only standard six and they left prison with a degree, sometimes two degrees and even three degrees.

There were men who went to prison who had master's degrees, even doctorates obtained in overseas universities. These were men of ability, committed to the values of liberty and freedom, and I have complete trust in them. But the dictum is that power corrupts and it corrupts absolutely. And history knows some of the passionate freedom fighters who, once they became members of the government, forgot that they were put in those positions by the masses of people, some of them illiterate, inarticulate, but who wanted a shelter over their heads, work to bring up their children and clothe them in dignity. And power can make the people who once promoted those values to forget that mandate.

It is for the press to keep the ideals of liberty alive, to ensure that public figures carry out their mandate, and we use—the press must be used as a mirror from which public figures can see whether they are on the right track. And I therefore jumped at the opportunity of attending this meeting and addressing you.

Returning to my written speech, may I first express my profound and heart-felt appreciation for the honor of being here today before this distinguished gathering of American journalists and other eminent guests.

I would like also to express our collective thanks, as South Africans, for the support to which our struggle for democracy received from the United States media as a leading component of international media. In the darkest days of apartheid and political repression, when our organizations were banned and thousands of South Africans faced imprisonment, torture and even death, and when our local media was severely censored, the international media laid to bare the terrible conditions in our country and kept the world alive to the issue of apartheid.

When our voice was silenced, you lent your voices to our demand for freedom of expression and information, and gave support to South African writers, artists and journalists who were persecuted for daring to use their skills against tyranny and in support of freedom.

The South African media, journalists and publishers alike, are indebted to you for that sustenance. Our media now enjoy rights that democratic societies like yours have taken for granted for many years. These rights are written into our constitution. The constitution also guarantees that all media financed by or under the control of the state shall be regulated in a manner which ensures impartiality and the expression of a diversity of opinion.

Our experience of repression and our persecution has only strengthened the commitment to the rights of freedom of information, freedom of expression and freedom of the press, not merely as constitutional rights, but as a daily reality.

If you will excuse me, you will find me now and again wiping my eyes. There is nothing wrong. This is my unique way of attracting attention to myself. *(Laughter, applause.)*

Our country has come a long way from the dark days of oppression and conflict. An enduring national consensus has been forged, founded on a deep and shared conviction that the only way forward is to unite our people on the basis of reconciliation and reconstruction. The interim constitution and reconstruction and development program reflected that consensus in clear and concrete terms. It is on these basic principles that the legitimacy of the Government of National Unity is founded. Among our most urgent tasks in South Africa is consolidating democracy. However, unless we successfully start addressing the question of economic growth, development and the equitable distribution of wealth and income to end the inequities of apartheid, we would not in any convincing manner be able to speak of social stability and justice.

Yesterday, before Congress, I thanked the United States for its generous assistance with the reconstruction and development in South Africa, but I also made it clear that, while such aid does make a valuable contribution to our development, it cannot solve our economic problems. We are not looking for handouts. Rather, we seek to build a partnership with the United States administration, business and other sectors to benefit both our nations.

Our economy has started to show signs of recovery, and all indications are that this will be sustained. This is in great measure a result of the political achievements we have made, particularly the setting up of legitimate structures which are a fundamental departure from the era of apartheid and mismanagement. This, however, will not be easy. But precisely because our programs are based on sound economic policies, including the expansion of our economic and fiscal base, they are bound to give a spur to economic growth.

The government is creating, with a great measure of success, an environment in which a small and a big business can thrive. We are committed to fiscal discipline and prudent management of natural resources. Our efforts are underpinned by the commitment to involve society as a whole in reconstruction and development. We are therefore building an enduring partnership among all social structures, including government, business and labor.

This is a partnership that should see to the restructuring of our industries to make them more competitive in international markets, improve the productivity in the workplace and imparting of skills to all employees. It is a partnership to which not only the government but also organized business and labor are committed, and which underwrites our uniform national economic development and labor council. The council, involving government business and labor, will be the blast furnace of joint strategies for sustained economic growth and equity.

I address this because it is something that has been left out of the picture which has been portrayed by some sections of the media. According to this one-sided picture, South Africa is buckling under the weight of labor unrest. In actual fact, the reality is that the collective bargaining system in our country is a healthy one and that most strategic industries have this year resolved their disputes without resorting to strike action. Besides, in bringing our labor legislation up to date with the new political realities, emphasis will be placed on efficient and effective dispute resolution mechanism.

Now, some people judge what is happening in South Africa on the surface without delving deep and to see the real underlying reasons for the industrial turmoil that sparked off around about June, July. You may not be aware in our country that whites, white workers who are doing the same job, identical job, with a black worker—that is, an African, colored or Indian—white workers received between three to five times more wages than black workers. And the workers are fighting to close this gap, and that is why we are fully behind them, because that is a just struggle.

And if the government of the country has allowed a situation to develop where blacks can see their white counterpart doing the same jobs enjoying incomes far out of proportion to those received by blacks, you will agree that every democrat will support the struggle of the workers to come to the same level as white workers. But the labor movement in our country is led by a highly talented and seasoned group of leaders who know how to think and that to relate their problems to the welfare of the country as a whole.

I spoke to them. I called the whole leadership of the Congress of South African Trade Union and I said to them, "We have just taken over the government of this country, but at the present moment we merely occupy a political office. We do not exercise a real political power. To acquire political power is not something that can be achieved overnight. It is a process. It is going to take a year, two and even as much as five years. We are here to end all discrimination in all of its ramifications. But don't embarrass us in that task because you have got an army of five million people unemployed. We want business to respond in order to absorb this five million people. We also want investments. Growth from inside and outside the country and if the environment for investment is not there, we are not going to get investments."

Having addressed the leadership, I then went to their national conference and put forward this message, and because we are dealing with people who can think, who have fought for liberation, who have won political power even though they still occupy merely political office, they realize the importance of discussing their problems with labor without coming into the open and disrupting our economy. That is the situation, therefore, about the labor unrest of which many people have made a mountain from.

We also know that through the complex filters of international media, the public in the United States may have a perception of a country as one in which crime and lawlessness loom large. Crime is indeed a serious problem and one which concerns us deeply. But the most important development in this regard is the transformation of the police force, regarded by most South Africans as illegitimate, into one based on community policing. Impressive progress, which has multiplied the success of our police services, has been made.

We have already, in a very short time, transformed the police force which was set up, built and developed on the basis of supporting apartheid and color repression. They were told that any political demonstration by blacks against white supremacists, no matter how constitutional, how peaceful, how non-violent, is a declaration of war against white minority rule. It must be brutally suppressed.

For the last 45 years, the police force in our country concentrated not on suppressing ordinary crime; they concentrated on suppressing the liberation movement. In the process, criminals organized themselves into powerful syndicates, and in some areas they virtually took over the running of the life of the community. And, especially because the previous government had no interest in protecting its black citizens, of the police force of our country only 20 percent was deployed in the black areas, and that is a vast population—a population of 41 million, in which there are only 5 million whites. The rest of the police force was deployed in white areas, and only 20 percent in black areas. And the members of the police deployed in black areas were working under the most difficult conditions, where they had no transport of their own. They had to use public transport, each policeman, each detective, investigating at one time as much as 60 different cases.

You can see, therefore, in that situation the criminals formed the powerful syndicates. It is those syndicates that we are busy now dismantling, throwing those hardened criminals behind bars. We have already reduced the level of crime considerably. But, of course, because these criminals had become so powerful that they actually recruited even members of the police into their syndicates, we have to clear the police force of elements who are involved in this corruption, drug smuggling.

But having said so, I must tell you that the overwhelming majority of the police were nonetheless men and women of integrity who did their work according to law and who helped to ensure that these elections take place and that there is this move for transformation. And we must, therefore, not get a distorted picture of what is happening with our security forces.

However, in the overall, what is required is deliberate speed in implementing the reconstruction and development program to remove the causes of the instability and mistrust of the past. This the government has started undertaking in earnest, in close cooperation with all sectors of the population. The logic of the changes through which South Africans are going demands of each and every institution an examination of the part that it can play. This naturally includes the media and, if I may suggest it here, includes the international media.

I was struck by a recent remark of a leading American businessman in South Africa. He said that there were two things that bred an extraordinary caution in potential U.S. investors in South Africa. They know all about South Africa's past. They know what the country has been through to achieve this miracle, but they also know the history of Africa.

It is crucial that an objective and even critical appraisal of South Africa and Africa as a whole should not be based on a pessimistic reading of the past. Rather, it should be a full and accurate reflection of the hopes, the aspirations, and optimism of the present. It should also be a reflection of the of the fears, and even the apprehensions, as they currently prevail. In this way, the magnitude of the achievements South Africans have made will come out in bold relief.

In fact, many problems that we may have would fade into insignificance against this background. They will be understood in the context of the real miracle playing itself out on the southern tip of the African continent. The international media can play as crucial a role in the rebuilding of South Africa and the rebirth of Africa as they did in the struggle for freedom and democracy.

During the course of my visit, I touched on the multilateral interests South Africa takes in international issues. These include the following: prevention of the proliferation of weapons of mass destruction, promotion of democracy and human rights, economic development based on mutually beneficial relations, prevention of the international trafficking in narcotics and global environmental issues. During my visit to the United Nations on Monday, I had occasion to sign a number of treaties on human rights and socio-economic issues. In this regard, South Africa is taking her rightful place among the community of democratic nations.

With regard to the U.S. in particular, I should emphasize that we have made great progress during the course of this visit regarding issues such as trade, joint efforts to mobilize funds for investments in South Africa, assistance to black entrepreneurs, cooperation in matters of human rights, including the judiciary and so on.

In other words, a new partnership is being born between our two countries and governments. We are indebted in particular to the Clinton administration for the unprecedented cooperation and understanding evidenced before and during the course of our visit. We in South Africa are determined to succeed in our endeavors, and we are confident that with the assistance of the international community we will do so. I leave the United States of America with many fond memories and confident that we have laid the basis for full and mutually beneficial relations.

I thank you. (Applause.)

MR. KLEIN: Thank you very much, Mr. President. That was excellent. We have, of course —many, many questions have come up in just a little time, so let's get right to it—a lot of interest in you personally, of course. The first one is: During your long ordeal of imprisonment, what gave you the strength to keep body and mind alive, vital and ready for the new challenges of freedom? Where do you draw your strength?

PRESIDENT MANDELA: Well, I wish I could be able to hate and to revenge for the injustice that was done to me, but my country and the world are giving me little opportunity for retribution. *(Laughter.)* There is a lot of work to be done. And you must remember that you pass through this world but once, and if you commit yourself to a particular approach, you will be judged by that approach. It is better to commit yourself to those things which are constructive, which help to put sunshine in the hearts of men and women. And I have found that approach to be extremely important.

And, by the way, I must tell you that here, I am no exception. I shared prison with wonderful comrades who perhaps are far better than me in forgetting the past and working to unite a nation, to bring happiness to the people of South Africa, the people of our continent, and to humanity as a whole.

We have to acknowledge the support which we have received throughout the democratic world. As I said the other day, it matters little to us which government is in power in a particular country, because all of them condemn racial oppression. And the trust that is vested in us demands a sense of responsibility which is higher than merely being free to do what you like. We are expected to deliver the goods. And if you rely on the support—which has been there before I came out of prison—if you rely on that support, it is possible for us to solve the most sensitive problems. And I, therefore, have no time to think in terms of bitterness, of retribution. *(Applause.)*

MR. KLEIN: This questioner asks: If the South African economy fails to meet the reasonable expectations of the black people, what political consequences do you foresee, and how much time do you have?

PRESIDENT MANDELA: Well, the rest of the question is actually irrelevant. *(Laughter, applause.)* It is the first part that is important. Our people are perfectly entitled to have unreasonable expectations, because, as I have said, whites in our country enjoy rights and privileges which are tied to the majority, and our people can see in our neighboring countries discrimination of all kinds having been removed. Their own country, where they have been responsible for producing the wealth in that country, is shared by a tiny minority, and therefore, they are entitled to have unrealistic and exaggerated expectations.

But in the run up to the elections, those who are students of South African politics, they will notice that in practically every meeting in the run up to the elections I said to our people, "We have a strategy, a master strategy: the reconstruction and development program. It is intended to better the lives of all South Africans without exception—to build houses, to create jobs, to build hospitals and clinics, schools, to bring in electricity because the overwhelming majority of our people have no electricity, to bring in running water. Our people in the countryside in particular have no running water. And this is the object of this master strategy."

But I pointed out that, "Don't think this is an event that when you return from the polls on the 27th of April you'll find a job waiting for you and a Mercedes for you to ride." *(Laughter.)* "It is going to take a number of years before we can deliver. But the important point is that from the 28th of April we will be coming back to you to report to you what we plan to do in order to solve the problems that face you. We will come back and tell you we have already, in spite of the formidable problems that we face, made a great deal of progress."

President Nelson Mandela greets NPC member James Parks at private reception with unidentified secret service agent standing by. October 7, 1994.

There was an examination—both in the national and international press—what we had achieved in 100 days, because some American president started that tradition. *(Laughter.)* They forget that in the United States you had an infrastructure throughout your public life. In our country we do not have that infrastructure to bring about those changes. We introduced, as from the first of September, free medical treatment for children under six and for pregnant mothers. The response of the community was overwhelming, but because we have few hospitals, few clinics, few doctors, few nurses, the crowds and the queues were terribly long, and sometimes we had to ask people to go back and come the following day because we don't have the infrastructure.

In education, we have already started feeding about a million where there is need, but again we are faced with the question of the infrastructure. You mobilize resources, you buy food, and the first difficulty you have, there is no accommodation where you can put this food, because in the countryside, in particular, people are living under hunger, starvation. When they see food, the first thing that this person thinks of is his own stomach, not the stomach of the children. And so we have to find some shelters, some buildings where we can keep the stores, the supplies, where they can be kept under lock and key and so that they can reach the children for whom they are meant.

These are the problems that are facing us, the question of infrastructure, and to have expected us to have brought about changes which were brought about by President Roosevelt within the first hundred days is completely unrealistic in terms of our situation. But nevertheless, we are making progress. And the masses of the people are responding very well.

I am now in the process of going around the country reporting to our people what we have done since the 27th of April, and the jubilation, the ovation—the standing ovation—when they hear the plans that we have, the small beginnings that we have made, the question therefore of impatience of our people does not arise. Because in these meetings which I have addressed, people understand that socio-economic issues take a long time before they can be addressed. (Applause.)

MR. KLEIN: I understand that you're going to go from here and meet with President Aristide of Haiti. What advice can you give him in terms of how to bring about reconciliation and nation-building?

PRESIDENT MANDELA: Well, I'm very reluctant to discuss with the media what I'm going to discuss with the president of a country. (Laughter, applause.) It is a matter of respect to a head of state. There is enough time for us after we've had our discussion to agree with him as to what press statement we should issue. This is the proper approach. But, of course, you are the media. (Laughter.) And I know how cross you're going to be if I don't tell you, if I don't take you into confidence. I don't know if the media can be taken into confidence about anything—(laughter)—but I'm sure President Aristide, who is, by the way, my friend—I'll be meeting him now for the third time—I'm sure he will not mind when I say that he requested to see me and I gladly agreed, because I can see the problems he has in his country, and I am prepared to share with him the humble experience we have had in our own country.

In our own country, we realized that, as such hopelessly divided society characterized throughout the centuries, especially during the last four decades, by conflict and turmoil, it was necessary for us to have a strategy of involving all political leaders, even those who had about 50 or 25 members. We felt that they should be involved in negotiations. At one time, because of our caution to ensure an all-embracing process, we had no less than 26 different political parties, and what we relied upon is not the majority which the ANC commanded; it was the question of consensus, of persuading people through the strength of your argument.

And that method succeeded. In this, this long-drawn process of negotiations, not once have we ever used a vote where our majority would prevail. We appealed to the power of reasoning of human beings, and that, whatever political party they belonged, there are good men who will embrace a good argument, a solid argument. And we succeeded in that.

Then we came to the question, now what to do with people who had committed crimes during these last 45 years. It was not an easy matter because we are dealing with cases where people have lost their beloveds and we had to look at the matter from both sides. But we said, the opponents of apartheid—that is, ourselves, people who were in exile, like the foreign minister here and like my speech writer, who is somewhere around here, Joe Natajensa— they were in exile. They came back. They were asked to apply for an indemnity, and they were told to explain precisely what offense, what crime, they had committed for which they wanted indemnity. We did that.

Now, we wanted those who defended apartheid also to do the same thing, and we want them to do that because we want to be even-handed, and those people who committed offenses such as we committed, those must be indemnified.

Now, that process of being even-handed has brought about unparalleled unity in our country because now, having pardoned people who committed offenses in the course of implementing their own political objectives, as members of political organizations, that amnesty, that indemnity, has helped to inspire confidence that the country is led by people who want to forget the past.

But, of course—and that is what I want to say to the president. But, of course, there are cases where we say we cannot give any amnesty, that is, of highly-placed officials who sat down to plan the killing, the assassination of innocent civilians who were no threat at all to white supremacy, who were eliminated simply because they wanted equality with whites and nothing more, who were never involved in the armed struggle. Now those—we are saying that they must be brought before a commission, a commission of truth and reconciliation.

And we are saying this body is not going to be a court of law. It won't have any power of arresting and charging anybody. All that it's going to do—it is going to address the concerns of the victims of his crimes, because indemnity and amnesty addresses the concerns of the perpetrators of the crimes, and that truth and reconciliation commission is going to address the case of the victims. The parents, the next of kin are going to know what happened to their beloveds, and when they know, then it will be easy for them to forgive.

And if anybody has committed an unpardonable crime, the police are free to charge, and if sufficient evidence, the courts can convict them. That is our approach, and that is the information I'm going to share with my friend. *(Applause.)*

MR. KLEIN: Starting to get close to the end, but I want to ask one more question before I get to the last question, which is what do you see as the role of South Africa in the rest of the continent, especially as a peacemaker in places like Angola?

PRESIDENT MANDELA: Well, the continent of Africa has produced wealthy sons and daughters of caliber—talented people who have been trying to address these problems in their individual capacities, and sometimes collectively. I am not keen to get caught up in the problems of any country, either in our region or elsewhere in Africa, unilaterally. Individual responses in these cases are not as effective as an organized and disciplined machinery to address problems.

We are members of the United Nations. We are members of the Commonwealth of Nations. We are members of the Organization of African Unity. We are members of the Non-Aligned Movement. And our approach is that we should work through structures which have been set up and which have resources to address problems. That is our approach. We will try as much as possible to avoid unilateral action. But, of course, we have been asked at times to be entrusted in trying to address the problems in a particular country.

For example, the special representative of the secretary general of the United Nations, Mr. Bayer, visited my country and asked me to help in bringing about peace in Angola. In that regard, I was not acting unilaterally; I was acting as one who was supporting an initiative taken by the United Nations, and therefore, I was able to save President dos Santos, President Mbuto and President Chissano of Mozambique, and to discuss how we could bring about a solution in Angola. I also invited Dr. Savimbi to come. Although he sent his emissaries to prepare for the visit, I'm still waiting for him to come.

We have been able to get involved in Lesotho, which is a small kingdom surrounded by South Africa, when the king of that country had dissolved a democratically elected government which had swept all districts in the election two years ago. Well, we condemned the action of the king, but we didn't stop there. President Mugabe of Zimbabwe, President Ket Masire of Botswana and myself got interested in this and had discussions with both parties, the deposed prime minister as well as the king. I invited them to Pretoria, and we were able to resolve the matter. There is peace now in that country.

In that way, where I am acting through existing structure, I am prepared to play my role. But I am not prepared alone to try on big solutions to the troubled areas. *(Applause.)*

MR. KLEIN: Just a reminder that Mr. Mandela will have to leave in a hurry after we're finished here, and we ask you all to remain seated until he has been able to get out of the room.

Before asking the last question, of course, I'd like to present you with a certificate of appreciation for appearing here, and now that you have joined the pantheon of world leaders, you have to have your own National Press Club mug. *(Laughter, applause.)*

PRESIDENT MANDELA: Well, thank you very much.

MR. KLEIN: The last question is: We know that you are an avid boxing fan. What did Muhammad Ali tell you yesterday about the outlook for the next heavyweight bout?

PRESIDENT MANDELA: *(Laughs.)* Well, Muhammad Ali is one of my heroes. *(Laughter.)* He is a man who brought a new dimension to boxing, and many of you, especially those who have got white hair, will remember some of the colorful statements he made. He said before one fight, "I will float like a butterfly"—*(laughter)*—"and sting like a bee." And on one occasion he said, "I am so handsome"—*(laughter)*—"that my face should be declared a natural resource." *(Laughter.)* And he talked about another boxer whose name I won't mention, and he says, "So and so's face is so ugly that it should be donated to the Bureau of Wild Life." In fact, he was talking about a handsome gentleman who is also my friend.

While we didn't have the opportunity—I met him last night—I didn't have the opportunity of discussing the matter with him, even if I had and he told me his opinion, I wouldn't repeat them, certainly not to the press. *(Laughter.)* And I supported the best boxer in that fight. *(Applause.)*

Well, and I say I have received a check for $1,000, and I will read the accompanying letter and respond positively. But we have friends in many parts of the globe and that donation is an indication of how the people of the United States care. It will go to the children's fund which I have established in order to address the question of street children, children in jail—about 20,000 of them—one of almost 13 years, are languishing in jail and some of them have been there for two years and then abused children. I have established a fund for that purpose and this amount will go to that fund.

Thank you.

NATIONAL PRESS CLUB

LUNCHEON
October 7, 1994

$\mathcal{S}$PEAKER

PETER LYNCH
*Vice Chairman of Fidelity Management and
Research Company*

MODERATED BY: Monroe Karmin

HEAD TABLE GUESTS

STEPHANIE OVERMAN
HR Magazine

EDWARD KEAN
Knight-Ridder Financial News

GREG ROBB
AFX News

ROBERT BRUSGE
Chief Economist at Nikko Securities

STAN CROCK
Business Week

CAROLYN LYNCH
Spouse of our Speaker

VINEETA ANAND
*Pensions and Investment and the member of the National Press Club
Speakers Committee who arranged today's luncheon*

JAMES JOHNSON
Chairman and CEO of Fannie Mae

REPRESENTATIVE EDWARD MARKEY
*Democrat from Massachusetts and Chairman of the House Subcommittee on
Telecommunications and Finance*

LEE SHEPPARD
Tax Notes

DAVID VISE
Washington Post

Monroe Karmin

MODERATOR

ood afternoon, and welcome to the National Press Club. My name is Monroe Karmin, and I am the vice president of the press club, and editor-at-large at Bloomberg Business News. I'd like to welcome club members and their guests in the audience today, as well as those of you watching on C-SPAN, or listening to the program on National Public Radio, or the Internet global computer network.

There's one thing you have to understand about our luncheon speaker today: Sometimes Peter Lynch may look as if he is going out for a sandwich at lunch; but what he's really doing is trying to figure out if Au Bon Pain is a good investment. Lynch is always on the prowl for a good stock. One friend says that if you came to him with the best widget in the world and the queen of England were sitting on one side of him and Cindy Crawford on the other, he would ignore them and inundate you with questions about the widget maker's management.

His intense interest in anything that would produce a good return is one reason few people have had a greater impact on the investment world. In fact, the market dropped about 40 points one day when a compressed version of his market views went over an online computer service. He had said that if you looked at markets over a 20-year period there were ups and downs. But that got translated into the headline, "Lynch predicts market correction." *(Laughter.)*

But the Lynch legend is based more on what he has done than on what he has said. He helped transform investing by giving individuals access to a mutual fund that steadily outperformed the market and competitors for more than a decade. His performance at Magellan earned the appreciation, unintended, of many Americans who paid for their kids' college through Magellan's growth. When Mr. Lynch became portfolio manager for Magellan in 1977, it had less than $20 million in assets; by the time he retired in 1990, to spend more time with his family, Magellan was the largest mutual fund in the world, with more than one million shareholders and approximately $14 billion in assets.

It's easy to see what attracted shareholders to Magellan. The share price had risen 28-fold since Mr. Lynch had taken the helm, with annual increases averaging 29 percent. Even more remarkable, though big funds are supposed to have more difficulty than smaller funds in outperforming the market, in the last five years of Mr. Lynch's stewardship, Magellan outperformed 99 percent of all stock funds.

Given his golden touch, it is no surprise that Mr. Lynch's books, "One Up on Wall Street," and "Beating the Street"—I have one here—have been best-sellers. His message is really rather simple, if he'd allow me to paraphrase it. He thinks anyone can get rich in the stock market if they do two things: Use their powers of observation and do their homework.

Still, Mr. Lynch knows how to lose money, too. The Magellan fund lost about $2 billion—maybe more—in a single day in 1987 when the stock market crashed. I personally hosted Mr. Lynch once before, a few years ago, and he was discussing his views on the stock market, and I asked him to give me some examples of stocks he liked at the time. He suggested Sbarro, the Italian fast food chain, whose price rose remarkably over the past few years, and he also recommended Texas Air, which dropped, crashed, to nothing. So I think he would agree that he is not infallible, too.

A native of Boston, Mr. Lynch is a 1965 graduate of Boston College and received his MBA from the University of Pennsylvania's Wharton School of Business Administration. He served as a lieutenant in the Army before coming to Fidelity in 1969. He currently serves as vice chairman of Fidelity, sits on the boards of Morrison-Knudsen and W.R. Grace, and is heavily involved in charity work. Will you please welcome Mr. Peter Lynch. *(Applause.)*

PHOTO, MARTIN KUHN

PETER LYNCH

Thank you very much. It's a pleasure to be here. I love this town.
And it's a thrill to be here with Jim Johnson, who did so much for Fannie Mae. That was the greatest single stock in my life, and it is still my largest position, and if anybody wants to talk after about how to make money, I'll tell them how to buy more Fannie Mae. And now I've added Freddie Mac to the list too.

And Congressman Ed Markey, who was a—went to Boston College and also Boston College Law School, and has done a great job in Congress for everybody in this country, but especially people in his district in Massachusetts.

But the great honor is to have my wife, Carolyn, right here—my sweetheart, my great stock picker, who found L'Eggs and a bunch of other good stocks.

What I am going to try to do today briefly is—I don't know what I'm supposed to do with this gavel. I've never had one of these things before. *(Laughter.)* But I'm going to try and say some words on the things I've used over the years when I was an amateur, when I ran Magellan, and I still use today. I think they make sense, I think they make a lot of sense for investors. And I frankly think it's a tragedy in America that the small investor has been convinced by the media—the print media, the radio, the television media—that they don't have a chance, that big institutions with all their computers and all their degrees and all their money have all the edges. And it just isn't true at all. And when they're convinced, when this happens, when this occurs, people act accordingly.

When they believe it, they buy stocks for a week and they buy options and they buy the Chile fund this week and next week it's the Argentina fund, and they get results proportioned to that kind of investing. And that's very bothersome. I think the public can do extremely well in the stock market on their own. I think the fact that institutions dominate the market today is a positive for small investors. As institutions push stocks to unusual lows, they push unusual highs. For someone that can sit back and have their own opinion and know something about industry, this is a positive, it's not a negative. So that's what I want to talk about.

And the single most important thing to me in the stock market for anyone is to know what you own. I'm amazed at how many people own stocks, they would not be able to tell you why they own it. They couldn't say in a minute or less why they own it. Actually, if you really press them down, they'd say, "The reason I own this is the sucker is going up." And that's the only reason—*(laughter)*—that's the only reason they own it. And if you can't explain—I'm serious—if you can't explain to a 10-year-old in two minutes or less why you own a stock, you shouldn't own it. And that's true, I think, of about 80 percent of people who own stocks.

And this is the kind of stock people like to own; this is the kind of company people adore owning: It's a relatively simple company. They make a very narrow, easy-to-understand product. They make a one-megabit SRAM CMOS bi-polar RISC floating point data I/O array processor with an optimizing compiler, a 16 dual-port memory, a double-diffused metal oxide semi-conductor monolithic logic chip with a plasma matrix vacuum fluorescent display that has a 16-bit dual memory, that has a UNIX operating system, four whetstone megaflop polysilicone emitter, a high band width—that's very important—six gigahertz—*(laughter)*—

double metalization communication protocol, an asynchronous backward compatibility, peripheral bus architecture, four-wave interleaf memory, a token ring interchange backplane, and it does it in 15 nanoseconds of capability.

Now, if you want a piece of crap like that—*(laughter)*—you will never make money. Never. *(Laughter.)* Somebody will come along with more whetstones or less whetstones or a bigger megaflop or a smaller megaflop. You won't have the foggiest idea what's happened. And people buy this junk all the time.

I made money in Dunkin' Donuts. I can understand it. *(Laughter.)* When there were recessions, I didn't have to worry about what was happening. I could go there and people were still there. I didn't have to worry about low-price Korean imports. I mean, I just didn't have—*(laughter)*—you know, I could understand it. And you laugh. I made 10 or 15 times my money in Dunkin' Donuts. Those are the kinds of stocks I could understand. If you don't understand it, it doesn't work. This is the single biggest principle.

And it bothers me that people are very careful with their money. The public, when they buy a refrigerator they go to Consumer Reports; they buy a microwave oven, they do that. They ask people what's the best kind of radar range or what kind of car to buy. They do research on apartments. When they go on a trip to Wyoming, they get a Mobil travel guide—or California. When they go to Europe, they get the Michelin travel guide. People hear a tip on the bus on some stock, and they'll put half their life savings in it before sunset. *(Laughter.)* And they wonder why they lose money in the stock market.

And when they lose money, they blame it on the institutions and program training. That is garbage. They didn't do any research. They got a piece of junk. They never looked at a balance sheet. And that's what you get for it. And that's what we're being driven to, and it's self-fulfilling. The public does terrible investing, and they say they don't have a chance. It's because that's the way they're acting. I'm trying to convince people there is a method. There are reasons for stocks to go up.

Coca-Cola—this is very magic, it's a very magic number, easy to remember—Coca-Cola is earning 30 times per share what they did 33 years ago. The stock has gone up 30-fold. Bethlehem Steel is running less than they did 30 years ago. The stock is half its size from 30 years ago. Stocks are not lottery tickets. There's a company behind every stock. If the company does well, the stock does well. It's not that complicated.

People get too carried away. And first of all, they try to predict the stock market. That is a total waste of time. No one can predict the stock market. They try to predict the interest rates. If anyone could predict interest rates right three times in a row, they'd be a billionaire. Considering there's not that many billionaires on the planet, it's very—you know, I had logic, I had syllogisms and studied these when I was at Boston College. There can't be that many people who can predict interest because there'd be lots of billionaires.

And no one can predict the economy.

I mean, a lot of the people in this room were around in 1981 and '82 when we had a 20 percent prime rate with double-digit inflation, double-digit unemployment. I don't remember anybody telling me in 1981 about it. I didn't read it. I study all this stuff. I don't remember anybody telling me we were going to have the worst recession since the Depression.

So what I'm trying to tell you, it would be very useful to know what the stock market is going to do. It would be terrific to know that the Dow Jones Average a year from now would be X, that we're going to have a full-scale recession or interest rates are going to be 12 percent. That's useful stuff. You never know it though. You just don't get to learn it. I've always said, if you spend 14 minutes a year on economics, you've wasted 12 minutes, and I really believe that. *(Laughter.)*

Now, I have to be fair. I'm talking about economics on the broad scale—predicting a downturn for next year or the upturn, or M1 and M2, 3B and all these M's. I'm talking about—economics to me is when you're talking about scrap prices. When I own auto stocks, I want to know what's on the used car prices. When used car prices are going up, it's a very good indicator. When I own hotel stocks, I want to know hotel occupancies. When I own chemical stocks, I want to know what's happened to the price of ethylene.

These are facts. The aluminum inventories go down five straight months, that's relevant. I can deal with that. Home affordability I want to know about when I own Fannie Mae or I own a housing stock. These are facts. There are economics and there's economic predictions, and economic predictions are a total waste.

Interest rates—Al Greenspan's a very honest guy. He would tell you that he can't predict interest rates. He could tell you what short rates are going to do in the next six months. Try and stick him on what the long-term rate will be three years from now. He'll say, "I don't have any idea." So how are you and the investors supposed to predict interest rates when the Federal Reserve can't do it?

So I think that's—but you should study history, and history's the important thing you learn from. What you learn from history is the market goes down. It goes down a lot. The math is simple. There's been 93 years this century. This is easy to do. The market's had 50 declines of 10 percent or more. So 50 declines in 93 years—about once every two years the market falls 10 percent. We call that a correction. That's a euphemism for losing a lot of money rapidly. *(Laughter.)* But, you know, we call it a correction.

So 50 declines in 93 years, about once every two years the market falls 10 percent. Of those 50 declines, 15 have been 25 percent or more. That's known as a bear market. We've had 15 declines in 93 years. So every six years the market's going to have a 25 percent decline. That's all you need to know. You need to know the market's going to go down sometimes. If you're not ready for that, you shouldn't own stocks.

And it's good when it happens. If you like a stock at 14 and it goes to six, that's great. If you understand the company, you look at the balance sheet and they're doing fine, and you're hoping to get to 22 with it, 14 to 22 is terrific, six to 22 is exceptional. So you take advantage of these declines. They're going to happen. No one knows when they're going to happen. People tell you about it after the fact that they predicted it, but they predicted it 53 times.

So you can take advantage of the volatility of the market—if you understand what you own. So I think that's the key element.

Another key element is that you have plenty of time. People are in an unbelievable rush to buy stock. I'll give you an example of a well-known company. Wal-Mart went public in October of 1970; 1970 it went public. It already had a great record. It had 15 years' performance, a great balance sheet. You could have waited 10 years. Say you're a very conservative investor; you're not sure this Wal-Mart can make it. You want to check. You've seen them operate in small towns. You're afraid they can only make it in seven or eight states; you want to wait until they go to more states. You keep waiting. You could have bought Wal-Mart 10 years after they went public and made 35 times your money. If you'd bought when they went public, you would have made 500 times your money, but you could have waited 10 years after Wal-Mart went public and made over 30 times your money.

You could have waited three years after Microsoft went public and made 10 times your money. Now, if you knew something about software—I know nothing about software—if you knew something about software, you would have said: "These guys have it. I don't care who's going to win—Compaq, IBM—I don't—who's going to win Japanese computers. I know Microsoft MS-DOS is the right thing." You could have bought Microsoft.

Again, I'm repeating myself, stocks are not a lottery ticket. There's a company behind every stock. And you can just watch it. You have plenty of time. People are in an amazing rush to purchase a security. They're out of breath when they call up. You don't need to do this. *(Laughter.)*

You need an edge to make money. People have incredible edges, and they throw them away. I'll give you a quick example of SmithKline. This is a stock that had Tegamet. Now, you didn't have to buy SmithKline when Tegamet was doing clinical trials. You didn't have to buy SmithKline when Tegamet was talked about in the New England Journal of Medicine or the British version, Lancet. You could have bought SmithKline when Tegamet first came out, a year after it came out.

Let's say your spouse, your mother, your father—you're a nurse, you're a druggist, you're writing all these prescriptions. Tegamet was doing an amazing job of curing ulcers, and it was a wonderful pill for the company, because if you just stopped taking it the ulcer came back. So it would have been a crummy product if you took it for a buck and it went away. But it was a great product for the company. But you could have bought it two years after the product was on the market and made five or six times your money.

I mean, all the druggists, all the nurses, all the people—millions of people—saw this product. And they're out buying oil companies, you know, or drilling rings. *(Laughter.)* You know, it happens. And then three years later or four years later, Glaxo, even a bigger company—this is a huge company, a British company—brought Zantac, which was a better, at that time, an improved product, and you could have seen that take market share, do well. You could have bought Glaxo and tripled your money.

So you only need a few stocks in your lifetime. They're in your industry. I think people, if you'd worked in the auto industry, let's say you were an auto dealer for the last 10 years, you would have seen Chrysler come up with the minivan. If you're a Buick dealer, a Toyota dealer or a Honda dealer, you would have seen the Chrysler dealership packed with people. You could have made 10 times your money on Chrysler a year after the minivan came out.

Ford introduces the Taurus/Sable, the most successful line of cars in the last 20 years. Ford went up sevenfold on the Taurus/Sable. If you're a car dealer, you only need to buy a few stocks every decade. When your lifetime's over, you don't need a lot of five-baggers to make a lot of money starting with $10,000 or $5,000. So in your own industry, you're going to see a lot of stocks. And that's what bothers me. There are good stocks out there looking for you, and people just aren't listening; they're just not watching it.

And they have incredible edges. People have big edges over me. They work in the aluminum industry. I see aluminum industry's coming down—inventory's coming down six straight months. I see demand improving. In America today, you know, it's hard to get an EPA permit for a bowling alley, never mind an aluminum smelter, so you know when aluminum gets tight you just can't build seven aluminum smelters. So when you see this coming, you can say, "Wait a second, I can make some money."

When an industry goes from terrible to mediocre, the stock goes north. When it goes from mediocre to good, the stock goes north. And when it goes from good to terrific, the stock goes north. There's lots of ways to make money in your own industry. You could be a supplier in the industry. You could be a customer. This thing happens in the paper industry. It happens in the steel industry. It doesn't happen every week, but if you're in some field, you'll see a turn. You'll see something in the publishing industry. These things come along, and it's just mind-boggling—people throw it away.

One of the things that I find a rule—a couple rules I want to throw out that I find useful is a lot of times people buy on the basis the stock has gone down this much, you know, how much further can it go down? I remember when Polaroid went from 130 to 100, and people said here's this great company, great record, if it ever gets below 100, you know, just buy every share. You know? And it did get below 100, and a lot of people bought on that basis, saying, "Look it's gone from 135 to 100; it's now at 95, what a buy." Within a year it was 18. And this is a company with no debt. I mean, this is a company that was just so overpriced it went down.

I did the same thing in, I think, my first or second year of Fidelity. Kaiser Industries had gone from $26 a share to $16. I said, "How much lower can it go at 16?" So I think we bought one of the biggest blocks ever on the American Stock Exchange of Kaiser Industries at 14. I said, you know, "It's gone from 26 to 16. How much lower can it go?" Well, at 10 I called my mother and said, "Mom, you've got to look at this Kaiser Industries. I mean, how much lower can it go? It's gone from 26 to 10." (Laughter.) Well, it went to 6, it went to 5, it went to 4, and it went to 3.

Now, I am fortunate this happened rapidly or I would probably be still caddying or be working at the Stop 'N Shop, but it happened fast so I was able to—it was compressed. And at 3 I figured out, you know, there's something very wrong here because Kaiser Industries owns 40 percent of Kaiser Steel. They own 40 percent of Kaiser Aluminum. They own 32 percent of Kaiser Cement. They own Kaiser Broadcasting. They own Kaiser Sand & Gravel, Kaiser Engineers. They own Jeep. They own business after business. And they had no debt.

Now, I learned this very early. This might be a breakthrough for some of you people. It's very hard to go bankrupt if you don't have any debt. (Laughter.) It's tricky. Some people can approach that. (Laughter.) It's a real achievement. But they had no debt, and the whole company at 3 was selling at about $75 million. At that point it was equal to buying one Boeing 747. I said, "There's something wrong with this company selling for $75 million."

I was a little premature at 16, but I said, "Everything's fine and eventually this will work out." And what they did is they gave away all their shares to their shareholders. They passed out shares in Kaiser Cement. They passed out shares in Kaiser Aluminum. They passed out their public shares in Kaiser Steel. They sold all the other businesses, and you get about $50 a share.

But if you didn't understand the company, if you were just buying on the fact that stock had gone from 26 to 16 and then it had gone to 10, what would you do when it went to 9? What would you do when it went to 8? What would you do when it went to 7? This is the problem that people have, is they sell stocks because they didn't know why they bought it, then it went down and they don't know what to do now. Do you flip a coin? Do you walk around the block? You know, what do you do? (Laughter.)

Psychiatrists haven't worked so far. I've never seen them running into—the psychological/psychiatry fund I've never seen solicited with the SEC to make it through with a mutual fund. So they haven't seemed to help. I've tried prayer. That hasn't worked. So if you don't understand the company, you have this problem when they go down.

"Eventually they always come back." This one doesn't work either. People think RCA just about got back to its 1929 high when General Electric took it over. Double-knits never came back. Remember those beauties? (Laughter.) Floppy discs, Western Union. The list goes on and on, people saying it'll come back. Well, it doesn't have to come back.

Here's another one you hear all the time. "It's $3. How much can I lose?" I've had people call me up saying, "I'm thinking of buying this stock at 3. How much can I lose?" Well, again, you may need a piece of paper for this—(laughter)—but if you put $20,000 in a stock at 50, or your neighbor put $20,000—that fool—at 50 into the stock and you put $20,000 in at 3 and it goes to zero, you lose exactly the same amount of money: everything. And people say,

"It's 3. How much can I lose?" Well, if you put a million dollars on it, you can lose a million dollars.

Just the fact that a stock—this may be a reason to research a stock, but the fact a stock is 3 down from 100 doesn't mean you should buy it. And, in fact, short sellers, people that really make money in stocks, they don't short Wal-Mart. They don't short Home Depot. They don't short the great companies—Johnson & Johnson. They short stocks down from 80 to 7. They'd like to short it at 16 or 22, but they figured out at 7 this company is going to go to zero. They just haven't blown Taps on this thing yet. It's going to zero. And they're selling short at 7; they're selling short at 6, at 5, at 4, at 3, at 2, at 1¼. And you know, to sell something short you need a buyer. Somebody has to buy the damn thing. And you want to know who's buying this thing? It's these people saying, "It's 3. How much lower can it go?" *(Laughter.)*

Now, here's a subject that you probably all talked about—

MR. KARMIN: Getting close.

MR. LYNCH: Getting close? Getting close. All right, we'll drop that one out. *(Laughter.)* It's getting very close, so it—everybody has to go somewhere. So the important thing is you can't get too attached to a stock. You have to understand there's a company behind it. You can't treat this like your grandchildren. You know, you have to deal with the stock and say, "I understand the company," and if they deteriorate, there's a fundamental slip, you have to say goodbye to it.

One rule you want to remember is the stock does not know you own it. *(Laughter.)* This is a breakthrough. So don't get—you know, you have to understand it and say, "They're doing well, and as long as they keep doing well"—my best stocks have been my fifth, sixth, seventh year I owned them, not my fifth, sixth, seventh day. So you have to understand that and stay with it.

I'll switch through to my long shots. Avoid long shots. I've bought about 30 long shots in my life. I've never broken even on one. The ones that are really bad are called whisper stocks. And if Arthur Levitt was here, he'd appreciate these stories, because these are the times that somebody calls you up and says, "Hi, Peter. How's Carolyn? How are the kids? And I'd like to talk to you about International Blivit. And what they have in this company is they have—(speaks gobbledy-gook)—earnings. Are they going to be big? Small? Three dollars? One dollar a share." And they keep whispering.

And I always say, "What are you talking about? I don't understand it." *(Laughter.)* Now, either they're so surrounded by people that are going to run out and buy this stock because it's so exciting or they think the SEC is listening in and they'll get a shorter term. *(Laughter.)* You know, they'll get six months in the camp rather than two years in the camp. But whisper stocks don't work. *(Laughter.)*

And then I want to conclude with there's always something to worry about. If you own stocks, there's always something to worry about. You can't get away from it. What happens—in the '50s people were worried about—the only reason we got out of the Depression was World War II. We had another recession in the early '50s that said, "We're going to go right back into a depression."

People were worried about a depression in the '50s and they were worried about nuclear war. I mean, back then, you know, the little warheads they had then, they couldn't blow up McLean, West Virginia—or McLean, Virginia, you know, or Charlestown. Now all these countries that end in "stan"—there's nine of these "stan" countries that have come out of Russia—they all have enough warheads to blow the world up and no one worries about it.

When I was a kid, people were building fallout shelters, and we used to have this civil defense drill. Remember this in high school? You'd get under your desk. I never thought even then that was a particularly good thing to do. (Laughter.) You know, they'd blow a whistle, somebody would put on a hat, and we'd all get under our desks, you know. (Laughter.)

But in the '50s people wouldn't buy stocks. Except for the '80s, the '50s was the best decade this century of the stock market, and people wouldn't buy stocks in the '50s because they were worried about nuclear war and they were worried about depression. Then people—remember when oil went from 4 to 40 and it was going to go to 100 and we were going to have a depression? Remember that one? Well, about three years later the same experts, now higher paid, oil is now at 10, and then they said it was going to 4 and we're going to have a depression.

And then the Japanese—remember how the Japanese were going to own the world? Remember that one, and that we're going to have a depression? And then about two years later we're all worried about Japan collapsing. This is the most absurd thing I ever heard of. This is a country with a 20 percent savings rate, incredible workforce, incredible productivity, and people were saying, "We're going to have a depression because Japan's going to collapse." And, you know, on their prayer list they lowered Mother Teresa and crippled children and they were praying for Japan at night. (Laughter.)

You know, it's unbelievable. I mean, the LDC debt—remember the LDC debt? Remember that one? All these countries—Chase had lent their network to Brazil, Chile, Peru and all these other countries. And the LDCs said they were not going to pay it back and we were going to have a depression. It always ends that we're going to have a depression, or "the great depression"—we're going to have "the great depression." I never could understand that adjective in front of depression, "the great depression," or "the big one." "The big one's coming."

But all these countries—and now I understand, you know, these are called the—then they were called less—developed countries. We used to call them underdeveloped countries. Those are all wrong terms. Those are not politically correct. You have to call these emerging countries. You can't use "less developed" or "underdeveloped" because that's—in fact, the other day I heard the politically correct term for somebody that's overweight is "laterally challenged." (Laughter.)

So there's always something to worry about. And the key organ in your body in the stock market is your stomach. It's not the brain. If you can add 8 and 8 and get reasonably close to 16, that's the only level of math you need to know. You don't need to know the area under the curve. Remember that quadratic equation in integral calculus and the area under the curve? I mean, whoever cared what was under the damn curve? (Laughter.) But you had to study this. You don't need this in the stock market.

So all you have to know is you're going to see—it's always going to be scary. There's going to be always something to worry about. And you just have to forget all about it, cut it all out, and own good companies or own turnarounds, study them and you'll do well. And that's all there is. And I'm ready for questions. (Applause.)

MR. KARMIN: Okay, thank you very much. When managing a portfolio, do you pay much attention to the activities of Congress and the regulators? *(Laughter.)*

MR. LYNCH: Did Ed Markey put this one up? I'm not sure. *(Laughter.)* I spend zero time thinking about what's happening down here in Washington, and I spend little time thinking about what's going on in Russia or China. I just deal with facts. *(Laughter.)* When the economy is going down, when the economy is going the wrong way, I can deal with that.

This whole health care reform bill drove a lot of drug stocks down to low levels. And I could say to myself, "Well, 60 percent of Johnson & Johnson's earnings are outside the United States. Their pharmaceutical drug business is all on patent. Nothing's coming off patent. They only have 5 percent of sales from one product, which is Tylenol, which is already an over-the-counter drug and is growing overseas." I said, "Why has this stock gone from 58 to 36?" And these companies are already dealing in Japan and overseas with—they already have the government controlling pharmaceutical prices. They've dealt with it.

So I deal with facts. This year I thought it was very likely you'd have a bill passed on health care. It didn't happen; it drove the stocks down. But I think the stocks would have rebounded anyway, even if the health care bill was passed. So I don't deal with what's happening in Congress or what's going to happen in the future. I just deal with what's happening in the economy and what's happening in the companies I call.

MR. KARMIN: Thank you. How useful is the financial reporting in the general daily press to you, and how useful should it be to investors in general?

MR. LYNCH: Okay. It has improved dramatically, not just in the press but also company reporting. Ten years ago companies didn't have interim balance sheets. It's hard to imagine. They only gave their balance sheet to you once a year. Now they show quarterly what's happened to their inventories, what's happened to receivables. And now in the major newspapers they'll even show types of funds. I think there's 2,500 companies in the New York Stock Exchange. There's over 5,000 different mutual funds. So there's twice as many mutual funds as there are stocks. At least in the paper today it explains what kind of fund this fund is. So I think reporting has improved; the report earnings.

But again, I think if you own auto stocks you shouldn't be reading the financial part of the newspaper. On Wednesday the local newspaper, or Tuesday some places, or on Saturday, they have a whole four pages on automobiles and they talk about new models and they say, "This one stinks and this one's outstanding." They really—if you own auto stocks, that's the part of the newspaper you should be in.

You shouldn't be calling your broker four times a day to get stock quotes. It doesn't work. Getting up in the morning to look to see how your stock did yesterday is not useful. All this stuff is just a waste of time. If you're adding up how much your stocks are worth—absolute waste of time. You should be looking at the company. When you get the quarterly reports, you should—if you're at the mall—imagine if you were in the retailing industry or if you're in the restaurant industry, you would have seen Taco Bell, you would have seen McDonald's, you would have seen Toys 'R Us—I mean, you would have seen all these companies do terrifically well. You would have seen Bombay. You would have seen Tandy with Radio Shack. And you would have seen Radio Shack roll across the country, and pretty soon there were, you know, 25 Radio Shacks in every major city and you said, "There's not much room for them to go." But they had a 20-year great run.

That's what you're dealing with. You're not dealing with the minutiae of today. You're dealing with what's this company doing two years, three years, four years, five years from now?

And if you're dealing with a cyclical and business is turning around, you wait for signs that business is slowing down, and when you see it, you move on to something else.

MR. KARMIN: Are you concerned about the volatility in the financial markets today? Do you think something needs to be done to reduce it?

MR. LYNCH: Okay. I love volatility. *(Laughter.)* I remember when in 1972 the market went down dramatically and Taco Bell went from 14 to 1. They had no debt. They never had a restaurant close. And I started buying at 7, but I kept on to it and it went to 1, and it was the largest position in Magellan in 1978 when it was bought out at $42 by Pepsi Cola. And I think it would have gone to 400 if they didn't buy it out. I think volatility is terrific.

I think these collars are very important. I don't think the market going up 80 points one day and down 80 the next is a good thing for the public. I think that's not a very good thing. But I think all of these collars and all these other things to keep the volatility down each day is important. But the market is going to go up and down.

Human nature hasn't changed a lot in 25,000 years, and some event will come out of left field and the market will go down or the market will go up. So volatility will occur and markets will continue to have these ups and downs. I think that's a great opportunity if people can understand what they own. And if they don't understand what they own, they can own mutual funds, try and figure out mutual funds they own, and keep adding to it.

Basically, corporate profits have grown about 8 percent a year, historically. So corporate profits double about every nine years. The stock market ought to double about every nine years. So I think the next market is about 3,800, today 3,700. I'm pretty convinced the next 3,800 points will be up; it won't be down. The next 500 points, the next 600 points, I don't know which way they're going. So the market ought to double in the next eight or nine years. It ought to double again in the eight or nine years after that, because profits will go up 8 percent a year and stocks will follow. That's all there is to it.

PHOTO, MARTIN KUHN

Peter Lynch, Vice Chairman, Fidelity Investments (at the Hotel Washington). October 7, 1994.

MR. KARMIN: We're in the month of October. Beware of the month of October, the witching month for the stock market. What do you see as the outlook for this month? And when do you think the Dow will hit 4,000?

MR. LYNCH: October has always been a special month. I remember in 1987, you know, I was very convinced the market was not in trouble and I didn't worry about things. And Carolyn and I had planned this great golf vacation to Ireland and we were going to visit one course and stay at a little house and then visit another, go all along the west coast of Ireland and play golf.

And we left on a Thursday night and the market went down 55 points that day, which was not too good. *(Laughter.)* And the next day we got to Ireland. Because of the time difference, we had completed our day and I got back to the hotel and I called in. The market had gone down 112 on Friday. And I said to Carolyn, "You know, I think if the market goes down on Monday, you know, we're going to have to go back. And so we might as well"—we stayed there for the weekend.

And on Monday the market went down 508 points and my fund went from, I think, $12 billion to $8 billion. And that gets your attention, you know, in two working days. You know, I said by the end of this week I'd have no fund. Now, there wasn't a lot I could do. I mean, here I was on Monday, because the market didn't open—you know, by 12:00 in Ireland it was still 7:00 in New York. So we did spend that day, and we played a round of golf in the morning and then we went somewhere and sort of watched the market deteriorate. *(Laughter.)*

And I did come back. There was nothing I could do, I mean just nothing I could do about it. But I think my shareholders, if they called up and they said, "Well, what's Lynch doing?" and they said, "Well, he's on the sixth hole and he's"—*(laughter)*—"you know, he's even par up to now but he's in a trap"—*(laughter)*—"you know, this could be a triple bogey here, this could be a big inning," I don't think that's exactly what they want to hear, as though I could do something about this damn thing.

So I came back home and suffered with everybody else. And fortunately, I was very consistent. The market went down. When I ran Magellan, in 13 years the market went down nine times. And every time the market went down, Magellan went down. I was nine for nine. And, you know, it's very important. There's another one of these numbers you ought to write down. If you put $1,000 in a stock, all you can lose is $1,000. And I've done that several times. But if you're right, you can make $5,000, $10,000, $20,000.

So in this business you don't have to be right one out of two times. You can be right one out of four. The times you're right, you know the company's doing well, you know they're doing a great job, and you add to it, or at least you don't sell it, which is a terrible tragedy. So you can make more money on the upside, so I just rode those out.

And I will now flip a coin to tell you when the market will go to 4,000—this year or next year. Heads means it goes up—it is a two-headed coin—*(laughter)*—the market will go up in the next year. That's all I ever know about the stock market. *(Laughter.)*

MR. KARMIN: Well, we have, as you can imagine, many questions about where people should put their money. I'm going to divide it into two parts and you can address it. This questioner intends to put $1,000 yearly into my 4-year-old daughter's education fund. Where should I put it? Investment one.

MR. LYNCH: Okay.

MR. KARMIN: The other just covers everybody else. What are some of your current market favorites and why?

MR. LYNCH: Okay. Well, on the first one, and this is important whether you're investing for a 4-year-old, a 14-year-old, or a 74-year-old, you have to say, "What am I going to do when the market goes down?" Because I've had audiences like this, large audiences, and I'll say,

"How many people in the room are short-term investors?" I've never had anybody ever raise their hand.

I mean, everybody in the world is a long-term investor until the market goes down like in '90—I remember 1990; 1990 was so much scarier than '87. In '87, the market just fell down, and when you called a company, they said, "Our business is terrific; we're about to announce a stock buy-back or we're already buying back our stock. Business is great, and we can't figure this out."

But in 1990, you had Kuwait invaded, you had the banking system really on the ropes, I mean really close. You called up a company and they said that business was slowing down. We sent 500,000 troops to Saudi and we were about to fight what people thought was the—remember this? It was the fourth-largest army in the world and they were the toughest army in the world, and this was going to be a terrible war and that we ought to sit them out. Remember the big theory—there were a lot of people in this city saying, "We ought to wait them out." You know, we'd still be waiting there at 120 degrees with our 500,000 people. (Laughter.) I mean, I think Bush made an incredibly brave decision on the information he was getting to go in there and knock them out, or we'd still be there.

But that was an ugly time and that was very scary. And the public stood up—some people learned from '87 and they stood throughout that and said, "I'm confident about the next five, 10, 15 years for this country," and they hung in there.

So I would say if you want to buy a small growth fund or you want to buy a balanced fund that's part bonds and part stocks and you put so much money in, put more in every year, you'll be very pleased in 10, 20, 30 years. Stocks will beat the hell out of money markets, they're going to beat the hell out of bonds. No group of—you think of it. Any corporations—McDonald's, any of these great companies, Marriott, you name it—they've never gotten together and said, "Geez, you know, we're really doing well; why don't we raise the coupon on our bonds? Those bond holders are really loyal, you know?" (Laughter.) "You know, we've been giving 8 percent; why don't we raise it to 9, you know?" (Laughter.)

But companies like Automatic Data Processing, they do payrolls. An amazing, prosaic company—32 years of higher earnings, 32 years of double-digit earnings growth. We've had recessions, we've had wars, we've had changes in Congress, changes in the Supreme Court—32 years of up earnings. So I mean, that's what you're relying on—Johnson & Johnson, 30 years of up earnings; General Parts, 42 years of up earnings; Emerson Electric, 38 years of up earnings. You don't see companies like this in other parts of the world.

So I think that's what you buy when you buy a fund, you buy a bunch of good companies. And the second question was what again?

MR. KARMIN: Just your—

MR. LYNCH: Oh, the stocks. Well, I think the financial area has been hurt heavily in the stock market. I think that's an attractive area. Stocks like Chemical or Travelers' or Citicorp or Bank of Austin or Fleet or Shawmet, Fannie Mae, Freddie Mac—these stocks have all come down. Their business is terrific. They've improved their balance sheets. They're selling at multiples half or one-third lower than the general market.

I think the cyclicals—I think we have a chance for the cyclicals for the first time in a long time—the steels, the papers, the aluminums, the chemicals. I mean, it's their turn to come to the plate, and it's going to be a good time in the next—we seem to have the economy recovering in Latin America. Brazil is turning around. These are facts again. When you hear these facts, these countries are really—India, I've visited India. Things are really improving in India. Europe had the worst recession since the Depression. There's 18 million people out of work. Eighteen million people out of work in Western Europe right now, and the economy is starting to slowly turn. Japan has bottomed.

So I think you're going to see a demand, and commodity prices have been—aluminum prices got to a 30-year low; now an ingot has almost doubled. You're going to see the same thing with liner board. So you're going to see a very good time for cyclical stocks, and I think the auto stocks are also extremely cheap at four or five times earnings.

I think the economy's going to be—my opinion, from the companies I've talked to, in the businesses I look at, things are not off trendline. These are not extraordinary times. Housing is very affordable. It's not as affordable as it was two years ago, but on a 20-year basis, housing is very affordable. Automobiles are very affordable. Consumer durables are very affordable. I think people are going to—and we've added, as you know—I still don't understand what people—we hear the job growth. We've added—in the recession, we lost 1.8 million jobs, and now we've added back 5.8 million, 4.5 million in the last 19 months. So we've lost 1.8 million and we've added 5.8 million back. We're 4 million to the good. The tough part of it is we dropped about 600,000 manufacturing jobs, and we've only brought back 100,000 manufacturing jobs. But there are a lot more people working, and I think that trend's going to continue.

And the decade of the '80s—I think this is key. The decade of the '80s—this is what you hear from the press. This is what you hear from TV. In the decade of the '80s, the 500 largest companies eliminated 3 million jobs. Three million jobs. But there was 2.1 million businesses started in the 1980s, and if they just have 10 people each, that's 21 million jobs. This is an incredible job machine we have in America. So that's what happened in the '80s; these 2.1 million businesses created all of the jobs.

In the decade of the '90s, the top 500 companies are going to eliminate another 3 million people, and all you ever hear about is "Company X lays off 5,000 people in Hartford" and "Company Y lays off 5,000 people in Rochester" and somebody doesn't buy a sofa in Scottsdale, Arizona, because they read in their newspaper about all the layoffs in the Northeast. (Laughter.)

I mean, that's the nature. These companies have to do it to stay competitive. That's our business. And we've had, in the last two and a half years, a phenomenal—this has been a great thing for our country—we've had 1,750 companies come public. They've raised over $100 billion. There's only 2,500 companies on the New York Stock Exchange. Seventeen hundred and fifty companies is a lot. They're going to put this into research and development. They're going to put it into more plant, more efficient equipment. This is a fantastic thing for these companies. So I think the situation is excellent.

The banking system, for the first time since the early '50s—a lot of people follow the banking industry—the banking system today has more investments on the left side of the balance sheet. You talk about the governments—they own the mortgage-backed securities, then they have loans, for the first time ever since 1951, and they're only making 50, 20, 30 basis points and so say they love to make loans. The banking system has the highest equity of assets in 45 years. The banking system is ready to go. There's lots of liquidity around.

I don't know why people are so depressed about people getting hired all the time. I can't quite figure this out. I don't know. I have never met a banker or anybody in business that likes recessions. I have yet to find these people, you know. So I think it's very good the economy's doing well.

MR. KARMIN: Well, speaking of banks, are you concerned about banks being allowed to offer mutual funds and the confusion that creates among investors over whether bank deposits are insured or not insured or how much is insured or the whole question of deregulation?

MR. LYNCH: Okay. No, I think it's very positive banks are being allowed to sell mutual funds, because they'll probably sell a lot of Fidelity Mutual Funds. (Laughter.) That's very important.

No, but, seriously, I think it's very important that people understand when they own a bond fund, that bonds can go up and down—bonds are just about as volatile as stocks—and if they own a 30-year bond fund that you can lose 25, 30 percent of your money very fast even though they're government bonds. People have to understand this. There's an incredible rate of illiteracy in our public, and all they ever hear about is what happened today that Bristol-

Myers is going up $2 or $3. What happened to the Dow Jones? They don't get to learn anything about America.

And people at some point in their career are presented—they're near retirement and they're given $450,000, $500,000 because it's an early retirement, and they have no experience. They don't know what a bond is. They don't know what stocks are. And they have to make a decision in 30 to 60 days or they have a big tax consequence. These people have no experience learning about the stock market. It's a tragedy.

So I think anything we can do to educate the public—if you can convince people, if they understand the volatility of the stock market—I'm not saying anybody should buy a stock. I'm just saying if you purchase a stock, you ought to do certain things. If you purchase the stock and do certain things, you will do better. If you're not ready to do those things, you should keep your money in the bank, keep your money in a money market fund.

Some people aren't willing to do the homework, they don't have the stomach for it. They should stay out. They're not doing anybody any good by taking half their life savings and putting it in the stock market, or they've been lucky enough to save $50,000 or $60,000 to send their kids to college and one's going to start in a year and they're going to take all that money, and put it on an equity mutual fund with a one-year horizon? That's doing no one any good.

So I think the more—whether it's the banks that explain it, the brokers that explain it, anybody that does—and we're working on this at the SEC; the SEC's working very hard on this—to explain to people the nature of these products. If they understand them, they'll do better with it. The more information, the merrier.

Fidelity's launching a major study that'll be out at the end of this year on retirement. We've interviewed over 1,600 people; over 300 experts. We're going to put a major study on trying to explain to people about the nature of retirement and how they can best understand how they should invest their assets. We're not going to mention Fidelity, at all, of course. It may be subliminal in it, but—*(laughter)*—we're trying to help. And the more that we can do this now—and there's been an incredible push by the SEC to do this, and I think it's a very positive element.

MR. KARMIN: A couple of questions about that. What do you think of the SEC's proposal to require mutual funds to adopt a quantitative rating scale for riskiness, number one, and what effect do you feel that the new shareholder rights proposals for more open disclosure and communication are having on companies and the markets?

MR. LYNCH: Okay. On the second one—I'm not too familiar with the first one—on the second one, I think you have to be careful in crossing the bridge on how much we get involved in managing companies. I think there should be disclosure of what people are getting paid, there should be disclosure of how many shares they own, but I don't think we should be deciding whether they should make this acquisition or whether they should expand this plant.

When you get too involved in running a company, it's very complex, and a lot of great companies have made a lot of decisions you haven't heard about, because they decided not to do something. Some of the best decisions they didn't do was to not do something. And if they're under all this pressure from shareholders of what to do and what not to do, they're going to take their eye off the ball and they're not going to be able to run the business.

And companies are doing well because they look—the companies that do well look out five, six, seven years, and some decisions they make may not be the right thing for the next year. The more and more we concentrate on what they're doing and we keep commenting on as outsiders, it's going to be run by an enormous committee and we'll get committee results. So I don't think that's going to help anybody.

But disclosure of relevant facts of how many options people have or the options at the market, what they're being paid, I think that's important—how many shares they own, what the company's doing with it. I think this—they used to have a letter. I mean, it's not that recently that you have comments by the chief executive at the stock end report. They never used to have them make that. There was a letter saying what happened. I mean, it really is a very valuable piece of information. You don't realize the company has spent a lot of time on this. This is a very serious document. I think it's very helpful to shareholders. The quarterly shareholder reports are excellent.

And also, I'd stress everybody in America can get hold of a company. It's not Fidelity and Putnam and Dreyfus. You can get hold of a company. If you own a hundred shares, you can call the company and somebody will talk to you about it. And people don't take advantage of that. These companies are willing to talk.

On this quantitative and qualitative risk ratings, I think if it could be done, I think it might be positive. I'm a little confused on it. I'm not that up to date on it, but I think people should understand, you know, that certain stock funds, emerging growth funds, and investment companies that have $50 million in sales are very small and much more volatile than when you're buying major quality blue-chip growth companies, and that long-term bonds are more volatile than medium-term bonds, which are more volatile than one-year bonds, and I think these are things that should be explained to people. People should get a menu like you get at Howard Johnson's.

MR. KARMIN: Well, before we run out of time, and for Mr. Johnson's benefit, several people in the audience ask: How do you view Fannie Mae's stock and options today?

MR. LYNCH: Okay. I think I'd broaden it to Freddie Mac, too. I think both these companies, you know, have a great business, and I always look at the stock market. I think of it more—people study chess. This would be not a good game to study for the stock market, because in chess an outstanding player will beat a good player 1,000 times in a row. Everything's in front of you. All the moves are known. It's all technique.

In poker or in bridge, there's a lot of uncertainty, there's a lot of things you don't know. You can play a hand exactly right and lose. You say, "But I played it right. If I do it again over a night, over a month, I'll do it." That's the stock market. The stock market is much closer to poker than it is to any other game, and I think that's what's the important thing to know.

And what the hell was the question? *(Laughter.)* Oh, Fannie Mae. Fannie Mae has been sort of like a 27-card stud poker game—*(laughter)*—you know, over 12 years. Cards keep getting turned over like, "We're not doing so well in Houston," and this is 10 or 12 years ago, and, with these 5 percent downs that a lot of people had in mortgages, and people move there for jobs and the job—they brought their spouse along, and the job left. They had no ties to those communities, and they left. Or in Oklahoma or in Alaska. So when that card turned over, it was kind of ugly. And then they were losing a million dollars a day; that was easy to remember. *(Laughter.)* That wasn't too pleasant. And what they finally figured out was "We have very good business, we're extremely low cost, and if we can match our liabilities and our assets—make a very small spread, but we have very low costs—we could have a pretty good business."

Then a card would come over like, "Real estate prices start to go down in California." They started to go down in the Northeast. So then you had to say, "Well, I'd better keep checking to see what foreclosures are going to be like." And you may mean someone that doesn't own any Fannie Mae. So anyway, all these things—if you keep watching the story, every year you get a chance to buy this again. Something will come up.

People were worried that rates were going to go down, so stock went down because rates were going down. And now interest rates are going up, the stocks are going down because interest rates are going up. And Freddie Mac and Fannie Mae are still doing great and I think they're going to be terrific stocks. I mean, they're not going to quadruple, but I think they're about 25 percent undervalued now and I think they'd be good stocks to own for five years.

MR. KARMIN: It's my pleasure, Mr. Lynch, to present you with a National Press Club mug—

MR. LYNCH: Oh, thanks.

MR. KARMIN: —and a certificate of appreciation before I ask the final question.

MR. LYNCH: Uh-oh. Do I drink coffee?

MR. KARMIN: This fellow has a problem. He says, "Well, if the real secret of your success is following your daughters to the shopping mall to shop for stock tips, what do we bachelors do?" *(Laughter.)*

MR. LYNCH: Well, I think on the weekend—I think one of the reasons people get so depressed is they get away from children. On the weekend, they read all these magazines, they read the newspapers and they become economists and they get so depressed. I mean, they're bullish if they take their lunch to work on Monday, you know. *(Laughter.)*

And I think you need to rent a 12-year-old on the weekend just to—*(laughter)*—because they don't know about the problem of the ozone layer disappearing and all the problems of, you know, all these terrible things that we think about all the time, you get so depressed about, and how second basemen and shortstops that are getting paid $4 million and they can't throw it to first base on a bounce, you know. *(Laughter.)* So I think you need to find a 12-year-old and rent him for the weekend and follow this boy or girl around and see where they're shopping.

And our kids loved Body Shop, you know, and I bought it and I think it's going to be a good stock. And our oldest daughter, Mary, liked Ann Taylor, and she had to dress up to go to work at—she was working a summer at a consulting firm, and she thought Ann Taylor's prices were good and the quality was good and it was a great stock pick. And my wife, Carolyn, who was—until we had these three kids, she was an extremely good shopper. She almost got a black belt in shopping. *(Laughter.)* Because of the children, she didn't quite finish that, but she's a very good shopper, and, you know, she's given me some great tips, too, So I think you either have to use your spouse or you have to go out on your own.

I had this—the biggest position in my fund one time was Hanes, which owned L'Eggs, and was a huge stock, and it was bought eventually by Consolidated Foods, and it was in the Best division of Consolidated Foods. But it was my biggest position, and they had a monopoly on this L'Eggs, and L'Eggs was a really big hit, and I knew somebody would come along with a new product, and it was. Kaiser-Roth introduced No Nonsense.

And I was worried that this thing was better, and I couldn't quite figure out what was going on, so I went to the supermarket and I bought 62 pairs of No Nonsense—different colors, different shapes, everything. They must have wondered what kind of house I had at home where I was going back. *(Laughter.)* But I brought it in and I brought it to the office, and I passed it out to anybody, male or female, anybody who wanted these things. *(Laughter.)* Just take them home and tell me how it is, and they came back in about three weeks, and they said, "It's not as good."

And that's what research is. That's all it was. But I held on to Hanes and the stock was a huge stock, so that's what it's about.

Thank you. *(Applause.)*

NATIONAL PRESS CLUB

LUNCHEON
December 16, 1994

$\mathcal{S}$PEAKER

MARIO CUOMO
Governor of New York State

MODERATED BY: Gil Klein

HEAD TABLE GUESTS

DAVID HAWKINGS
Thomson Newspapers

ROBERT NOVAK
Syndicated Columnist

STEPHEN LABATON
New York Times

JOHN HALL
Washington Bureau Chief of Media General News Service

MONROE KARMIN
*Editor-at-Large of Bloomberg Business News and Vice President and
the President-elect of the National Press Club*

REGINA BLAKELY
CBS News

RICH OPPEN
Washington Bureau Chief of Knight-Ridder Newspapers

CHRISTY WISE
Freelance Journalist and Chairwoman of the National Press Club Speakers Committee

ALAN EMORY
Washington Bureau Chief of Johnson Newspapers of New York

CARL MALAMUD
President of Internet Multicasting Service

JONATHAN SALANT
*Congressional Quarterly and President of the Washington Chapter of the
Society of Professional Journalists*

AMY BARRETT
Business Week

CARL PISANO
Newsday

GIL KLEIN

MODERATOR

(Sounds gavel.)

*g*ood afternoon. Welcome to the National Press Club. My name is Gil Klein. I am the club's president, and a national correspondent for Media General Newspapers, writing for the Richmond Times-Dispatch, the Tampa Tribune and the Winston-Salem Journal.

I'd like to welcome my fellow club members in the audience today, as well as those of you who are watching us on C-SPAN, listening to us on National Public Radio or the Internet global computer network.

Today we are pleased to have with us Governor Mario Cuomo of New York. Few political figures have been asked more often than Governor Cuomo if he'll run for president of the United States. He played an electoral game of hard-to-get in the last three presidential elections, leaving a curious public pondering the Mario scenario. *(Laughter.)*

We all recall the drama of 1992: Just before the New Hampshire primary, the supporters poised on the final filing day, the airplane waiting on the runway in Albany, even Vice President Dan Quayle saying he was anxious for the fight. *(Laughter.)* But the plane never took off. Governor Cuomo said he was too busy being governor of New York to take on the presidency. The silver tongue of the consummate liberal was lost that year.

In the hard-charging 1980s, when Reagan was king and making money was all the rage, it was the governor of New York who had enunciated the plight of the poor and the disappearing middle class. When George Bush demonized the "L" word, Governor Cuomo embraced it. It's ironic, then, that halfway through a presidency of his own party, a president for whom he delivered the Democratic Convention's keynote address, that Governor Cuomo found himself struggling to fend off a conservative backlash in his bid for a fourth term. He even offered to put the death penalty up for a vote. The struggling middle class that he claimed to champion apparently wasn't buying it. We all know the outcome. In a sure sign of the changing times, Governor Cuomo's successor, George Pataki, has appeared on David Letterman's "Late Show," even reading a Top-10 list of ways to mispronounce his own name, including "Gapkakis" and "Boutros Boutros-Taki." *(Laughter.)*

So is this the end of liberalism as Republicans sharpen their budget axes and eye the Department of Housing and Urban Development and the Energy Department, the Education Department, the Interstate Commerce Commission? Is the notion that government can solve the nation's problems washed up?

Here to tell us about his concept of perfecting the union, please join me in a warm press club welcome for Governor Mario Cuomo of New York. *(Applause.)*

MARIO CUOMO

Thank you very much. Thank you very much. There are a lot of things I wanted to say immediately, just in quick response to Gil Klein's introduction. The truth about 1992 was that Klein, or somebody like him, just before that plane took off, over the wire came a story in which I was referred to as a consummate liberal. And that did it. I decided to stay behind in New York State. *(Laughter.)*

And I must say this, although I was going to say nothing at all, because I don't want to use up the 25 minutes they gave me, there's a lot I do want to tell you. I did note with some interest that the two biggest laughs from this rather difficult-looking group were for the postmaster general and Dan Quayle. *(Laughter.)*

I am going to do something unusual now in this, what appears I think to be the last time I'll be able to speak as a public official, because nothing is going to happen over the next couple of weeks, and that didn't strike me until I sat down and started making some notes. But maybe, especially because it is the last opportunity, there is a whole lot I want to get in. And because of that I'll stay close to my notes, closer than I usually do, and I'll rush a bit, if you don't mind, because I want you to have time to do the questions and answers.

You know by now that I was elected a private citizen—*(laughter)*—effective January 1st. It wasn't my first choice. Abraham Lincoln's familiar line in a similar situation, which I think the president used the other day, comes to mind. He said he felt like a young boy who had just stubbed his toe; it hurt too much to laugh, but he was too old to cry. The temptation, you should know, is to whine, you know—*(laughter)*—at least a bit. Why not? You served 12 years, you're entitled. And I caught myself doing that.

I began pointing out to people that ever since the Republican landslide on November 8th, it's been getting dark outside a little earlier every day. *(Laughter.)* You notice that? *(Laughter, applause.)* But whining is not what we need, so let me talk to you about some of the things I learned on the way back to private life, and there's a lot. Let's talk just a bit about America and how together we can make her stronger and sweeter.

Founded by the most optimistic people in history, in just 200 years, as we all know, we have become the most dominant military and economic machine, and the greatest engine of opportunity that the world has ever seen. But recently, say, within the last 15 years, we have made some terrible mistakes as well. We produced two devastating recessions that stripped from millions of our middle-class families the basic promise of the American dream, and even the simple security of steady work; mistakes that for millions more have produced lives of sheer desperation, dependence and despair.

Government did not create all these problems, but government didn't solve them either. And the people know that. Many of them are frightened, resentful, even angry. The conservative Republicans measured that seething unhappiness with polls, then designed some painless home remedies which they strung together in a new political agenda that they call now the "Contract With America." And they tell us it will solve our problems. I don't think so.

Some of the agenda puts the spotlight on relevant issues, at least for the moment. But the truth is the contract fails to deal substantially with the fundamental problems we face.

It's not a plan. It's an echo of selected polls. It adds nothing to the opinion surveys. It makes absolutely no demand on our political leadership other than that they set sail in whatever direction the political winds appear to be blowing at the moment. It offers a kind of plastic populism, epitomized by its bold promise of a balanced budget that will bend or probably break when tested with the full weight of our real problems.

We need something much sturdier. We need an agenda that deals with our real problems, all of them, especially the toughest ones, and proposes real, concrete solutions, even if they are politically inconvenient. The truth is, and I think we all know this, too, America is faced with a double-barreled challenge to our future. The most significant is an economy that is rewarding investors for sure, but at the same time threatening our workers. You tell a $30,000-a-year factory worker in Georgia or California that this is a growing economy, this third-wave economy, and see what reaction you get.

The second challenge is the frightening cultural corruption of drugs, degradation, violence, and children having children that's deteriorating our cities, crippling much of our potential work force, and alienating many of us from one another. And it is cultural. It is a cultural problem.

But the conservative Republican contract deals only superficially with our economic challenge and offers us little more than castigation and negativism with respect to our cultural weakness.

Now, Democrats should show America that we can do better. We should start by reaffirming our fundamental democratic principles, beginning with the confidence that this country can provide opportunity for everyone willing to earn it. And the first mistake would be to give up on that aspiration, to believe that somehow we are not as strong as we thought we were—we can't do it. Take up the gangplank—we can't afford them! That would be a mistake, an excuse if not a mistake, a cynical excuse for not making the tough decisions that will make it possible for us to realize what is our obvious, enormous potential strength still unused.

Our strong suit as Democrats has always been our concern for the vast majority of Americans who must work for a living. That's where we come from. That means we are committed to creating good jobs in a strong free-enterprise system, and to making sure that every working family in this country can earn enough to live with a reasonable degree of security and comfort. We believe that as part of the democratic bargain every American has responsibilities. Everyone who can work should work, instead of expecting others to pay their way. Businesses that thrive should share the rewards with their workers fairly. Business has a responsibility as well. And government should help create jobs, not discourage them, nor should it burden the rewards of work with unreasonably heavy taxes.

Now, we believe in law and order. I have built more prison cells than all of the governors in the history of New York State before me put together. But we will insist on fairness, and privacy and civil rights.

We agree with Lincoln that we should have only the government we need. But we agree with Lincoln, as well, that we must have all the government we need. We must have all the government we need. And so a balanced budget that fails to meet the basic needs of the struggling middle class or the desperate poor would be an emblem of failure.

We believe in the common-sense value of sticks, but we also believe in the common-sense power of carrots. We believe that prevention is always a good idea, and almost always cheaper. We'd rather preserve a family than build an orphanage. We believe that we're too good as a people to seek solutions by hurting the weakest among us, especially our children. And at our wisest, at our wisest—and it's not always true, it is probably not true at this moment—but at our wisest, we believe that we are all in this together, that Jeremiah was right, thousands of years ago, that we will find our own good in the good of the whole community.

Now this is not the time or the place to give all the details of what we can and must do to deal with the challenges and opportunities while living up to these principles. But we should reflect on enough of them, and I have the responsibility to give you at least enough of them so that you can see that the agenda offered by the contract is obviously incomplete and utterly inadequate to this moment in American history.

Most of all, we need to generate more jobs. We'll accept that—jobs that pay a living wage and make hope a possibility. In a global economy where labor often costs less in other places in the world—and that's the key—this is a complex challenge. But the Republicans would have us believe that the solution is remarkably simple.

Now, you know how hard it is. Taiwan and that part of the world—in China, Mexico—they can make things a lot cheaper than you can. That puts an enormous pressure on your manufacturing.

How do the Republicans deal with this problem? That's why the $30,000-a-year factory worker is scared to death. He knows it. He knows the investors are getting richer, and everybody is downsizing here, and the competition is enormous all over the world—a competition that I grew up without having to face.

Well, their proposal, the Republican proposal, is right out of the permanent conservative Republican playbook: cut the tax on capital gains, boost the defense budget, amend the Constitution to enforce a balanced budget, but let's not get bogged down in the awkward details about what we'd actually have to cut. Cut the taxes, boost the defense budget, and then provide a balanced budget. Does it sound familiar to you? Do you remember hearing that before? Cut your income, raise your expenses, and promise the bank that, this time, you're sure you can make ends meet. Does it sound familiar? It's nothing more than deja voodoo. *(Laughter.)*

In the early '80s, the conservative Republicans promised huge tax cuts, a huge military, and a balanced budget. And we wound up, as we all know, with a deep recession and $4 trillion more in debt.

Now, why is it different now? Why would it work any differently now? Has something changed? Has there been some kind of cosmic alteration? Only the language has changed. In the '80s, they talked about the magic of supply side. Now they have thought up a new way to count. It's called dynamic scoring. Do you know what dynamic scoring means? It means that for every basket they put in the hole, they get 10 points. That's dynamic scoring. And it would be wonderful if it were as easy as that—free up the wealth in the hands of the wealthy and it will eventually take care of all of us.

Now, this country tries that every so often. We tried it in the '80s, the early '80s. But then the truth reemerges. Life is more complicated and harder. It includes bothersome details, like a national deficit, leashed in by President Clinton but ready to run wild at the least relaxation or provocation. Life includes popular entitlement programs that won't be around for our children at all if we cannot bring ourselves to make intelligent, but different sacrifices now. Everybody in this room knows it.

In every conversation in Washington or New York or the capitals in the country, where people know what they're talking about, they all say the same thing. "You must do something about Social Security." We all know that. "You must deal with Medicare. You can't deal with our deficit problem without doing something about Social Security and Medicare. However, it's political poison, so we won't do it." But didn't you just tell me that if we don't do something about it we're in terrible trouble? "Yes." And then you tell me that it's going to be very difficult to deal with it politically. "Yes." And what do you prescribe then? "Keep yourself alive politically, and let the country die."

Am I exaggerating? Do you hear it differently? You write about it. You write about it glibly. Everybody comments on it, most of the time snidely, but nobody changes it. Warren Rudman leaves. Paul Tsongas creates a group. Peter Peterson writes books. Everybody is saying the same thing, and all the people who are bright, saying they're right, and admitting at the same time we do not have the will to change it. Why don't you at least say this to the American people. Why don't you say, "Look, let's get this clear, because I have the obligation to tell the truth." Who knows? Maybe there is a heaven. Worse than that, maybe there's a hell. *(Laughter.)* Maybe I'm going to be accountable. Maybe I'd better tell you the truth. So I'm going to take a chance.

Ladies and gentlemen, all the tax cuts in the world won't save you. They're popular, but we need a double bypass and they're talking about giving you cosmetic surgery. And the reason we're doing that is it's too tough to give you a bypass. We have to cut with a knife. That's very expensive. It's very costly. It's unpleasant for you. We have to do Social Security. We have to do Medicare. You have to apply a needs test of some kind. Everybody knows it.

Now why, therefore, don't the Republicans tell you that? Well, because they're into popularity. Why don't we tell you that? Because we're into popularity, too. *(Laughter.)* But we're going to say this to you: As long as the Republicans are in power in the Congress, and as long as it's absolutely clear that they will have a Pavlovian response to whatever you tell them in the polls, start telling them in the polls that you've finally awakened. You know they have to do something about Social Security and Medicare. Please do Social Security and Medicare. They will write a new Contract with America—addendum to the Contract with America. We've seen the latest poll. It just came in over the Internet. Okay. You can have Social Security. *(Laughter, applause.)*

There is another inconvenient truth, and that is that you have to make investments if you want to get returns. The Republicans especially should know that. And that means if we want to be the high-tech capital of the world—which you have to be, because if you're going to compete with cheap labor, how are you going to do it?—you're going to have to make things with exquisite high-tech capacity and superb productivity so that you can make things better and faster and different from the things that they can make even with cheaper labor.

How else do you do it? The only other way is to expand a whole other thing beyond manufacturing, make exquisite improvements in services. We're doing that. We're the service capital of the world already and we will stay that way for a long time, especially as long as New York stays strong, because you have banking, investment banking, and a lot of that there—publishing, et cetera. We're doing fine with services.

On the manufacturing side, you can't do it without high-tech. You have to do what we're doing in New York State: make a unique lens that we just sold to the Japanese. And when I complained to the University of Rochester about selling a unique lens to the Japanese, who are so good at replicating our products and producing something cheaper, they said, "Don't worry about it. We're working on a second lens." *(Laughter.)*

Making a new mammography machine on Long Island through high-tech, a mammography machine that solves the problem that the woman has with the old machine, where she has to press herself up against this plate, where there's constriction, discomfort and a poor picture. This one inclines. Bennett X-Ray. You incline and gravity does the work. And there's a full picture. And my daughter, the radiologist, loves it. And the woman is pleased by it. And the physician who has to operate feels better about it because he has a better picture. And we sell it to the Germans who make surgical instruments.

And when I say to Bennett X-Ray, "I created a center of high technology. Now you take this wonderful product, you send it to the Germans. How long before they replicate it?" He says, "Five months." I said, "Well, what are we going to do about that?" He said, "Don't worry about it, Governor. We're working on digitalizing it. We're taking the digital engineers from Grumman, who have gone down because they're no longer making planes, they're coming here, they're working on our mammography machine."

We have to stay one step ahead of them in high-tech. That's the way you became great the first time around. You used to make all the things of value in this world. You were the makers and the sellers, the creditors and the bankers. That's how we became dominant. You can't get out of that business now because you're in a global economy. You have to make things. That means high-tech. That means research. That means investment, investment, investment. And someone has to pay for it.

There are plenty of good ways of making our workers better equipped too, and you can't do that. You can't leave that factory worker where he is now, or she is now, at $30,000, and say, "Look, in this high-tech world where we have to be smarter and slicker than they are, I'm afraid you're going to fall behind because you don't have the training." The GI Bill is a good idea for workers. Training vouchers is a good idea. Head Start is absolutely essential, learning technologies.

Is there any way you can explain how every kid in the United States of America doesn't have the opportunity to learn at a computer? How do you explain that to yourself? The richest place in world history, with all the tremendous wealth you have, how do you explain to yourself that there are kids who never see a computer in my state, where people have Porsches parked, or BMWs parked next to Jaguars? How do you explain it when you're selling the airwaves for billions of dollars that you didn't even expect to have? Vice President Al Gore is right. Let's take some of that money and invest it in learning technologies. Tax cut—hell of an idea. Learning technologies—an even better idea.

Make your children the smartest in the world. Everybody knows that that's the avenue to the future. You write tracts about it. Kids write essays about it in the 8th grade. But we're not doing it. That's the real world. It means investing, then capitalize on the most extensive higher-education system in the world, promoting its strength in research and making sure that it becomes accessible to everybody.

It means infrastructure. There is no money for infrastructure. Have you heard any Republican step forward and say, "And another thing we're going to do is we're going to build the infrastructure." Why, infrastructure is an arcane word. You get no political points for infrastructure. I wish I could think of some sexy way to say roads, bridges, telecommunication, fiber optics. Infrastructure. Forty percent of the roads and bridges are in trouble.

Overseas, they spent $6 billion—Maglev, they're way ahead of you. You cannot succeed economically unless you invest in infrastructure. Where are you going to get the money? They didn't even mention it. How could you not mention it? Is there anybody alive with any brains at all, who knows anything about the economy, who would not say to you that, "Of course, we must invest more in the infrastructure." Or do they get challenged? Does the public rise, up after they have heard somebody on television, say, "Well, I'll never vote for you. You never even mentioned—what was that—infrastructure." Infrastructure. *(Laughter.)*

Those conservative Republicans cannot deny that all of these investments are essential. They simply ignore them because they're politically difficult truths, and because the polls don't give you points for arcane things like infrastructure. They know America needs a double bypass, and they know they're only suggesting cosmetic surgery. But as long as it's popular, that's what they're going to give you.

Now, massive tax cuts of any kind would surely ring the popularity bell. But would you insist on them if it meant that local tax rates would explode across the country, which they could, if you cut back programs that the states are going to have to pay for instead? Would they insist on tax cuts if they knew that bridges would collapse, that the deficit might go up again, that you were failing to meet your educational needs? And if we can afford to lower taxes, would you give 70 percent of the immediate benefits to people who make $100,000 a year, or would you give 70 percent of the immediate benefits to the ordinary families across America? And as long as you Republicans are so quick to point out that the people have spoken, who told you? The poll. Why don't you take a poll on it?

"Mr. and Mrs. America, we're going to give you a tax cut. What do you want? A tax cut, the immediate benefit of which goes to—70 percent of which goes to the people above $100,000, or one that goes to people under $100,000?" What do you think the poll would say? How about this one: "Mr. and Mrs. America, would you like to shorten the congressional session and cut everybody's salary in half—senators and congressmen?" What do you think

PHOTO, MARTIN KUHN

they'd say? *(Laughter.)* Last time I looked, it was 82 percent said yes. I didn't see a single Republican hold up, "The people have spoken." *(Laughter.)*

Of course, Democrats respect and believe in the efficiency of capitalism. A capital gains tax cut, in some circumstances, could be a very, very good thing. Deregulation—a very, very good thing. I did a lot of it in my own state. But if our system works only for investors and leaves millions of our people without the skills or opportunity to do more than tread water against the tide, our system fails.

Now, if they're silent on these important things, what are they loudest on? Now, I'm really going to have to rush and it's a shame. Welfare. Why? Because it's popular. Don't you see what's happened? They've turned the middle class against the crowd beneath them. In the Depression, you know, when everybody was angry, in 1932, whom did they blame? They blamed the power. The people who made it happen. The bankers. The government. Everybody turned on the government, and they were right.

And what's happened this time? Now they've turned the middle class downward. Instead of looking up at the people with the wealth, they're looking down at the people who are the victims. And who are you blaming? The immigrants. That's easy. They have no political power, really, to speak of. Forget the fact that everybody here is an immigrant and that we all started by killing the only real entitled people to the place, the Native Americans. We butchered them. We savaged them. Everybody else is an intruder by your popular current definition. Forget that, because I'm lucky to be here now. It's the immigrants who are our problem.

It's that baby who's making a baby. Forget about the fact that you allowed her at the age of two to be a toddler in streets surrounded by pimps and prostitutes and every kind of disorientation, that you allowed her to be seduced by somebody with a crack pipe when she was only nine years old. Forget about that, that you allowed that society, that you allowed it to happen. She's the problem. Punish her. Punish the mother. No benefits for that child. Stick the child in an orphanage.

You really think that's the answer? I don't. In New York State we have problems, but we have answers, too, and they're not orphanages. We can show you ways to bring down teenage pregnancy dramatically, and we have with the new "Avenues to Dignity" program in New York. That's not as popular as Draconian devices, like what they want to do with welfare or the death penalty.

In the end, behind nearly every one of the Republican proposals lurks the same harshness and negativity. And I think we need better from our leaders than to have them distill our worst instincts and then bottle the bitter juices and offer them back to us as a magic elixir. We need a cure, not a reaffirmation of our distress.

We must understand that our great social problems are not visited upon us like earthquakes and floods. They are uniformly avoidable disasters. And with intelligent and timely action, we can prevent them before they pull our children down. Punishment has its place, of course. But prevention requires more than fear.

In New York, the movement toward prevention is the strongest element in our approach to health care. Incidentally, that's what reforming health care should be all about, prevention. The reason you need to cover those 39 million people is not compassion. It's not that they're not getting health care. They are getting health care. In my state, everybody gets health care, even the people without insurance. They fall down in the street and they're taken to the emergency room, or they come with a terrible pain in their belly that would have been nothing if they had been insured and been to a doctor early, but now is acute, and we take care of them.

What would we do, let them die? "You have no Medicaid. You have no insurance. Lay here and die." Of course not. We operate. You can find in the hospitals of New York City women and men on machines being kept alive for nobody knows how long, except God, without any insurance, without any name, and we take care of them. You can't afford that. Health care costs are going through the roof everywhere except in New York State. And they're high there, but we're the lowest-growing in the United States of America. That surprises a lot of people.

You have to do something about those 39 million people. And if Congress closed its eyes because it couldn't find a proper solution last time, you can't simply say, "This is too difficult; leave the problem there." You will go bankrupt. Really? Of course. You all know that. It's not just Ira Magaziner. You can't make it go away by saying, "Well, it was very unpopular."

So do something else. Do something like what we're doing in New York. At least let the children of working people get insurance, get them into plans. We subsidize them to get them into plans. Why? Prevention. If you can vaccinate them, it's cheaper than trying to deal with their disease.

So, too, with drugs. What is the answer to drugs? Look, you can build all the prisons you want. You can contrive all the draconian punishments you want. You can say what the Republicans say—that more police, more prisons, more executions and reversing the ban on assault weapons will take care of the drugs and take care of the crime. It won't. Forget all about the complicated talk.

Imagine this, imagine a village, imagine a village where the young people are drinking at a poisoned lake. And it makes them mad, and they come in every night to the village and they commit mayhem, and they rape and they kill. And you arrest more and more of them and you stick them into jails in the village, and the jails are getting bigger and bigger, and you have more and more village police and the villagers are complaining because they can't afford it. And the generation of criminals keeps pouring out of the hills, having come from the poison lake. Wouldn't somebody with some brains say, "For God's sakes, let's dry up the lake. Let's find another source of water." Of course you would.

But why aren't you doing it here? Why doesn't it occur to you that unless you stop the generation of these drug-ridden people who become criminals and then violent criminals, your biggest problem now in terms of crime, children with guns. You're not going to get at that. Take it from me. I told you, I've built more prison cells than all the governors in history before me put together, and it's not going to work. Ask any policeman. Fifteen years ago they would have told you something else. You have cultural problems.

I'm going to have to end it now, and it really is a shame because I'm leaving out a lot of the good stuff. (Laughter.) I really am. But let me leave with maybe the largest point, and maybe the largest point that I have learned in public life, and it's something that I kind of intuited before I was in public life. It's something I spoke about in my first speech before I ever even ran, and this was up in Buffalo in 1973, and I was talking about mama and papa and what was important about mama and papa and what they taught me—these two illiterate people—what they taught me by their example.

And what they taught me, basically—and then a Vincentian priest, you know, added to it, and then good books, you know, taught you most of all—that you're going to spend your whole life learning things and experiencing things, most of all disappointment and occasionally moments of joy. But in the end, you've got to find some raison d'etre. You have to find some reason for living. You have to find something to believe in. And for it to work, it has to be larger than you, that you will discover that you are not enough to satisfy yourself.

Now, you might get to be 70 years old before you figure it out, but sooner or later you'll figure it out, that you must have something larger than yourself to hold onto. Where have you gone, Joe DiMaggio, Bobby Kennedy, Martin Luther King, Jr.—some great cause, some great purpose?

The Second World War did that. I remember a little bit of that. The Second World War was a horrid thing but it unified everybody in America. They were evil, we were good. They were Satan, we were doing God's work. And everybody got together—the men, the women, the blacks, everybody; forget about poor, forget about middle class, forget about everything else. There's a grander purpose here. There's a greater truth here, something we can give ourselves to, and we'll fight like hell. And we did.

We haven't had anything like that since, and you don't have it now. You're turning those white factory workers all over the country against people of color. You're turning them against the immigrants. They're blaming them. And I understand why they're blaming them. Their life is vulnerable. They say, "You're doing nothing for me, everything for them." That's the truth of it. You know it. We all talk about it. We don't all write about it that clearly, but you know that the society is being fragmented.

It used to be the middle class against the rich, but now somehow, I think with a little encouragement from some of the politicians, you have turned the middle class to look downward instead of up. And they're now pitted against the poorest. So here are the least powerful people in your society, the least fortunate, squabbling with one another.

Ladies and gentlemen, unless we find a way to put this whole place together, unless we find a way to see that your interest depends upon your seeing the child in South Jamaica, that Latina, that little Hispanic girl who just had a baby, that little black girl who just had a baby, as your child, or unless you see that factory worker in Georgia as your father about to lose his job, unless you understand that it's not as a matter of love, not even at Christmas and Hanukkah time; I wouldn't ask that of anybody in a political context. It's too much to use the word compassion. Forget that. You'll lose.

As a matter of common sense, you cannot afford the loss of productivity. You cannot afford the cost of drug addiction. You cannot afford it. We will not make it in this country unless we invest in dealing with those problems. And to deal with those problems you have to give them other avenues to dignity instead of streets of despair. You will not frighten them into being good. You will not punish them into stopping drugs. You have to teach them. How to teach them? Have a crusade—not just a rhetorical crusade, a real crusade. Invest in it. How would you teach children not to have sex too soon, to treat it as a great gift; not to be violent; not to take the drugs? How would you teach them? How do you teach anybody?

Well, at home their family is broken. In school the teacher is too busy. In the church, the temple, the mosque if they went there, it wouldn't be a problem. How do you teach them? Let the government teach them with laws. There's a role there, yes. What's the best teaching instrument you have? Television. Yes, that's right. Why don't we teach them every night on prime time?

Well, we have a Partnership for a Drug-Free America. Once every week or two weeks they'll see those great commercials by the Partnership for a Drug-Free America. You read the New York Times this week. Drug use is up with teenagers. Why? Part of the reason, Partnership for a Drug-Free America isn't being seen enough. How do you explain that to yourself? You know it works. You know the best thing you can do is teach the children not to take the drugs. The best way to teach them is television. Why aren't you on prime time? How can you settle for once a week or once every two weeks?

If you were a mother of a child in South Jamaica, my neighborhood, and you knew that they were out there, going to tempt her with a pipe, a crack pipe, and you had to go to work, would you settle for a stick-it note on the refrigerator once a week saying, "Hey, dear, if they come at you with a pipe, make sure you don't take it. See you tonight, Mother." Would you settle for that? We're settling for it as a society.

You want to talk about tax cuts? You want to talk about all these nice things? Talk about the real problems. Talk about how to invest in your economy, how to create jobs, how to invest in a real crusade that would have to put up some money, buy some time, sit down with Tisch and NBC and all the others, say, "We'll put up five billion bucks, we want you to do the same." Let's saturate the place. Let's have billboards. Let the National Press Club write about it. Let all the community groups talk about it. Let's go at this problem for real because it's killing them and it's killing us.

Look, I lost an election. I've lost more than one, but I've learned a whole lot on the way, and I haven't forgotten any of it. And I'm telling you that I am absolutely certain we are not being honest about our problems. And the person who stands up and is honest with America and reminds America that they're now in charge—politicians used to think of themselves as shepherds. That's all over now. Now the politicians are following the sheep.

Read the polls. They'll tell you where they should go to pasture. And as long as you know that, you had better send the right signals to your government, because if you tell them you want the death penalty, you'll get it. If you tell them you want tax cuts, you'll get it. If you tell them to take up the gangplank, you'll get it. If you tell them to ignore sick people, you'll get it. If you tell them to ignore the poor, you'll get it. If you tell them to victimize young children, you'll get it. Be careful what you ask for, because they're listening for you. And ask for the right things. Ask for the truth. Ask for the real solutions to the real problems. I learned that. I won't forget it.

Thank you for your patience. (*Applause.*)

Mario Cuomo, right, clowns with Sarah McClendon.

MR. KLEIN: Thank you very much, Governor. It so happens that the last time you spoke here, in 1991, I was the moderator. You gave a similarly impassioned speech. And my first question was how, after giving a speech like that, can you deny that you're running for president? I won't ask that question this time. The question is, how did the Republicans seize the—in your mind, how did the Republicans seize the public mind for their program and the Democrats could not?

GOV. CUOMO: Well, I probably would quarrel with you about their program. What program? *(Laughter.)* No, let's be clear. What program? What economic plan? Capital-gains tax cut? What else? Line-item veto? What do you want to bet they don't let President Clinton have the line-item veto? Term limitations? The first thing they did is to say, "But not for me." The gag rule? Susan Molinari got rid of that. Three-fifths vote? Gingrich said, "Well, yeah, three-fifths if you vote for taxes, but not for income—but only for income taxes." "Oh, you mean, you can tax us a thousand other ways?" Yeah.

What are you talking about? A balanced budget? How? We're now in a debate between this tax cut and that tax cut. That's terrific. You know, I'm about to set a record for New York State governors, especially those who have served 12 years. That's a lot. January 1st I'm going to be both homeless and unemployed, it looks like, which is an all-time record. So I'm not thinking much about things like picking cars.

But if I were thinking about picking cars, I could see the similarity to this tax cut. They're talking about "Do you want this tax cut or that tax cut?" The first thing I would ask, if I were going to pick a car, is, "How much do I have to pay for it? And how do I pay? You know, what is this, Park Avenue, Park Royal, Park Caprice, whatever it is? It's nice. I like the chairs. I like the bags. I'll be comfortable in this car. But how much does it cost me, and how do I pay for it?" And that's true about these tax cuts, too.

So they haven't told you anything. They said they're going to balance the budget in six years, seven years, whatever it is. You heard that before. What would a balanced budget amendment do? Whose programs would it kill? I'll tell you who it'd kill—the most vulnerable people. It would destroy the states. This notion, the program we're going to swap with the states, don't you remember the New Federalism? Don't you remember Stockman telling you what that was all about? Shift it to the states. Let them pay the burden.

You know what that means? Go from the progressive tax, which taxes people on the basis of wealth—that's federal, the income tax, the biggest tax—to sales taxes, real estate taxes, property taxes, which tax the people with lesser wealth. It is a progressive to regressive taxation. The Republicans love it. But that's what would happen. So what program?

If the American people knew everything that you know, they would laugh at this contract. I'm not even sure they're not laughing because they don't know about it. One poll said that 75 percent of them didn't know anything about the contract, which is kind of ironic since they were taking credit for having, you know, dished out the contract over Rush Limbaugh or something, and that's why they got all the votes. I don't think that's why they got the votes. I think the reason they got the votes is the reason the Democrats are now stronger. They got the votes because the Democrats are in power. The president was a Democrat, the Senate was Democrat, the House was Democrat. Things are lousy, get rid of the power, right? So they kicked us out. That was the principle.

I was the mega-incumbent, 12 years. I went the way other incumbents did. Not everyone, but basically it was an attempt to get rid of the power. Not a bad notion, but as soon as they got rid of us, we got stronger. Why? Because now they are the power, they have to produce.

We have now the glory of being dissenters because we're in the minority, and when you're in the minority, you can afford to be irresponsible because you don't have to produce a result.

I hope we resist that temptation, but not totally. (*Laughter, applause.*)

MR. KLEIN: Are you saying that President Clinton is being dishonest with the American people by proposing this tax cut?

GOV. CUOMO: No, because he's also proposing money for infrastructure. He's also proposing money for investment in education. That tax deduction is a very, very good idea.

He also proved himself on the deficit. He reduced the deficit. Who did that before him? What Republican can say that? So he's done most of the things I'm talking about. There is no question that my assessment of the truth, as I've described it to you in abbreviated form today, if that's the truth, what I've described to you, President Clinton is much, much closer to that than the Republicans even pretend to be.

Now, look at the Republican agenda. The Republican agenda is, "We'll do whatever we have to do to win power. If it is popular, we will do it."

Now, he who lives by the polls should die by the polls. You know what some of you should do? Take some polls. (*Laughter.*) Take some polls on this question: Should you raise corporate and business taxes instead of any other taxes? Sixty percent will say yes. Incidentally, I don't think that's a good idea, but the polls will.

Here's one: Do you think you should have to prove O.J. Simpson's guilt, or should O.J. Simpson have to prove his innocence? What do you think the poll would say? I know. Sixty-five percent would say the defendant should prove his innocence, despite the Constitution.

What? Oh, yeah. Do you want to live by the poll? How about cutting Congress' time and cutting their salaries in half? How about this one: Should anybody in Congress get a pension that is higher than the average pension of the average working person in the United States of America? (*Laughter.*) What do you think the poll would say? Isn't there something eclectic, kind of disgracefully eclectic by making arguments as Republicans say, "Well, the people have spoken." How do you know? "Here is the poll."

He who lives by the poll, you know, will die by the poll.

MR. KLEIN: This questioner says: Didn't we try to purify the poison lake with the Great Society and now it's still poisoned?

GOV. CUOMO: No, we didn't. (*Laughter.*)

Well, hey, the Great Society gave you Social Security. I don't hear anybody complaining. It gave you Medicaid. That's not enough. You have to have jobs. You have to have jobs and opportunity in the ghettos. What did the Great Society do for you in the ghettos? What jobs and opportunities? You should have had laws that stopped people—you have zoning laws, right—on the assumption since—at least since 1925, Euclid against Amber—U.S. zoning laws that say people shouldn't be living on top of one another. It's bad for them. It's like in a hospital, when people are ill, you have to have a certain number of square feet for each bed because there needs to be space.

How did you let people live on top of one another, poor people, live in these huge high-rise apartments that became so disgraceful that you had to blow one up at Pruitt-Igoe in the middle of the country? How did you let that happen in the middle of the Great Society? Jam all the poor people into these little spaces where there are no jobs, there aren't enough teachers, there aren't enough police—just get them away from me.

No, we didn't do it well in the Great Society.

MR. KLEIN: Why did you turn down the opportunity to serve as a justice on the Supreme Court, and do you now have second thoughts?

GOV. CUOMO: Well, there was nothing I could have imagined 20 years ago that I would enjoy more or regard as a higher honor than being on the Supreme Court. I mean, the notion of—first of all, the notion of being governor for three terms was kind of mind-boggling to me, but as a lawyer, and as a lawyer who had been a clerk in my own highest court, it would have been wonderful.

I really felt that this is a unique moment in the modern history of the country, that we are challenged in a way that we haven't been for a long, long time; that it is a question of very basic belief, it's a profound question about the soul of the people, that the United States, that New York State, about whom E.B. White said this: "The role of New York is the same as the function of the white church steeple in the village. It is a visible symbol of aspiration and faith. It is the white plume saying, 'The way is up.'"

Now, that's what he said about New York and that's how I feel about New York, and I thought this would be the moment to be governor, this four years when everybody is turning away from what I think the level of civility should be. Everybody is retreating from the level of aspiration I think we should have for all of us; that so many people are hiding from this notion of family—that we are connected, we are interconnected, not as some theological truth, but as a practical necessity. No man is an island—no woman, no city, no state, no village, no nation either. That is the central truth that's taught to you by the whole progression of the universe, from the slime to the sublime. Things are getting more complicated and integrating, and as they integrate, they get smarter, better, sweeper, until you get to the pluroma, if you will.

That's the lesson, and that's what we are trying to say in New York, and I thought that New York State would be the one place that could deliver that message when the country needed it most, so I wanted to win and do it. I lost, and lost the opportunity to do that. I regret that very much, but I don't regret the decision to try. *(Applause.)*

MR. KLEIN: How much was President Clinton a factor in your defeat and the Democratic defeat in general?

GOV. CUOMO: I don't think he was a factor in my defeat. I brought him in? No, I didn't bring him in—I asked him to come in a few times, and he did. He was probably much more generous in his time in New York than he could have afforded to be, really, because he had a lot of other places to go. We had Hillary more than a couple of times. I think they were very good for us. I think my state is very proud of them.

In New York City, where they came most of the time, I did better than I did in any previous election. I won overwhelmingly. We were beaten upstate in what are basically Republican precincts, by a huge turnout—in one place, 92 percent turnout. If there had been anything like the historic patterns of turnout, we would have won very comfortably. I don't believe President Clinton was anything but a plus for me. I was very grateful to him for coming, and I'm grateful still. *(Applause.)*

MR. KLEIN: A couple of questions about what you might do in the future. One is will you run for the U.S. Senate against Senator D'Amato? *(Laughter, applause.)* Did you ever consider assuming the position of DNC chairman?

GOV. CUOMO: Well, I wouldn't consider DNC chairman. I mean, I think they have some candidates and that's very good. As for the future, I have no idea what I'm going to do. I don't have a job yet, which is a little inconvenient when you make an application for a cooperative, I've discovered. *(Laughter.)* It's very hard to explain, you know. They don't care about what you did 20 years ago.

Anyway, I don't know what I'm going to do. I know this: That my children and I have learned an awful lot in a full life in New York, where there is every problem and every potential. There's nothing that happens in this country that doesn't happen in our state, and much of it happens there first. So you live a lifetime, as we have, and if you go from, you know, the very bottom rung to a comfortable life, as we have, and then you were governor for 12 years during that and a public official for 20 in your state, then you have to know a whole lot about what's happening in this country. And we want very much to share that where it's useful, so I'm looking for opportunities to do that.

I've been invited to speak in various places. I'll do that. I want to get into an academic context where I can study more and keep up, because you've got to know what you're talking about. I mean, too much of this is superficial and you have to make sure you don't slide into that and start saying the easy things, the popular things.

Incidentally, I did not—if I may say so, because this is an important point—I did not change any position on the death penalty. I did not ask for a vote on the death penalty. My position on the death penalty has been the same for all of my life, and I had three people sentenced to death and I had the next-to-last person sentenced to death in the electric chair. And I have debated it all over the world, literally, and I'm absolutely certain that this is a kind of symbol of what's happening in the nation—this lust for executions, despite the plain evidence of all the years that it not only does not deter, it probably promotes barbarity.

Of the seven states that went back to it in recent years, I think five of them have higher rates of homicide and violence than New York State, that did not go back to it. What do you think you're going to say to your children when, finally in New York State, and God forbid it should happen, you have your first execution? "We just fried our first guy in years," and everybody stands up and cheers, "Well, we finally did it! We finally got the death penalty."

"What does that mean, Mama?"

"We killed somebody."

"Yeah, but why'd you do that, Mama?"

"Well, because he was bad and he killed somebody."

"But, Mama, what happens if you were wrong, if you made a mistake?"

"Well, every once in a while you'll make a mistake, but that's all right, because we had to let them know."

"Let them know what, Mama? I mean, if they rape me, are you going to rape them?"
Anyway.

MR. KLEIN: We are unfortunately about out of time, although there are many, many more questions.

I would like to present you with a certificate of appreciation for appearing here.

GOV. CUOMO: Do I get a mug?

MR. KLEIN: Do you get a mug? *(Laughter.)* Not to be missed, the National Press Club mug, which you can put pencils in; you can hold out, if you don't get a job, you know, on the street. *(Laughter, applause.)*

GOV. CUOMO: Thank you. That's great.

MR. KLEIN: And if you really have a hard time getting a job, you come back here. I think with your political skills, we might get you—Bud Karmin is already going to be president, but, you know, we'll get you on the board, you know. *(Laughter.)*

Now, you were, of course—had a short career as a professional baseball player in the Georgia-Florida league. The question is, if you could have hit a curve ball, would your career have been different? *(Laughter.)*

GOV. CUOMO: Well, as I've proved in politics, I probably would have struck out once in a while, anyway. *(Laughter, applause.)*

MR. KLEIN: Thank you very much, ladies and gentlemen. That concludes our program for today. You all have a happy holiday.

NATIONAL PRESS CLUB

LUNCHEON
April 7, 1994

$\mathcal{S}$PEAKER

GARRISON KEILLOR
Humorist

MODERATED BY: Gil Klein

HEAD TABLE GUESTS

CAROL BYRNE
Minneapolis Star Tribune

MASAMICHI FUJITSUKA
Kyodo News Service

MICHAL MAINWARING
Freelance Journalist and member of the Board of Governors of the National Press Club

STEVE THOMMA
St. Paul Pioneer Press

SONYA HILLGREN
Washington Editor of the Farm Journal and Chairwoman of the Board of Governors of the National Press Club

DOUG TURNER
Washington Bureau of the Buffalo News

ELEANOR CLIFT
Newsweek Magazine

CHRISTY WISE
Freelance Journalist and Chairwoman of the National Press Club Speakers Committee

DORIS MARGOLIS
President of Editorial Associates and the member of the National Press Club Speakers Committee who arranged today's luncheon

BJORN HANSEN
Norwegian Broadcasting

PAT MCGRATH
Fox Television

JACK CUSHMAN
New York Times

ROBERT DOUGHERTY
Reuters News Service

HAROLD STAR, JR.
Foreign Correspondent for the Lake Wobegone Harold Star

GIL KLEIN

MODERATOR

*g*ood afternoon. Welcome to the National Press Club. My name is Gil Klein, I'm the club's president and a national correspondent for Media General Newspapers, writing for the Richmond Times-Dispatch, the Tampa Tribune and the Winston-Salem Journal.

I'd like to welcome club members and their guests in the audience today, as well as those of you who are watching us on C-SPAN or listening to us on National Public Radio or the Internet global computer network.

Now today, we are honored to have Garrison Keillor, creator of public radio's "Prairie Home Companion" and one of the premier story tellers in America today. I've been a fan of Mr. Keillor for years—not quite as long as Sonya's mother, perhaps, but a long time. The problem was that his show would come on the radio while I was driving somewhere, and I'd want to keep listening to it even after I had arrived.

I would slow down, drive around the block a couple of times, then I'd just park and listen. But in my neighborhood in Arlington, if you spent a lot of time sitting in a parked car, people get suspicious. Oh look, they'll say, it's another CIA agent waiting for a pay-off. So I solved that problem by buying tapes of Mr. Keillor's performances, and now I can drive for hours on long trips with the kids in the back seat yelling, "Play the baseball song, Daddy! Play the front-porch song!"

After a few years of listening, you feel like you know Lake Wobegon and the people who live there. Take the three generations of the Krebsbachs and Myrtle, who are getting on in years, but they still enjoy fighting with each other. Florian once left Myrtle at the truck stop on the interstate heading for St. Cloud; and their son Carl, who sometimes wishes he wasn't so handy, because people are always calling him to have a look at something—and Carl's daughter, Carla, the beautiful homecoming queen, who could only be worshipped from afar by an unnamed, shy, gangling youth. *(Laughter.)*

It's that shy, gangling youth, of course, who created this little universe where you can get a cup of coffee from Darlene at the Chatterbox Cafe or stop by the Sidetrack for a beer and a bump with a Norwegian bachelor farmer.

A native of Anoka, Minnesota and a Graduate of the University of Minnesota, Mr. Keillor launched "A Prairie Home Companion" on Minnesota Public Radio in 1974. Thirteen years later he closed it and moved to New York City to begin a new show called "Garrison Keillor's American Radio Company."

But the name didn't stick, and he returned to his roots and brought back "A Prairie Home Companion." Now Mr. Keillor has come to the press club to announce he is not running for president in 1996. We in Washington know what that really means. The woods of New Hampshire are filled with politicians, mostly Republicans, who claim they are not running for president. So what do we know of Mr. Keillor's politics? Not much. We know he's a liberal, but then he's from Minnesota, so what do you expect? But I want to leave it to Mr. Keillor to explain his politics and why he has seen fit to come to Washington to announce his non-candidacy.

Ladies and gentlemen, please join me in a warm press club welcome for Mr. Garrison Keillor. *(Applause.)*

GARRISON KEILLOR

SPEAKER

hank you very much. Thank you very much, and it's so good to be able to get all of these Norwegians sitting up at the head table here. *(Laughter.)* Ordinarily, Norwegian people would naturally take a seat towards the rear of the room, and it's good to get them up here in the bright light. I want to begin by sending congratulations and love and best wishes to a fellow Minnesotan, Justice Harry A. Blackmun, after his announcement yesterday that he's stepping down from the Supreme Court, and to thank him for his years of service to our country.

I would love to be 85 years old some day if I could be 85 in the way that Mr. Justice Blackmun is 85, and we will miss him.

I'd like to thank you for inviting me today. Ordinarily, the National Press Club invites newsmakers to speak; men and women who, on account of the awesome power they wield, cannot speak in simple, declarative sentences for fear that it will unsettle the bond market. *(Laughter.)*

And then, once in a while, the press club invites people like myself, a humble journalist, like you, who's dedicated himself to telling the truth to the American people without fear or favor, no matter the personal cost. *(Laughter.)* Including the terrible truth that the press tries to keep from the American people, which is that the country is actually going along pretty well. *(Laughter.)* There is pain and danger and misery in America, and yet people still do get up in the morning and go to work; even in New York they do this.

It's the role of the press to scare us with stories about bears, and we enjoy this. We know that the roaring we hear outside the tent is not from bears, but it is from respected journalists crouched in the grass and hollering into culverts. *(Laughter.)* And so we get up in the morning and we go to work. America gets along pretty well.

I came up with this when I was in London for a couple of weeks in March, and I was explaining America to the British people, as I do, and that thought just sprang to my mind.

America gets along pretty well. You can learn a lot about America by explaining it to other people. *(Laughter.)*

Now before I go any further in my speech, and I did come here to talk about 1996 and my plans, I just want to say that the statement that I gave to U.S. Customs at Newark Airport when I returned to this country is a statement that I still stand by. *(Laughter.)* And that the total value of goods brought into this country by me at that time was $800, on which I paid a duty of $40, which is 10 percent of the amount over $400.

It's true that I estimated the value of those items on the plane as it was making its final descent. *(Laughter.)* And once I had claimed my baggage, I did not open it and check price tags and try to make an absolutely accurate appraisal, and perhaps in retrospect, I should have done that. *(Laughter.)* So I would say, in my own defense, that most of these items were gifts for friends and colleagues, and so the price tags had been removed. *(Laughter.)*

Nevertheless, I would be the first person here to say that that $800 was an estimate. It was my best estimate. But if the estimate should turn out to be low, I will pay the additional duty that would be required of me. Thank you very much. *(Applause.)*

As for the gifts, and I'm sure you're curious about them, it is true that one of the gifts went to a friend of mine who is a public employee at a state mental hospital in Minnesota. *(Laughter.)* And if that appears to be an inappropriate gift, I regret it. But, in my own mind, I was not looking for personal favors. *(Laughter.)* I have not patronized that hospital to the best of my knowledge at any time in the past 20 years.

Now, I was not going to come down here and talk about Whitewater, but then I thought that if I did not talk about Whitewater that you would assume that I know something about it. *(Laughter, applause.)*

The only way for me to prove that I don't know anything about it is to talk about it at great length. *(Laughter.)* And I'm willing to do that. It's been a quiet week in Whitewater. *(Laughter.)* This morning's New York Times was devoid of any news. It's hard to find the one item in the Washington Post. But there is surely more to come on this, because an audience is still waiting to hear.

With any shaggy dog story like this, whose point is its pointlessness, people become fascinated by the fact that they are still standing and listening to the story—*(laughter)*—though they don't know what it means. It's a long, winding, circumstantial joke, a shaggy-dog story, that the teller keeps complicating by tossing in new, unrelated elements. Characters keep coming in, and sudden, inexplicable events that one assumes must be related in some way, and the storyteller's voice then becomes hushed.

And we all lean forward, and now there are men with watermelons on their heads in this story, and there's buried treasure, and there's a naked lady on a horse, and there's a dog with very long hair whose name is Fred. And the dog's hair gets longer and longer, and the audience now realizes there is not going to be a punch line at all—*(laughter)*—and that the joke is that the teller has kept them hooked on an utterly inconsequential story. And then the shaggy dog speaks, and the dog says "Woof"—*(laughter)*—and that's the end.

The difference with Whitewater is that it is not going to end—*(laughter)*—and you are going to be writing about this for much longer than you really want to. The Whitewater story has run for months on the power of suggestion, things we don't know that may be true, and if they were true, then other things might be true as well. And it's now a story about itself and whether the press should be devoting so much time to this, and what does this say about politics, and would this story have gotten so big if it weren't that people distrusted the president anyway? And now this week the story dwindles a little bit as we are low on fresh facts. We just have scraps of stories about inconsistencies in statements about things that nobody ever suggested were wrong to begin with. But the American people are still sitting on the bleachers, under the tent, and we are waiting for the elephant to come out, and all we see are the guys selling cotton candy. These guys are you. *(Laughter, applause.)* This is a lousy way to run a scandal. *(Laughter.)*

In Britain they know how scandals ought to be done. Scandals should be big; they should be sudden; they should be fascinating; they should, if possible, involve sex; they should be on the front page for three days; and then they should be gone. *(Laughter.)* When an American goes to London, it is fun to open up the morning paper; you know there will be a prize in there for you. *(Laughter.)* There will be a story about a woman and her lover accused of trying to kill her husband with a lawn mower. *(Laughter.)* Yes. And there will be a story about a man who is on trial for assault for biting a woman twice on the right buttock in a bar where he was celebrating his engagement to a woman who was not the woman he bit. *(Laughter.)* You don't get news like this in America. *(Laughter.)* We never seem to get down and bite people on the buttock. There are any number of stories about shootings in barrooms, but you could read 10 of them and they wouldn't be nearly as interesting as this one buttock-biting incident.

The man was drunk, of course, he knelt down, he raised the woman's skirt, described in the story as short—*(laughter)*—and he bit through her pantyhose and left a mark and did it twice. *(Laughter.)* I don't know how we came to think of British people as a tasteful people. *(Laughter.)* Maybe because their grammar is so good.

There was a story about a conservative member of Parliament who was found naked and dead in his kitchen, an accidental death in the midst of a very unusual sexual act that you should never try except with adult supervision. *(Laughter.)* This was a typical British political scandal. It entertained millions of people for a few days at absolutely no public expense. There were no hearings, there was no special prosecutor, there were no tapes, no computer disks to be gone through, subpoenas, no mountains of financial records to sort through, just the fact that a politician who had always stood for old-fashioned family values evidently had a rich fantasy life as well. *(Laughter.)* It was all in the papers—in the better papers—in great detail for two days, and then it was over.

A scandal is a revelation of the humanity of famous people. Famous and powerful people can be amazingly human. A man can be a United States senator, knowledgeable about foreign policy, tax law and dozens of other things, and also be capable of lunging at a woman whom he barely knows and kissing her on the lips against her will, which is a pretty dumb thing to do. *(Laughter.)* And he can do this again and again over the years, grabbing women, hugging them, saying dumb things to them—a dreadful experience for the women, and they are right to expose him and it ought to be in the papers. But how much time should the U.S. Senate spend on this? How much attention does this deserve? How much should this man spend on legal counsel? A quarter of a million dollars? Should he spend a half a million dollars? And wouldn't it be better to simply say that any senator or congressman who lunges at a woman and kisses her against her will or grabs her should pay her $50,000? Just let it go at that. Skip the hearings, let it be in the paper for a couple of days. One more dumb thing done by somebody you didn't think would do it. Have him pay the money and we all go on to something else.

To hold Senator Packwood up as a pariah is not attractive or becoming. It only shows our self-righteousness, and we already know how self-righteous we are. *(Laughter.)*

Now I didn't come to discuss scandal, I came to discuss 1996 and the tremendous pressure that I've been under to consider a run for the presidency. But you seem to be interested in scandal, so let me continue. *(Laughter.)*

During the time that I was in London buying, to the best of my knowledge, about $800 worth of merchandise—*(laughter)*—the British defense chief of staff was on the front page of numerous newspapers. He had been photographed in front of the Dorchester Hotel kissing a former mistress of his named Lady Beanvinida Buck. He is 60 years old, and she is, according to her best estimate, 32. *(Laughter.)*

According to the story, she had been his mistress for a couple of years, though she was married to someone else, and he was married as well. And now she had received a quarter of a million dollars from one of the tabloids to lure the man to this rendezvous and to kiss him in a place where the light was good—*(laughter)*—and also to turn over his love letters to her, which the newspapers also printed. And the next day the chief of staff resigned, which is sort of a tradition in Britain.

So the British newspaper reader got to see the literary style of a 60-year-old man who had spent his life in the military, and he wrote a pretty good love letter. It made me wonder how many men on the Joint Chiefs of Staff would be capable of—*(laughter)*—doing this. He wrote a letter that began, "My darling, my little one, my love, you have maturity beyond your years, yet the body of a young girl. Your face is serene, your eyes piercing, your mouth enchanting, your back elegant, your hands so graceful, your skin so very fair and satin to touch, your breasts so petite, your legs so gazelle-like, your smell so overpoweringly intoxicating. How I long to hold you in my arms and to envelop you in kisses." Now this is the sort of scandal a person can enjoy. *(Laughter.)* A distinguished public servant who becomes infatuated with a younger woman who then betrays him for money, brings him down in disgrace, and who then says through her publicity man that she revealed this affair to the newspapers not for the quarter million dollars, but so that she could, quote, "put it behind her and get on with her life." *(Laughter.)* That's a story.

Scandal ought to have something operatic about it. *(Laughter.)* And futures trading is nothing that's particularly operatic compared to your eyes piercing, your mouth enchanting, your smell so overpoweringly intoxicating. Puccini could have set that to music. *(Laughter.)*

One thing that I've never seen anyone say in print in Mr. Clinton's first year, and so I'd like to say it today, is this: I like this President and I think most people in the country do.

He is a soulful man and he is remarkably cheerful and optimistic, and these are good qualities. He got himself elected without scaring people, and he enjoys his work. He likes politics, he likes being around his fellow Americans, and he loves to talk. It's amazing to have a president who can face any audience, large or small, without a script, and speak in sentences —(*laughter, applause*)—sometimes gracefully, about any subject whatsoever.

In my lifetime, presidents always have been pretty well guarded and managed, and you seldom saw them without a TelePrompTer or without notes in their hand. But here is one who can walk out and talk. A good thing in a democracy. (*Laughter.*)

This year, he has succeeded in moving so many wrenching public issues into the political arena, and he has done this with remarkable good humor. He's faced even this long, dreary story of Whitewater with about as much good humor as a person possibly could.

A democracy like ours needs a certain good humor to keep bumping along. Government as a profession tends to attract people who have a lot of time to kill—(*laughter*)—and the proceedings of government tend to be long and verbose. And a democracy, of course, always welcomes the people's complaints, and the people who do come and complain exaggerate their complaints in hopes of getting action. So there is a lot of grimness around in a democracy. And without some good humor, government would not be able to come to work in the morning.

A democracy is threatened by people's lack of faith in it. And when people lose faith in it because they would rather believe in conspiracies of powerful people manipulating the levers to thwart the will of the people, whether it be Wall Street, or Communist infiltrators, or liberal intellectuals or Arkansas vacation-home speculators, then democracy suffers from it.

Whereas the British relish a scandal in which the private life of the great is suddenly revealed in a burst of light, we prefer scandals about shadowy characters who are in cahoots with each other and flushed out finally through inspired detective work. But the truth is that ours is a pretty open and democratic society. The press was after this president for weeks to answer questions and when the president stood up to answer questions, he got questions like, "Who do you feel is responsible for this Whitewater story getting as big as it's gotten?" A dumb question. (*Laughter.*)

The person who tells a shaggy-dog story is responsible for that story. We're still waiting for the elephant to come out of the tent. The New York Times says there's an elephant in there. The Republicans say there is one. The Wall Street Journal. It hasn't come out yet.

A White House aide calling up somebody in the Treasury Department to ask and complain about a Republican being hired to look into the savings and loan out in Arkansas—that's not an elephant. (*Laughter.*) I'm still waiting to see the elephant. The president says he could do without the elephant, and he'd like the country to move on to something else. But I'd like to see the elephant. (*Laughter.*) And if the elephant doesn't come out pretty soon, I'd like to know why.

When scandal breaks and we get to see the humanity of the great and the powerful revealed, naked and dumb, in front of us, there's always a cry for new rules, or at least some new awareness that will prevent this from ever happening again.

We should be careful, though, not to make the world so fine and good that you and I can't enjoy living in it. A world in which there is no sexual harassment at all is a world in which there will not be any flirtation. A world without thieves at all will not have entrepreneurs. (*Laughter.*) A government in which there are no friendly connections or favors between politicians and powerful people would be the first in the history of mankind. (*Laughter.*) And a world without fiction, my friends, would be unbearable for all of us.

Thank you. (*Applause.*) Thank you. (*Laughter.*)

MR. KLEIN: You will notice, he did not categorically deny he was running in 1996. *(Laughter.)*

The first question is: What are they saying about Bill Clinton at the Chatterbox Cafe? Do they agree with you there? And do the people—what they say at the Chatterbox Cafe, differ at all from what they're saying at the Sidetrack?

MR. KEILLOR: Well, the people at the Chatterbox Cafe are, by and large, Scandinavian people. You have to keep that in mind. And so their view of other people—especially people far away whom they do not know, such as the president—tends to be dark. The Scandinavians take a dark view of human nature so that they will not ever be surprised by—*(laughter)*—anything that happens.

I would not care to trust my fate to the opinion of the people whom I find in the Chatterbox Cafe. *(Laughter.)* And I don't trust the president's fate to them either. You'd have to ask them what they think. *(Laughter.)*

MR. KLEIN: This questioner says: Since you prefer sex scandals, please give us your views on the stories quoting Arkansas state troopers about Mr. Clinton's affairs.

MR. KEILLOR: I saw a photograph of those state troopers in the newspaper. *(Laughter.)* They were both photographed in black and white, and I think I rest my case on the photograph. *(Laughter, applause.)*

Garrison Keillor and John Metelsky. October 20, 1987.

MR. KLEIN: There is a strong movement to relocate the nation's capital to Lake Wobegone. Are there any thoughts on how that would affect the country's future? *(Laughter.)*

MR. KEILLOR: *(Laughing.)* Well, they're not aware of this—*(laughter)*—strong movement at home, and they'll be seriously alarmed by it. One thing it would mean—if you moved the capital of our country to central Minnesota—is that for a long period of the year, when you had come to Washington, Minnesota, you would not be able to leave Washington, Minnesota. *(Laughter.)* And so, Congress would not be able to get off for weekends to meet with constituents and to go out and tell the truth to the American people. *(Laughter.)* The members of Congress would be pretty much stuck there in Washington, Minnesota, looking at each other over the weekend. I'm not sure if this would be good or bad.

Minnesota is a state, though, with a serious theology, and I think that would be good in government. We are a state where, three or four times in the course of a year, nature makes a serious attempt to kill us. *(Laughter.)* And so, I think we are less sanguine than people in Congress often seem to be, who seem to believe that someday, somebody's going to figure this out.

MR. KLEIN: You mentioned the theology in Minnesota, and you have the—Our Lady of Perpetual Responsibility and the Lake Wobegone Lutheran Church on the other side of the street. How do these people get along? Is there a chance this could break down like Yugoslavia at any time? *(Laughter.)*

MR. KEILLOR: No. I don't think so. We're not that well-armed, for one thing. *(Laughter.)* And the people who do bear arms in Lake Wobegone are not always in the condition to operate them. *(Laughter.)* We get along pretty well in Lake Wobegone, I think, on the basis of nearly complete misunderstanding of each other. *(Laughter.)* We look at people whose beliefs are basically different from ours, we look on them as being, really, beyond the pale. And so, we don't bother to try to win them over to our side. That's really where the big problems come in, in human relations, I think, is when we believe there's a chance for the other person to see the light. *(Laughter.)* That's where the problems come in.

But when you believe that the other person is dumber than dirt and—*(laughter)*—and hopelessly ignorant and not worth wasting your breath on, you get along with them pretty well. *(Laughter.)*

MR. KLEIN: Have the Lake Wobegone Whippets played their first game and, if so, who threw out the first ball?

MR. KEILLOR: This is just early April, and the Lake Wobegone Whippets don't even start thinking about training or getting in shape for about another six weeks. Their first game will be on Memorial Day weekend. I don't know why they choose this weekend, when we commemorate our valiant dead, to begin their season. But there's a long time yet. There are guys in the Sidetrack Tap who—they've got a long time to get into shape. *(Laughter.)*

MR. KLEIN: Can you please give a detailed of description of the Statue of the Unknown Norwegian? *(Laughter.)*

MR. KEILLOR: Well, the Statue of the Unknown Norwegian was constructed by the Sons of Knute Fraternal Lodge back in the—about 100 years—1870s, I believe—to commemorate the immigrants. The statue is called the Statue of the Unknown Norwegian because the man who modeled for the statue moved on West before anybody got his name. *(Laughter.)*

He was sculpted in marble in a heroic pose. He's pointing off to the West. And he is saying something heroic that, I believe, probably, if they hadn't spent all that money on that sculpture, they would have put an inscription on the base. *(Laughter.)* But they couldn't afford the base. So, we don't know what he's saying exactly. He looks as if—most of the year, he looks as if he is saying, "Onward toward yon setting sun, ye who have struggled so long for the dream, tire not, not weary, but pursue ever onward yon guiding star." *(Laughter, applause.)*

However, there is no base for this statue, so—*(laughter)*—he stands about the same height as the rest of us. *(Laughter.)* And so up close he doesn't look that heroic. When the Christmas tree is put up in the square there in front of him, he looks as if he's saying, "That's leaning a little bit to the left." *(Laughter.)* "Do you want to bring it back this way just a little?" *(Laughter.)*

We're fond of him. We grew up with him, and so we became so familiar with him that we didn't realize he exists. It's only when you move away from Lake Wobegone and stay away as long as I have that you are able to give this detailed description. *(Laughter.)* A person who is still living in Lake Wobegone couldn't tell you anything about the Statue of the Unknown Norwegian because they see it every day—two, three times a day. They're hardly aware that it's there. They might even be surprised to know it's in their midst. This is why writers leave home, so that you can have the necessity of remembering. Was that a complete sentence? I think that was a complete sentence. *(Laughter.)*

MR. KLEIN: Well, getting to leaving home, then—how did you like living in New York, and how would you compare it to living in Anoka?

MR. KEILLOR: Well, living in New York is something that a few ambitious people in Anoka dream of when they're 13 or 14 years old. I wanted something to happen to me when I was 13 or 14. I wanted the car to come along and pick me up and take me off where I imagined life was being lived with fervor and passion, by people who were not afraid to look foolish. New York is that sort of a place. *(Laughter.)*

And from the time I first saw it, when my father took me out there as a little boy, I was fascinated by it. Other people I grew up with preferred quiet and stately places—the deserts and the ocean—or they became sailors, or they wanted to move to remote rural areas. I never did. I like to live in a place where I'm safe, but when I'm tired of being safe, I can get to dangerous places in a hurry—*(laughter)*—and get down on the street and hear people yelling at each other and people exposing their lives, all within just a few blocks—and I live in a good neighborhood. There are other places where it's even more dramatic than that.

I'm very fond of New York. Of course, I moved there as a privileged person. I should say that, being a truthful journalist. And I had plenty of money when I moved there, and that's different. And I was in my late 40s, and I was a little bit too old to get into the sorts of trouble that I would have been anxious to get into when I was 14. *(Laughter.)* But still I enjoy it.

There are mornings in New York—I think of October, when the city is golden and suffused with light, when you wake up in the morning and shower and shave and eat your bagel and leave the house and you walk down to the subway and you head down the stairs and your steps quicken as you head down. About once or twice a year, you come onto that subway platform just as the train is pulling up and the doors are opening, and everything that you've done in your life up to that point seems exactly right and to have taken exactly the right amount of time for you to catch that train. It's for moments like that that a romantic person like myself lives. *(Laughter.)* And I'm well able to ignore all the rest of it.

MR. KLEIN: This just in from the Reverend Dabney over here, who, I think, is writing a book about the gospel according to Garrison Keillor. How important is that Minnesota theology or other regional theological variance to the way America is doing pretty well?

MR. KEILLOR: What was the question? How important is that Minnesota theology to the way America is going pretty well? Oh, I don't think so important. I know that other people around the country look on Minnesota as being crucial to the life of this country and being a source of wisdom. But we in Minnesota, we don't feel that way at all. We modestly take our place up there at the top and middle of America, defending the border against Canada. *(Laughter.)* And we just take it as it comes. No, I just can't assign too much importance to Minnesota or Minnesotans, not here in front of this audience. *(Laughter.)*

MR. KLEIN: This questioner wants to know what is the secret of the culinary success of the Cafe Boeuf?

MR. KEILLOR: Well, the secret of cooking at the Cafe Boeuf is the secret of—my secret as a cook and a lot of other people. First of all is cooking slow so that you have a chance to change direction. *(Laughter.)* And the other secret is cooking things that are really much simpler than the uninitiated realize. There are some things—puff pastry and souffles and so on—that I just won't touch because it's really hazardous to get into it. It'd be like singing opera. You really are exposing yourself to risk. But there are a lot of other dishes that the cook likes to do in private because they're really slick and simple.

Do I have time to share these recipes? No. *(Laughter.)*

MR. KLEIN: Is there such a thing as a Minnesota accent?

MR. KEILLOR: Yes, there is. There is. I've lost it because I wanted to. From the time I got into radio when I was 18, I wanted my listeners in Minnesota to think that I was from someplace else. I thought they would give me more credence if they believed that. I wanted them to believe—for a long time wanted them to believe that if I was not actually from the United Kingdom, that perhaps I was descended from people who were. *(Laughter.)* My descendants, however, left England in the latter part of the 18th century, so it was a long time.

Yes, there is a Minnesota accent. I could do it for you, but I would embarrass the Minnesotans who are sitting up here at the head table. *(Laughter.)*

MR. KLEIN: What would you do if you were editor of The New Yorker, assuming you would want the job?

MR. KEILLOR: Who sent this question up? *(Laughter.)*

MR. KLEIN: There's also a P.S.: "If you're not busy April 23rd and happen to be in Toledo, why not come to my wedding?" And there's no name. *(Laughter.)*

MR. KEILLOR: Is Mr. Newhouse here in the—*(laughter)*. I don't want to consider a hypothetical job offer. It just isn't good. If they want me to come and edit The New Yorker, I'm ready. And I'll be getting on a plane anyway this afternoon, so I can be up there towards the end of the day. But I don't want to show my hand too early. *(Laughter.)*

MR. KLEIN: What do you think of Hillary Clinton and her expanded role as first lady?

MR. KEILLOR: Well, her expanded role seems to have contracted very suddenly here—*(laughter)*—in the last month or two. And she's been rather secretive. I think an awful lot of her, and I wish her the very best. I was sorry to see her interview in People magazine the other day in which I had a feeling that the first lady succumbed to a kind of self-pity that's a real hazard, I think, for people in public life. She'll regret that. She'll regret that. She's really very lucky. And I hope that she feels lucky again soon. She should, because she is lucky. She's bright and full of idealism and enthusiasm and she's married to a soulful guy. *(Laughter.)*

MR. KLEIN: A lot of people want to know things about the show, of course, like how did you happen to create the "Prairie Home Companion"? And tell us about Tom Keefe. And does he really know how to speak French? And every program is so perfect. How long do you and your cast rehearse?

MR. KEILLOR: That's a lot of questions, but I'm going to answer each of them in tremendous detail. And I'm not going to withhold a single salient fact from you here, if we have to stay the afternoon. *(Laughter.)*

I created "Prairie Home Companion" as a way to avoid work—*(laughter)*—is the plain truth. I had been working for Minnesota Public Radio and doing a show that began at 6:00 in the morning and it went until noon. And as part of this, I had to do the news. I had to do all manner of things. And I worked out this other deal where I did one show on Saturdays and it was only an hour and a half to start. Now I'm doing two hours so I'm getting half an hour of overtime. *(Laughter.)* And it was on once a week, and they paid me more money to do this. This is a great deal, and I recommend this to you.

How and when did I meet Tom Keefe? He was a guy who was working in radio with me when we got up early in the morning and did the news and read the sports scores and advertised lost dogs and gave out recipes for oatmeal cookies. And then after I got this good deal, a part-time job that paid really well, I, of course, got him a place on my show where he plays a number of roles. He does the voices of all our animals, including cats and dogs and elk—*(laughter)*—a very difficult sound effect which I taught him myself. *(Laughter.)* Elk make a sound that is something like this. *(Mimics the sound of an elk call.)* I taught him that. *(Laughter.)* And that is also the sound made by moose and by wapiti. And elands, I believe, make a similar sound.

Does he really know how to speak French? He only knows how to speak French to people who don't speak French. *(Laughter.)* And to us, he speaks great French, really better than the original. *(Laughter.)*

How long does the cast of the show rehearse? We rehearse on Friday night. Today is Thursday. I go back up to New York. I start writing tonight and I write tomorrow morning and we rehearse it on Friday evening and then we do the show on Saturday. That is not a bad deal. That is a two-and-a-half-day-a-week job. And that's the secret of the good life, ladies and gentlemen—is a short work week. *(Laughter, applause.)*

MR. KLEIN: Well, we're almost out of time. Just a reminder that audio and videotapes and transcripts can be had by calling 1-800-500-9911. But first I'd like to present you with a National Press Club mug, which now you've been here three times so you've got three of them. We made this one blue so it would not be a matched set. There you go.

MR. KEILLOR: It works.

MR. KLEIN: And, of course, a certificate of appreciation for appearing here.

Well, let's see. There are a lot of good last questions here. There's one; they want me to ask about the red socks you're wearing, but I don't know. They're wonderful red socks. Maybe I can ask you about Guy's shoes. Are you wearing Guy's shoes? But why didn't Disney America—or should Disney America, instead of coming to Virginia—should they not move to Lake Wobegon? And is not that the real America? *(Laughter.)*

MR. KEILLOR: We'd much rather they stayed here. *(Laughter.)* And I believe that the American people would want Disney America to be in a convenient place where, having stopped in Washington to see the Smithsonian and be photographed on the steps of the Capitol with their congressman or congresswoman, they could then go off and take gondola rides through Civil War scenes—*(laughter)*—and see animated figures of American presidents speaking. I think it's just—they go together.

To put it in Lake Wobegon or Minnesota would be an inconvenience to the American people, and I am opposed to anything that would be an inconvenience for the American people. *(Laughter, applause.)*

MR. KLEIN: Thank you very much.

Thank you very much, Mr. Keillor. That was excellent. I'm sure everybody here will take your message to heart and go and write nice things about Bill Clinton this afternoon. *(Laughter.)* But I wouldn't bet on it.

Thank you all for coming. *(Applause.)*

NATIONAL PRESS CLUB

LUNCHEON
October 12, 1994

$\mathscr{S}$PEAKER

RALPH E. REED
Executive Director of the Christian Coalition

MODERATED BY: Gil Klein

Head Table Guests

Derrick DePledge
Copley News Service

Gill Tucker
Agence-France Press

Patricia Griffith
Washington Bureau Chief of the Pittsburgh Post Gazette

Alex Johnson
Knight-Ridder/Tribune News Service

Heidi Scanlon
Director of Government Affairs for the Christian Coalition

John Mulligan
Providence Journal

Jo Anne Reed
Wife of our Speaker

Rosemary Goudreau
*Assistant News Editor of Knight-Ridder and the member of the National Press Club
Speakers Committee who arranged today's luncheon*

Marshall Wittmann
Director of Legislative Affairs for the Christian Coalition

Sylvia Smith
Fort Wayne Journal-Gazette

W.C. Clough
UPI Radio

Julia Leiblich
Newshouse News Service

William Hershey
Akron Beacon Journal

Rachel Jones
Knight-Ridder Newspapers

GIL KLEIN

MODERATOR

ood afternoon. Welcome to the National Press Club. My name is Gil Klein. I'm the club's president and a national correspondent with Media General Newspapers, writing for the Richmond Times-Dispatch, the Tampa Tribune, and the Winston-Salem Journal.

I'd like to welcome my fellow club members in the audience today, as well as those of you who are watching us on C-SPAN or listening to us on National Public Radio or the Internet global computer network.

Now today, we are pleased to have with us Mr. Ralph Reed, the director of the Christian Coalition. Since its founding five years ago with the mailing list from evangelist Pat Robertson's presidential campaign, the Christian Coalition has grown to a political force that has drawn the ire of the Democratic Party and the supplication of just about every possible Republican presidential candidate.

The Coalition now claims a million members, organized in 872 local chapters in all 50 states. It has full-time staff in 20 states and an annual budget of about $20 million.

All of this is being organized by this cherubic-looking fellow on my right. *(Laughter.)* A graduate of the University of Georgia, with a Ph.D in history from Emory University, Mr. Reed has been immersed in politics practically from the cradle. He worked on his first congressional campaign when he was 15. Before he graduated from college, he was director of the College Republican National Committee, where he supervised a network of 100,000 members on 1,000 campuses.

He allied himself with Pat Robertson in 1989 to create the Christian Coalition. "What Christians have to do," he told the Religious News Service, in 1990, "is take back this country one precinct at a time, one neighborhood at a time, one state at a time. I honestly believe that, in my lifetime, we will see a country once again governed by Christians and Christian values." And that's pretty much what he's doing.

The Coalition reportedly controls or dominates nearly 20 state Republican parties, and has delivered the decisive vote in several off-year elections. At a recent national convention here in Washington, the Coalition attracted Dan Quayle, Phil Gramm, Elizabeth Dole, speaking for her husband, Bob, and Dick Cheney. The next time that crowd gets together might be in New Hampshire. *(Laughter.)*

Critics say the Christian Coalition is attempting to impose its religious dogma on a country that is founded on the principle of separation of church and state. They paint the Coalition as a highly motivated group of right-wing extremists. But opinion polls find Americans now are deeply concerned about decay in moral values. Political analysts say the party that addresses that concern will be the winner this year and in 1996.

Says Mr. Reed: "We're going to sweep from one side of this country to the other like a tsunami." Ladies and gentlemen, please join me in a warm press club welcome for Mr. Ralph Reed. *(Applause.)*

RALPH E. REED

hank you very much. Thank you, Gil, for that generous introduction. I only wish that we were having half the impact that you credit us with. I understand that today you are looking forward to an address by one of America's brightest young political operatives, who may play a role in the selection of the next President of the United States. But unfortunately George Stephanopoulos couldn't be here today, so I have agreed to fill in for him.

Anyone who is, as I am, engaged in the rough and tumble of American politics understands and has reflected upon the wisdom of our founders in granting freedom of the press and of speech, just as they did to freedom of religious expression. It is no exaggeration to say that the First Amendment to our Constitution, which was as you know, really an afterthought by the founders—it was really only included as a condition of ratification by Virginia and New York—which made it possible for the Constitution to be ratified—it was not in the original document—contains the two twin pillars of American democracy: on the one hand freedom of religious expression, which gives liberty to our spiritual lives, and on the other hand freedom of speech and the press, which gives liberty to our intellectual life and the life of our conscience.

The movement that I represent, the pro-family movement, is involved in a dialogue with you in the press, with the American people, about who we are, about what we really believe, and about what we want for this nation.

So, as part of that ongoing dialogue, it is a distinct pleasure for me to be here in this, one of the most prestigious citadels of American democracy.

In 27 days, the American people will go to the polls in what is almost certain to be one of the most consequential elections, not only of our lifetimes, but of the post-World War II American period. Twenty-seven days is an eternity in American politics, and it's far too early to make any predictions about the outcome of that election. But one thing I believe is certain, and that is that the religious conservatives that we represent are going to play a major role in these elections, and in American politics for years to come. So it behooves us not to stereotype them, marginalize them, or attempt to demonize their leaders. It is our responsibility to understand them, what caused them to get involved in politics, and what kind of America they believe in.

We know from extensive surveys that this is one of the largest voting blocs in the entire electorate, maybe the largest. VRS exit polls conducted in 1992 found that one out of every four voters personally identified to a conversion experience and testified that they went to church four times or more a month. In fact, a recent poll by Newsweek magazine found that the number may be as high as 31 percent, almost one out of every three voters that will darken the threshold of a voting booth 27 days from now will be a religious conservative.

We know that, contrary to stereotype, it is not a male-dominated movement; it is 62 percent women and 38 percent male. Indeed, according to the Newsweek poll, it is 68 percent female and only 32 percent male. And, by the way, half of those women work outside the home. Also contrary to stereotype, they are not poor, uneducated and easy to command. *(Laughter, applause.)* Sixty-six percent of them have either attended or graduated from college.

Fourteen percent have advanced professional or graduate degrees; that, by the way, is 3 percent higher than the general population.

In terms of party affiliation, a little less than half are Republicans, between a third and 40 percent are Democrats, and the rest are independents. Seventy-six percent are married, 66 percent have children, two-thirds are Protestant, a little more than a third are Catholic, or Greek Orthodox, or Jewish. And they are well-educated, middle-class baby boomers who are concerned primarily about the education, the health, the nurture and safety of their families.

We at the Christian Coalition believe that any group of voters that large and that diverse deserves a voice in our government that is commensurate with their numbers. And that is why the Christian Coalition, in the coming weeks, will distribute 33 million non-partisan voter guides. It is the largest voter education and get-out-the-vote effort in the history of our organization. We will do this not in order to endorse any candidate or political party, but so that voters can have the information that they richly deserve so that they can cast an intelligent and informed ballot on November the 8th.

The voter guides will tell where every candidate at every level of government stands on the key issues affecting our nation: crime and drugs, spending and taxes, education, term limits, abortion, and health care. They will be distributed wherever voters are to be found: in shopping centers and churches, in synagogues and in union halls, and at polling locations on Election Day. They will be given to any voter of both political parties and of all faiths who request it.

Between now and Election Day, we will continue to advance the issues that we care about, endeavoring to do so with grace, with dignity, and with respect for our opponents.

But we will not judge our success based on the outcome of those elections, because, ladies and gentlemen, there is an issue that is far more transcendent and profound in America today than the fortune of any single candidate or political party. That issue is the outcome of a debate about the role that religion should play in our public life and the role that religious people and religious values should have in influencing government policy.

There are, on the one hand, very optimistic signs. There seems to be an emerging consensus in America about the need for time-honored values in both our private and public lives. Nesting baby boomers are returning to the churches and the synagogues of their youth to find meaning for their lives and spiritual anchors for their children. Cable television has become an electronic bazaar, buzzing with the competing gospels of religious broadcasters and new age psychics.

Newsweek Magazine recently put Jesus on its cover. And in a remarkable cover story in April of this year, U.S. News & World Report found that 57 percent of the American people say that they pray every single day. That number, by the way, has been on the rise since Bill Clinton took the oath of office in January of 1994 *(sic)*. *(Laughter.)*

That same cover story found that 80 percent of the American people believe that the Bible is the infallible word of God. U.S. News concluded that the United States, apart from Israel, is the most religious nation in the history of the world.

You know, Winston Churchill once said, "The American people always do the right thing, after they have exhausted every other possibility." *(Laughter.)* And after the sexual revolution of the '60s, the cultural narcissism of the '70s, and the self-indulgent acquisitiveness of the '80s, the American people are clearly turning inward and upward to fill what Pascal called the God-shaped vacuum that is in every person's soul.

And this rediscovery of time-honored values is affecting our politics as well, I think in a positive way. A former vice president once ridiculed and lampooned and made the butt of jokes for warning America about the dangers of family breakup is now honored by a head-line on the cover of one of our most respected magazines with the provocative headline "Dan Quayle Was Right." Where once it was shock-jock Howard Stern and Roseanne Barr at the top of our best-seller list, today it is Bill Bennett and his "Book of Virtues" with over 2.1 million copies sold and still selling.

Jim Sasser of Tennessee, who is seeking to succeed George Mitchell as the Democratic leader in the U.S. Senate, used the first commercial of his campaign for re-election this year not to talk about where he stood on an economic issue or where he stood on a fiscal issue, but to reinvigorate and to make a commitment that he would vote for voluntary prayer in schools. Where once a Democratic candidate for president said, and I quote, "I'm sick and tired of politicians preaching to us about family values," that same Democrat today, President Bill Clinton, recently went to an audience in New Orleans and called for a return to morality and for a renewal of faith in God.

Yes, ladies and gentlemen, Americans are seeking once again to build personal as well as public lives that are enriched by faith and informed by values. And accompanying that search is a new appreciation for a very old public wisdom. That wisdom was summed up a century and a half ago by Alexis de Tocqueville, the great French observer, who I think was the best observer of the American character in history. And he came to this country, and as he put it, "Despotism may be able to do without faith in God, but democracy most assuredly cannot." He also said, and I quote, "America is great because America is good, and if America ever ceases to be good, she will cease to be great."

It is that aspect of the American character that Czech President Vaclav Havel was talk-ing about this past Fourth of July when he spoke at Independence Hall in Philadelphia and said, "Men and women can realize liberty only if they do not forget the one who endowed them with it."

My friends, it wasn't only Dan Quayle who was right—de Tocqueville and Havel are right. Religious values are not a threat to democracy, they are essential to democracy. Faith in God isn't what's wrong with America, it's what is right with America. And yet even as the American people are seeking to find those spiritual roots for their lives, as they always have, a strange hostility and scowling intolerance sometimes greets them when they bring those religious beliefs into the public square.

As Yale professor Steven Carter recently concluded in his book, *The Culture of Disbelief*, "We've created a political and legal culture that forces the religiously faithful to be something other than themselves, to act publicly and sometimes even privately as though their faith sim-ply doesn't matter to them. The result is a discomfort and a disdain for religion in our pub-lic life that sometimes curdles into intolerance."

Consider just the following: In Massachusetts this past month, an incumbent United States senator attacked his opponent not because of his voting record, not because of where he stood on the issues, but because he was once an elder in his church. How bitterly ironic, given who that senator was.

In South Carolina, a candidate for attorney general attacked another candidate, who hap-pened to be an evangelical, by saying, quote, "Your only qualifications for office are that you speak fluently in tongues and handle snakes." And a Washington columnist recently referred to politically active evangelicals and Roman Catholics as quote, "The American equivalent of Shi'ite Muslims," managing in a single breath to not only offend 40 million Americans, but 100 million Muslims around the world. *(Laughter.)*

And then there is Surgeon General Joycelyn Elders. She has become a symbol of this administration's insensitivity to religious values and religious people. She is the highest ranking medical officer in the United States, and yet she has used her bully pulpit of that office to do something that, as I understand it, has never been done before, and that's attack people because of their religious beliefs. She said in a speech in New York City that politically active people of faith were quote, "Un-Christian people who were selling out our children in the name of religion."

You know, the last time our nation confronted the so-called religion issue, it was when John F. Kennedy went to the Houston Ministerial Association on September 12, 1960, exactly 34 years and one month ago today. And he said in that speech, "If 40 million Americans have lost their chance to be president on the day they were baptized, then our whole nation is the loser, not only in the eyes of history, but in the eyes of our own people." He also said, and I am quoting, "The issue in this campaign isn't what kind of church I believe in, for that should matter only to me. It should be what kind of America I believe in."

Now, religious conservatives have to answer that same question. So let me describe the kind of nation that we believe in. We believe in a nation that is not officially Christian, Jewish or Muslim. We believe in a separation of church and state that is complete and inviolable. We believe in a nation in which any person may run for any office without having to worry that where they go to church or synagogue will become an issue in their campaign. We believe that there should be no religious test, implicit or explicit, for any office of public trust at any level of government.

We believe this not simply because the state needs protection from the church, but even more importantly, because the church needs to be protected from the state. I do not believe that the God that I serve is so feeble or insecure that he requires the agency of the government to win his converts or accomplish his purposes. Nor do I want to turn over the sacred tablets of my faith to the same government that has given us the Keating Five, the House Post Office scandal and hasn't been able to balance its budget since I was born.

We believe in a nation of safe neighborhoods, strong families, schools that work, a smaller government limited in its functions, lower taxes and in citizen legislators that rotate in and out of office and return back to the communities from whence they came so they can live under the laws that they've been passing for everyone else.

We believe in an America where every citizen is judged based on the content of their character and not based on their gender, their race, their religion or their ethnic background. We believe in an America where parents can send children to the school of their choice, the best school for their children, whether it be public, private or parochial, and be fully confident that that child is learning how to read and how to write, that that child is safe, and that that child is going to be able to master the disciplines of math, and science, and history and geography, far beyond their counterparts around the world.

I want to live in a nation in which I can send my five-and-a-half-year-old daughter to a playground three blocks from my home and not worry whether she's going to come back alive or not. We want to live in a nation in which more marriages succeed than fail, in which more children are born in wedlock than outside of it, and where children are counted both by families and by government as a blessing rather than a burden.

This is the kind of America we believe in. This is the kind of America we seek, not only for us but for our fellow citizens. It is a vision of an expansive future, not an intolerant past.

You know, I'm a little reluctant to use military metaphors to describe our movement. It's gotten me into a little trouble in the past. But I have found in the self-description of another religious movement, also criticized for bringing its moral beliefs into the public square, the embodiment of our hope for America.

It was, in the words of its leader, a special army. It was an army with no supplies but its sincerity, no uniform but its determination, no arsenal except its faith, no weapon except its conscience. It was an army that would move but not maul. It was an army that would flank but not falter. It was an army that would sing but not slay. It was an army whose allegiance was to God and whose strategy and intelligence were the eloquently simple dictates of conscience.

Those were the words that Martin Luther King used to describe his movement of conscience that forever transformed this nation. We can never know the violence, the indignity and the suffering that he and his movement knew. But in our own time, we have reluctantly entered the political arena based on a sense of what we believe to be right and wrong, animated by faith, motivated by conscience and seeking to impart dignity and life to a society that has grown increasingly callous and course.

We also understand, and this is important, that our vision for America, the vision that I've described, is not going to be achieved primarily or principally through political action. It must be achieved through how we live our lives, how we live privately as well as publicly. That is why, if you want to understand our movement, you must not simply cover our political activity or our political organizations, you must go into our churches, into our synagogues and into our homes. And you must see these decent people doing the things that they have always done, unheralded and unproclaimed, working in homes for unwed mothers, at crisis pregnancy centers, in prisons and in jails, teaching the illiterate how to read, in homeless shelters, in inner-city schools and in hospitals caring for the hurting and binding up the wounds of the brokenhearted. That is the work of faith.

As Emerson once said, "What we are is more important than what we say."

As I say in my new book, "Politically Incorrect," when Christ went into a village during his earthly ministry, he always met the needs of the people first. If they were blind, they saw. If they were lame, they walked. If they were hungry, they ate. If they were thirsty, they drank. If they were deaf, they heard. He met their needs first and preached later, and that made all the difference.

His life must be our model. We must seek not to dominate but to participate. Our goal must not be power, but protection of our homes, of our families and of the liberty that we all cherish. And we must seek to serve and not to rule.

The spark of our movement, the reason why we're involved is not because we seek power, but because, as an essentially religious, and private, and conservative people, we have reached the conclusion that we can no longer afford not to be involved in politics.

Why is that? It's because for 30 years government has waged war on social pathology. And my friends, the social pathologies are winning. We live in a nation in which one out of every three children born is born out of wedlock, and that number continues to rise. We have tens of millions of children in this country that do not have a father—that may not know anyone who has a father.

We live in a nation in which one out of every two marriages ends in divorce. We have the lowest rate of family formation of any nation in the Western industrialized world. We live in a nation in which one out of every three pregnancies ends in abortion, one of the most common surgical procedures in America. There are 30 million children since 1973 that will never know what it means to be held, to be loved, to be wanted, to be nurtured. That is an incomprehensible tragedy for all of us.

We live in a nation in which one out of every four high school students who walks across a graduation stage can't read the diploma that they were just handed. And in this city, our nation's capital, an African-American male under the age of 35 has a higher likelihood of being killed than an American soldier did in Vietnam.

You know, I have a friend of mine who teaches kindergarten at a school in inner-city Washington. This past year, six of her students—these are five-year-olds—have either been shot or they've witnessed the shootings of family members. She had one little boy who spent month after month in the hospital recovering from a gunshot wound, only to come out of a hospital and see a family member shot to death before their eyes.

She had a five-year-old who stole everything that he could get his hands on. Frequently, it was food. She learned that this crack-addicted family, this child's parents, did not feed him as he was growing up because they spent all their money on drugs. Imagine that—a five-year-old growing up learning to steal so he could eat.

And yet gazing out over that unchartable social chaos, there are still some people who honestly insist that the most dangerous thing that could happen in America today is for people with faith in God and moral values to get involved in our politics. My friends, I don't think we need less people with religious beliefs involved in our politics, I think we need more of both parties and all faiths.

One final thought. We are a growing movement. In the long train of history, 50, 60, 70 years, remember that the NAACP was founded in 1909; you didn't get the Civil Rights Act until 1964. This is going to be a long movement. It's going to take not a decade but a lifetime, and maybe beyond. And in that long train of history, we are still in relative adolescence. We have much to learn. We have much yet to communicate about who we really are and what we really believe. We don't have all the answers, nor should we lay claim to them.

It was Edmund Burke who once said, "Our patience will achieve more than our force." Ours is a movement, I believe, of decent and honorable men and women who are the backbone of this country and who are the social fabric of this country. But even we must admit that not all who share our faith have acted with our decency. When doctors who perform abortions are slain at the hands of disturbed and demented men claiming to act in the name of God, not only does our movement suffer but this entire nation suffers. And I wholeheartedly agreed with the U.S. Catholic bishops when they said, "To kill in the name of pro-life makes a mockery of the pro-life cause."

When a group of Christian leaders distributes a pamphlet which says that to vote for Bill Clinton is to sin against God, they are guilty not only of bad theology, but a manner of speech that I don't think is consistent with the democratic spirit of fairness.

When a prominent minister claimed some years ago that God doesn't hear the prayers of Jews, he raised the ugly specter of anti-Semitism that has no place whatsoever in our public life. We do not identify with these statements or actions, and we will avail ourselves of every opportunity to say so.

At the risk of stating the obvious, let me just simply observe that we are no different than any other social movement. We have elements that do not speak for us, nor we for them. But these individuals that I have mentioned do not represent the mainstream, pro-family movement any more than the terrorism practiced by the Black Panthers represented the mainstream civil rights movement in the 1960s. And the fact that a few, 30 years ago, carried their rage to violent excess in no way signaled the moral bankruptcy of the crusade for a color-blind society.

We live in exciting and challenging times. We live in difficult times. But no matter how difficult they seem, they in no way compare to the Civil War, when our nation was nearly torn asunder and when our experiment in self-government almost perished from the face of the Earth. At a particularly pivotal time in that war, just before the battle of Gettysburg, as brother faced brother across a thousand bloody battlefields, a clergyman, seeking to encourage Abraham Lincoln, sent him a letter and assured him, "God is on our side."

Lincoln replied as only he could. "I know that the Lord is always on the side of right," he said, "but it is my constant anxiety and prayer that I and this nation should be on the Lord's side, and not the other way around."

Lincoln's prayer must become our prayer, to be found on His side, not only in what we say but in how we say it, not only in public but in private, not only in word but in deed, not only in what we stand against but, even more importantly, what we stand for, not only in who we are but in what we seek to become as a people. If Lincoln's motto becomes our motto, and if his prayer becomes our prayer, and that is our goal at the Christian Coalition, then with God's help we can heal our land and we can restore this nation to greatness.

Thank you very much, and God bless you. *(Applause.)*

MR. KLEIN: Thank you very much, Mr. Reed.

MR. REED: Thank you, Gil.

MR. KLEIN: We have an awful lot of good questions coming up here, and I'll start with this one. From your remarks, it sounds like you have removed Christian from your Coalition. You talked about people running without—without their—excuse me here. You were talking about people running without having their religion being part of the test. Are you repudiating the statement that I read in the introduction, that you envisioned a nation run by Christians and Christian ideals?

MR. REED: We believe that no candidate should be judged or measured based on their personal spiritual belief. We think that's a matter of their private life. We think they should be judged on their voting record and their stands on the issues.

You know, I guess it was Martin Luther who said, "I would rather be operated on by a Turkish surgeon than a Christian butcher." *(Laughter.)* And what we're looking for is people in office who are qualified and capable.

With regard to that remark, I have to be honest with you, Gil, I've seen that quote that you cited, quoted in some publications by People For the American Way, but I don't know that I ever made that statement. It does not accurately reflect my views.

Let me say this, though, with regard to organizations like the Christian Coalition. We're not running for office. We're not candidates. And that's where I make the distinction. But I don't think we want to get into a situation where we say to American citizens, whether they be liberal or conservative, that you can no longer identify yourself in the public sphere based on your personal religious beliefs.

Let's remember that Martin Luther King called his organization "The Southern Christian Leadership Conference," and that was not an accident. He did that because he wanted to make it clear that, unlike some in the civil rights movement who were arguing against integration and who were arguing against desegregation, he wanted people to know that his movement was animated by Christian values and Christian beliefs, things like mercy and justice and love for fellow man, even those who mistreated him.

I also think that organizations like the American Jewish Congress, organizations like the Catholic Campaign for America, ought to be able to identify themselves based on who they are, based on their personal faith. I think that's part of the American tradition. I think it's one of the proudest traditions in our history, and we believe that we're part of that tradition. *(Applause.)*

MR. KLEIN: This questioner says, "I am a secular journalist, but, more important, an Evangelical who believe's in the authority of the Bible. I find the Bible pays much more attention to poverty, injustice, oppression, than to anti-abortion and gay rights. This seems the opposite of the Christian right's position. Why is that?"

MR. REED: Well, I don't think that's really accurate. And, as I said in my remarks, I think that all too often, and this may be as much our fault as some in the press, we focus only upon the political activity of these Americans who are animated by their faith. Right now, for example, Pat Robertson and the Christian Broadcasting Network is taking an L-1011 aircraft and at enormous expense, outfitting it as a fully mobile hospital with 70 surgeons that can go anywhere in the world, even places where there's no electricity or water, and perform surgery on people who are hundreds and even thousands of miles away from the nearest hospital.

My understanding is that, some time in December, that airplane is going to go to Zaire, and it's going to be there as a mobile hospital, operating on and caring for people in Rwanda and Zaire who are starving to death and who are dying from lack of medical attention. You never see a news report about those kinds of things that people of faith are engaged in. You often only hear about the political activity.

Another example is the Roman Catholic Church. About the only time you read about the Catholic Church is when there is a reference to their opposition to abortion, which I believe is a principled position based on the sanctity of human life and based on their notion of human rights, which I agree with. But in addition to that, the Catholic Church also operates the largest privately operated system of hospitals in the entire world. There are parts of the Third World that you can go to where the only hospital in that area is a Roman Catholic hospital, often subsidizing the care for the poor, the down-trodden and the needy.

We probably need to do more to talk about the things that we're doing in those areas, to do something about poverty and sickness and illiteracy. But I also think that there is a burden on the part of the journalistic community to seek those stories out and to report on them because they are going on.

MR. KLEIN: This questioner says, "Some people think family values has become little more than a sound bite for conservative politicians." They want to know more about how exactly do you propose we reduce the number of unwed mothers, how exactly do you propose restoring our inner cities?

MR. REED: Well, I think we have to do a number of things. I mean, number one, I think we've got to dramatically and totally reform welfare. And I think we need to do that by discouraging incentives to bear children out of wedlock. You know, we know from a vast body of social scientific evidence that there are three things that someone has to do if they're going to emerge from poverty. Number one, they have to get a high school diploma; number two, they have to not bear children out of wedlock, they have to wait until they're married before they have children; and number three, they have to get a job and keep it. If they do those three things, they have an 80 percent chance of not living in poverty.

Every one of those things that I just described, we discourage as a matter of government policy. And we subsidize the pathologies that we know have a tremendous likelihood of driving people into poverty. You only receive a subsidy from the government if you engage in three activities and forms of lifestyles simultaneously. Number one, don't get a job. Number two, don't get married. And number three, bear children repeatedly out of wedlock and you will receive a subsidy. That, we believe, is one of the reasons why the illegitimacy rate for African-American babies has gone from 22 to 67 percent since 1960, and why the white illegitimacy rate has gone from 5 to almost 25 percent, and continuing to rise. We have a permanent government subsidized underclass in America.

The second thing that we think we need to do is we need to start going after deadbeat dads. We have over $10 billion in back child support owed to women and children who have been abandoned. And I think we're going to have to look at some way to reform the laws so that if a man bears a child or sires a child, that man is held responsible for that child and the wife that he abandoned.

The third thing that we favor, that we think will do a lot for the inner city and for the poor—in fact, it will do far more for them than it will do for anyone in society—is experimenting with the privatization of school systems in the inner city that are often now run by government bureaucracies that have failed. I agree with Bill Bennett when he says that if you go into the inner cities of America, you see schools that are performing as if they were designed by the Ku Klux Klan. They are not doing their job. They are not meeting the needs of those children. Those children are not safe.

I recall, at one point, when Pat Robertson went to participate in a Virginia Heroes Day, where they had Arthur Ashe, and Doug Wilder and Pat Robertson. It was a bi-partisan deal, and they had various prominent Virginians. And they divided a group of sixth graders—these children were 11 years old—and they divided them into groups of 25, and each Virginia hero rotated and spoke to the different students. And at one point, Pat asked this group of sixth graders, "What is it you need in your school? What's the thing that you need that'll help you learn, that'll help you become educated?" They didn't say they wanted more books. They didn't say they wanted more computers. They didn't say that they wanted smaller class sizes. They all raised their hand and they said, "We need metal detectors. We need magnetometers at the doors to keep people from bringing guns and knives into our schools, because we don't even feel safe coming to school."

So, if we were to move towards some system of experimental privatization—in some places this is already being done—and secondly, if we provided those families with scholarships that could be redeemed at the school of their choice—private, parochial, home, or public school— and if we created the kind of free market in primary and secondary education that we have in higher education, where you can get a GI Bill and you can redeem it in Notre Dame and you can redeem it at Yeshiva University, or you can redeem it at Howard University. The government doesn't tell you where you can go to school. You can go to school anywhere you want to. And that's why our higher education system—not the only reason, but one of the reasons— why our higher education system is the envy and magnet of the entire world. There are people from all over the world who come to this country for one reason and one reason only, and that's to attend our colleges and universities. I think if we moved to a free market education system, especially in the inner city, people would be able to read and write, and we would also be able to do that with primary and secondary education.

MR. KLEIN: It has been reported that you are tempering your anti-abortion stance in order to appear more mainstream for the 1996 election. Is that true?

MR. REED: No, that is not true. Our position has been, is, and will remain that we believe that an unborn child has an inalienable right to life. We believe it's a sacred human right. We believe that it is secured by natural law. We believe it's codified in the Fourteenth Amendment of the Constitution, which says that, "No one shall be deprived life, liberty, or property without due process of law."

As I indicated in my remarks, we believe that it is an incomprehensible tragedy that that right to life is being denied to millions of children who will never know the light of day and who will never know what it is like to be held and to be nurtured.

We're going to continue to press because we believe that's the right position, we believe it's the correct position, and we also believe, coincidentally, that it is the politically right thing for candidates to stand for.

If you look at the VRS exit polling on election polling on Election Day 1992 or you look at the Worthlin poll, Worthlin found 16 percent of the voters voted solely on the abortion issue. The VRS exit poll was 12 percent of the voters cast their ballot on that issue, and among both of those groups, George Bush won that group of voters two to one.

It's been a winning issue for the Republican Party, but it's also a democratic issue, as well. It's not a liberal or conservative issue. We think it stretches to both parties, and that's why we took the step of inviting Governor Bob Casey of Pennsylvania—I think one of the most eloquent spokesmen in America for the rights of the unborn—to speak at our convention as an ethnic Catholic Democrat, to get up and speak to his party, as well as the Republican Party, about the need to have both parties respect that right.

We will continue to do so. We will do so in a way that we hope is unequivocal, and we will do so in a way we hope resonates with the American people.

MR. KLEIN: This questioner asks a follow-up a little bit on the question before that one. Are you saying that young women have children out of wedlock to get on welfare, and that eliminating that would lead to the end of the problem of unwed mothers?

MR. REED: No, I don't think it would end the problem of unwed mothers, but I do believe that if you could do two things—number one, take the vast, uncontrollable, Byzantine bureaucracy of our welfare system, which right now, if you take every family under the poverty level, they're spending $27,000 per family. That, by the way, is only 3,000 below the median income in this country, and yet we still have this permanent underclass.

What we're saying is two things: Number one, block grant a lot these functions to the states. Let them do it. Let the local communities do it. That's where it belongs. It shouldn't be a federal function, in our view. Secondly, we believe that we ought to allow states to enact tough restrictions on abortions—I mean, on welfare. Not only things like time limits, but also experimenting with eliminating welfare after a certain period of time or not allowing people who don't marry or don't engage in some kind of change of behavior to receive a subsidy.

We think that we are, in fact, driving people into poverty, subsidizing poverty. We don't think that that is how it should be done. I think that you should also encourage, through some means—perhaps charitable tax credits and so forth, perhaps through the block grant process—homes for unwed mothers and congregate care centers so that instead of a lot of our children not having fathers, not having intact families, they could at least be in congregate care centers where they are receiving love and nurture and fellowship.

MR. KLEIN: Can you talk about the Coalition's strategy of attracting non-religious conservatives to expand its base? Will appealing to issues that the non-religious conservatives find important, such as low taxes, take away from the emphasis on moral issues and cause the Coalition's core base to decline?

MR. REED: Well, you know, the interesting thing about that question is there is—the assumption in the question is that religious conservatives only care about two or three issues and all the other voters are concerned about things like the deficit, and taxes, and whether or not they live in a safe neighborhood, whether or not their child goes to a school that works or not.

The truth of the matter is, as I indicated in my remarks, these voters are your neighbors, they're your friends, they're your co-workers, they're the people you go to church or synagogue with. They care about the same things that we all care about. They want taxes to be lower, they want the economy to be creating jobs, they want tougher laws against crime and drugs, they want our government to be back to the people again, instead of controlled by special interests and career politicians and foreign lobbyists.

So what we are attempting to do is in no way retreating from the principled stands that we've taken on social issues, but we also want to speak to everyday concerns. That's why we've worked, for example, on behalf of a balanced budget amendment to the Constitution, because we believe that the government should have to live by the same rules that families do. My family has to balance its checkbook every month. Sometimes it's more difficult than other times. But the government should have to live by the same rule.

That's why we worked for term limits. We believe that if somebody goes to Washington, serves for a relatively brief period of time, comes back home, has to live with the citizens that they have just passed laws for, because of their intimacy and connection to the communities from whence they came, that we'll have better government.

That's really the way America was founded. In the early days, Congress was only in session for maybe a hundred to 130 days of the year, and it's only been with the rise of a big, bloated government and a welfare state that this has really turned into a career. It used to be a part-time vocation for average citizens, the way our state legislature is.

You know, I have—one of my good friends as my state senator, and I see him all the time. I mean, he's in Richmond maybe 40 days out of the year. The rest of the time, I see him around town, and it makes it easier for me to connect with that person.

That's what we want. I think that's what religious conservatives want. But I want to make something clear. We don't believe that working on those other issues in any way detracts from or weakens our voice on things like the traditional family or the sanctity of innocent human life. We're going to continue to work on those issues. We're going to continue to press on them. We did so during the health care debate. We opposed the Clinton health care plan because it would have included abortion in the basic benefits package and it would have subsidized abortion. We were opposed to it not simply because of our efforts, but because of a lot of other great organizations. It was stopped, and we're going to continue to do that as well.

So we think that it's a seamless web, that they actually work together and all these issues connect to our view of what kind of America we want to live in.

MR. KLEIN: This questioner says this summer a large group of clerics from many faiths organized the Interfaith Alliance because, they said, of their concern for the hatred and intolerance your group promotes. What is your reaction to that?

MR. REED: Well, I really don't have much of a reaction to it other than to simply state that they have a right to their view, and they have a right to organize as they see fit. We think that their criticism is unjust and unfair. We don't believe they're accurately characterizing our views or our organization. I think that the Christian Coalition is growing at a very large rate, about 8,000 to 10,000 new members and supporters a week, about 50,000 new members and supporters a month, and I think that that will continue, and I think we will continue to be engaged, and we're not going to allow organizations like this to throw us off our game or keep us from staying on our message.

MR. KLEIN: This questioner, who is not myself, although it's a "Times-Dispatch" person—your spokesman Mike Russell told "The Richmond Times-Dispatch" reporter that your organization had never taken money from the Republican Party. Didn't you take a $64,000 contribution from the Republican Senatorial Campaign Committee in 1990?

MR. REED: We're an equal employment opportunity organization that will accept contributions from the Democratic Party as well as the Republican Party. If David Wilhelm would like to meet with us and contribute so that we can distribute these non-partisan voter guides, we would accept his contribution.

We did receive one contribution in 1990, four years ago. After that, our board promulgated a policy that we would no longer solicit or accept contributions from either political party. So all of our contributions ever since then have come from average citizens. The average contribution is $19. We don't receive a dime of money from either political party.

I might just add, by the way, that the Interfaith Alliance, the organization that you just mentioned, its only contributor is a $25,000 check from the Democratic National Committee. So there are organizations out there that accept that money. We choose not to.

MR. KLEIN: There are some who associate themselves with your group's views who believe in the literal interpretation of the Bible. Do you, and how does that influence your view of U.S. aid and policy toward Israel?

MR. REED: Well, I believe, as I said in my remarks, what 80 percent of the American people believe, which is the Bible is the infallible word of God. My positions on the issues are based on my understanding of what is right and wrong and good for this country.

You know, one thing that we've never done at the Christian Coalition is back in the '80s, there was a thing called the Biblical scoreboard, and they would go out and score candidates based on whether or not they thought they were upholding what was right according to the Bible, which was fine as long as you dealt with things like capital punishment or abortion or so forth, because they could usually reference a verse about the death penalty from the Bible or something. But it was a bit of a problem when you got into SDI or aid to the Nicaraguan contras, because it was hard to reference a specific Bible verse.

We are a pro-family organization. We want policy to be friendly to the family again, and our positions on the issues are based upon what we think is family friendly. Clearly those views are informed by our faith, but we don't meet with a member of Congress and say, "Vote for this particular bill because of the following scripture verse." We meet with them and ask them to support a particular bill because it will have the following desirable and ascertainable effects on families and children.

With regard to my support of the nation of Israel, my support for the nation of Israel is based on the fact that Israel is the only true democracy in the Middle East, it is one of the best and most reliable allies that we have in the entire world. I've visited there. I was there in January of this year. It is a decent and good society that we believe is upholding democratic values consistent with what the American people would favor, and we want to support that nation wholeheartedly, and that's the basis of our support for Israel.

MR. KLEIN: We are about out of time, I'm afraid. I certainly appreciate your being here and I'd like to present you with this certificate of appreciation for being here and the ever popular National Press Club mug, which you can—I guess you have a bunch here. Pat Robertson's got one of those, I think, and Bill Bennett has a complete set. *(Laughter.)*

So anyway, I thank you very much for being here.

MR. REED: Gil, thanks very much. I appreciate it.

MR. KLEIN: Appreciate it. *(Applause.)*

Ralph Reed makes a point at NPC, October 12, 1994.

NATIONAL PRESS CLUB

LUNCHEON
September 30, 1994

PEAKER

BARBARA JORDAN
Chair of President's Commission on Immigration Reform

MODERATED BY: Gil Klein

HEAD TABLE GUESTS

JULIA KLEIN
Philadelphia Inquirer

MIKE DOYLE
McClatchy News Service

BETH SCWINN
San Francisco Examiner

RICK DUNHAM
Business Week

GARY MARTIN
San Antonio Express-News

MICHELLE KAY
Austin Statesman American

LAWRENCE FUCHS
Vice Chairman of the U.S. Commission on Immigration Reform

REGGIE STEWART
*Assistant News Editor for Knight-Ridder Newspapers and a member of the
National Press Club Speakers Committee*

MICHAEL TEITELBAUM
Vice Chairman of the U.S. Commission on Immigration Reform

DAN CARNEY
*Houston Post and the member of the National Press Club
Speakers Committee who arranged today's luncheon*

EILEEN SHANAHAN
New America News Service

STEVE McGONIGLE
Dallas Morning News

ROBERT SURO
Washington Post

TOM FERRIGER
San Jose Mercury News

GIL KLEIN

MODERATOR

ood afternoon, and welcome to the National Press Club. My name is Gil Klein. I'm the club's president, and I'm a national correspondent with Media General Newspapers, writing for the Richmond Times-Dispatch, the Tampa Tribune and the Winston-Salem Journal.

I'd like to welcome my fellow club members in the audience today as well as those of you who are watching us on C-SPAN or listening to us on National Public Radio or the Internet global computer network.

Now, today we are pleased to have with us former Congresswoman Barbara Jordan, who is chairman of the President's Commission on Immigration Reform as well as a fixture of American political discourse for more than two decades. Ms. Jordan is here to make news. Her commission is reporting its findings today following six months of study on a problem that has vexed America practically since its founding: How do we as a nation of immigrants control the flood of people desperately seeking to live here?

Shortly after accepting the chairmanship of the commission, Ms. Jordan outlined the problem quite starkly. She said the patience of the American people is growing thin toward those who are ignoring, circumventing and manipulating our immigration laws. She told the committee, "Unless this country does a better job in curbing illegal immigration, we risk irreparably undermining our commitment to legal immigration." Immigration is a hot political issue. Californians will vote in November on Proposition 187, that seeks to clamp down on illegal immigration by forcing illegal immigrants out of public schools, out of government health programs, and out of social services.

Ms. Jordan brings to this issue a stature born from nearly 30 years as a prominent political figure. In 1966, she became the first African-American elected to the Texas State Senate since Reconstruction, and the first woman ever to hold a seat there. But it was her performance as a congresswoman from 1973 to 1979 that catapulted her to national attention. As a member of the House Judiciary Committee, she gave a passionate and articulate case for impeaching President Nixon. Though she left Congress in 1979 and has settled into a life as a professor of national policy at the University of Texas, and also the honorary coach of the women's basketball team—*(laughter)*—she is often called on when a voice of authority is needed. It's her voice that draws instant attention. It's a cross between Shakespearean actress and southern preacher that instantly commands respect.

It may be no coincidence, though, that Barbara Jordan was the keynote speakers at two Democratic National Conventions.

MS. JORDAN: We won both. *(Laughter.)*

MR. KLEIN: You took my line! *(Laughter, applause.)* That's right. The only two times that the Democrats won the presidential election is because, just coincidentally, maybe.

Ladies and gentlemen, please join me in a warm press club welcome for Barbara Jordan. *(Applause.)*

BARBARA JORDAN

SPEAKER

hank you. Thank you very much.

You did not tell me that you were going to take seven minutes to introduce me. Does that mean that I don't have to stop until seven past 2:00? *(Laughter.)*

I thank you for the opportunity to come to the press club and report on the work of the U.S. Commission on Immigration Reform.

I have the two vice chairs of the commission at the head table. You have heard them introduce Larry Fuchs and Michael Teitelbaum, and there are other commissioners seated at the table over there, Warren Leiden, and Bruce Morrison, and Bob Hill and Richard Estrada. So we've got representation from the Dallas Morning News right there sitting at— participating in our proceedings, not that that has tainted his participation at all. *(Laughter.)*

The commission was created to assess the implementation and impact of the Immigration Act of 1990. We have been on a fact-finding mission. We have had expert consultations. We've identified major immigration-related issues. We have had all sorts of input—some expert, some inexpert—into our deliberations.

I delivered the copy of the report to the Congress today because the law said when it created us, "Present an interim report on September 30, 1994," and I went trying to find somebody to present it to. *(Laughter, applause.)* But seriously—*(laughter)*—seriously, we did get a good reception from the members of Congress who received the report, and it is a serious bit of work. And we submitted it to Congress this morning and we hope that they're going to give it serious attention, as they have indicated they would.

First, we set forth principles. The commission believes that legal immigration has strengthened the country and it continues to do so. Most people come to America because they are close family members, they have kinship ties, they want to be permanent residents, or they're needed by U.S. businesses. We strongly denounce—denounce—on our commission the hostility which seems to be developing around immigrants. That is not healthy when we seek to blame immigrants for all of our social ills. We cannot sustain ourselves as a nation if we condone divisiveness in this society of immigrants. At the same time, we disagree with those who label our efforts to control immigration as anti-immigrant.

Now, I recognize that our report is not unanimously applauded, but we did try to forge a consensus with which the country could live. If we are to preserve our immigration tradition and our ability to say yes to the people who want to get in and seek entry, we've got to have the strength to say no to the people who are not supposed to get in. We need to make deportation a part of a credible immigration policy.

The commission, nine of us, disparate views, yes, from one end of the political spectrum to the other. Mr. Klein, you introduced me as a fixture of American political discourse, and as chair of this commission, I felt like a fixture—*(laughter)*—placed there to receive all of the disparate notions and ideas that people have and have had about immigration. As one who is accustomed to preaching apple pie and motherhood, it has been a real awakening to get some of the people who are not so happy with what we've said. But we made some tough recommendations. We laid down first principles, we cut through the rhetoric, and that's the first thing that we had to do and tried to look for answers and not excuses.

I believe quite firmly that we can quiet and dampen the flames which are surrounding public opinion where immigration is concerned, because people on both sides of this issue have engaged in too much hyperbole. We have got to put the matter of immigration back on a civil course. We have got to know that immigration really goes to the heart of who we are as a nation. If we are confident enough as Americans in our culture we should welcome the legal immigrant. We should be able to accommodate diversity in our society. Are we strong enough to welcome those who ought to be in and retain a commitment to the rule of law by keeping those out who shouldn't get in?

The commission is convinced that immigration can be managed, and it can be managed in a sensible way and it can be managed effectively. We also believe that we can do this in a manner which will protect civil liberties and civil rights. As a nation committed to immigrants and the rule of law, we've got to do that balancing act.

The most urgent immigration problem we face today is the unauthorized entry of hundreds of thousands of illegals. That undermines our commitment to legal immigration.

Although the illegal alien may be generally law-abiding, and particularly in good economic times maybe we need the illegals, their entry and the violation of the law is a violation of our national interest. The problem of illegal immigration will not be solved easily, and the cure, the solution, is not cheap. But if we are serious as a country, we have got to commit more resources than we currently are spending to this issue.

We believe a credible approach to immigration must be comprehensive. We recommend a seven-point strategy. First, border management. We support a very simple view about border management: Prevent illegal entries, facilitate legal ones. Prevention holds advantages. It's more cost-effective than apprehension and removal after the fact. It eliminates the voluntary cycle of return and re-entry which so many exercise. We applaud Operation Hold the Line at El Paso, the brainchild of Sylvester Rejas, our impressive border control chief out in the area. Prevention requires a combination of additional personnel, improved technology and communications, data systems that permit quick identification of repeat offenders, additional equipment including vehicles, and a political commitment to this approach. We also support efforts to train border patrol officers so that abuses on the border can be reduced, and we hear reports of abuses.

Preventing illegal entries alone is insufficient in terms of effective border management. We've got to do more. We've got to do something at land borders and airports. People get in that way, too. We do know that whatever we do, we have got to continue to receive the benefit that we receive from trade and tourism from our immigration policies. We know our policies must support a strong national interest in trade and investment abroad.

The second part our strategy: Work site enforcement. This is the one which has generated most controversy. Employment, we believe, continues to be the principal magnet for illegal aliens coming into the country. As long as U.S. businesses benefit from illegals on their work force, they are not going to try to help us get on top of the problem. As long as U.S. businesses benefit, control of unlawful immigration will be impossible. We believe that employer sanctions must be made to work, and enhanced labor standards enforcement essential components of a strategy to reduce the job magnet.

As currently formulated, employer sanctions don't work. They're doubly flawed. Illegal aliens are able to easily circumvent these employers by presenting them counterfeit documents. Concerned about inadvertently hiring illegal aliens, employers discriminate against the people looking at them, and the employer looks at them and says, "Well, you look foreign and you sound foreign," and that could be a citizen of the United States of America. Employers should not be asked to make that kind of a subjective judgment. As a society, we cannot tolerate the fraud which is implicit in employer sanctions and inherent in employer sanctions, and we also as a society cannot tolerate discrimination.

At the heart of the problem is the system used to verify that workers are authorized to hold jobs in the United States. The commission's recommendations to improve the verification procedure has drawn great attention, and I understand that, but our report is 250 pages long, and there's more in it than worker verification, employee verification. The commission recommends a measured strategy for developing a new work authorization system. We believe, and we know others disagree with us, but we believe the most promising option for alleviating fraud and discrimination found in the workplace and in the current verification procedure is a computerized registry based on the Social Security number. All employees must already provide a Social Security number. That's not a new question. All employees are asked—all employees would be asked to tell us the number, then employer, you call the computer registry to verify that the number is valid and was issued to someone authorized to work in the United States.

Now let me be clear. We've recommended a test. The commission says test what we think is the most promising option. We want to find a simpler, more effective worksite verification system. It would not depend on a single document. It may not depend on a document at all. When you withdraw money from the bank with your PIN number, you don't have a document. And the way we value money, if we can get it with a PIN number—*(laughter)*—why can't we verify work authorization with a number?

Well, I hope this type of a system works, but if it doesn't, then let's test it and find out that it doesn't, and then go back to the drawing board and try to do something else. We are urging the president to carefully phase in and evaluate pilot programs testing this, what we say is the most promising option, we feel.

In setting up the pilot programs, special attention must go to ensuring that they fully protect civil rights and civil liberties. They must also include safeguards against fraudulent use by illegal aliens of that data base for other purposes or other use by unscrupulous employers.

The commission, along with others, will carefully monitor the pilots. We are not all going to quit once the recommendations are made and if the pilots get under way. During the next three years, the commission will still be in business. The authorization law says that we exist until 1997. We want to see whether these pilots meet our requirements for what, reliability, cost effectiveness and protection of civil rights and civil liberties. Should the results prove promising, as we hope they will and think they will, we expect they will, we recommend that they form the basis for implementation of a national verification system.

Now, let me say one last word about the computer registry. The registry will use data obtained from the Social Security Administration and the INS, the Immigration and Naturalization Service. Though it will be linked directly—the verification database will be linked directly to neither of these databases, we do not make that connection because we are trying to protect privacy.

One of the most troubling concerns I have heard expressed by everybody who objects to what we have said is that of the quality of the data in Social Security and INS databases. Some people believe we will never have sufficient good data in those bases, sufficient good records, to even try the registry. Others are afraid that, if we clean up the databases in INS and the Social Security Administration, that the government will have too much information to intrude upon our lives.

Now, if that is going to be your conclusion, then you must think that the great protection of liberty is for the government to make errors, to do the wrong thing. I would hope that Congress spends the money necessary to correct the data that is kept by Social Security/INS. The government needs good data, too. They do. *(Laughter.)* As someone who pays into the Social Security system, you should not have to worry that someone is fraudulently using your Social Security number. No American wants to see discrepancies in the Social Security records, and no immigrant should suffer because INS can't find their records. We can't run an agency of the government of the country that way.

The third part of our recommendations: immigrant eligibility for public benefits. That's a major one.

The commission believes that decisions about eligibility should support the objectives of immigration policy. Using these objectives as a measure of benefit policy, we come to the following conclusions.

First, legal, permanent residents should continue to be eligible for needs-tested assistance programs. U.S. law already bars entry into this country of those who are likely to become a public charge. Circumstances may arise after the person enters this country and they become a public charge, circumstances like an unexpected illness, injuries sustained in an accident, loss of employment or a death in the family. We are not prepared as a commission to lift the safety net out from under individuals who are here legally and, we hope, will become a part of our social community. We strongly recommend against any broad, categorical denial of eligibility of public benefits for legal people based on their alienage.

At the same time, the commission endorses initiatives to ensure that sponsors who say they are financially responsible for the immigrant who comes here have a legal obligation to support their charge after the charge is here. In the present law there is a moral obligation, but not a legal contractual obligation. Moral obligations work in church but they don't work very well for the law. Mechanisms should be developed which assure that sponsors provide the support they promised.

Our views on eligibility for benefits of illegal aliens are different from those benefits that are recommended for legal aliens. If an alien is in this country lawfully, he should receive whatever benefits a lawful resident receives, but if a person is here unlawfully, he should be entitled to no benefits, no benefits except where there is emergent need for specific assistance, such as emergency health care. Where there's a public health safety or welfare interest involved, such as immunizations and some type of vaccine to prevent the spread of communicable diseases, child nutrition programs, school lunch programs, that should be made available. If their eligibility is constitutionally protected, that benefit should remain available.

Why the distinction between the eligibility of legal aliens and illegals? Illegal aliens don't have the right to be here, they broke the law to get here, they never intended to become a part of our social community, and they are not entitled to benefits. They have no intention to integrate. As a nation, it is in our interest to provide a limited range of other services. Immunizations and treatments of communicable diseases fall into that category. If illegal aliens require other aid, then that aid should be granted in their own countries.

Even under this strict eligibility concept, illegal aliens can pose fiscal burdens on states and localities, and we are not unaware of that as a commission. And we say let us take care of short-term, identifiable, net costs to states and localities, but such impact aid should not become a part of the regular budget of the state or community. So for now, we are supporting short-term impact aid to help states with the costs of incarcerating illegal aliens. Those are measurable costs, they're temporary, and the requirement to cooperate with federal government poses no problem for these communities.

The fourth part of our strategy addresses the removal of those who have no right to be here.

The fifth element is emergency management. We have seen most recently immigration emergencies: Cuba, the Haitians. That is the fifth element of our strategy.

The sixth part of our strategy addresses the statistics on immigration. We are going to seek reliable data because reliable data is a necessary ingredient of credible policy.

And lastly, much as we support enhanced enforcement efforts of this country, the commission also believes that unilateral action on the part of the United States is not enough to sufficiently curb illegal immigration. Effective deterrence of unlawful immigration must include attacking the root causes in the countries of origin. This will require cooperation with other countries.

Now, what about the future? The commission is at mid-point in its work. In our longer-term agenda we will assess and discuss and inform of the implementation and impact of the Immigration Act of 1990. We encourage the country that we know and love to realize that much has changed on the face of the world, and we must make adjustments which will address those changes. There are now economic arrangements like NAFTA, GATT, I suppose, if we get it. We know that racial and ethnic tensions abound in our own neighborhoods, and we know that serious attention must be addressed to health and welfare problems.

We are going to continue as a commission to look systematically at all of the issues which attend the volatile issue of immigration, and we are going to report to the Congress on the kinds of policies it should be considering for the 21st century.

I hope in these remarks that you hear the commission is working hard and continues to have a full agenda. We've had a good staff. We've got an executive director, Susan Martin, who knows more about immigration than anybody who ever knew anything about immigration. And we have a staff which worked around the clock to meet that September 30 deadline for the interim report on immigration. And we hear so much negativism about people who do governmental kinds of work, but you can't compensate for the kind of quality care these people have given, staff and our executive director, to make this report possible.

Immigration remains a cornerstone of American tradition, and I believe that it remains a cornerstone of the definition of us. And I think we are confident enough and secure enough in our identity as Americans, committed to immigration and the rule of law, to make these proposals work.

Thank you very much. I'll take your questions. *(Applause.)*

MR. KLEIN: Thank you very much, Ms. Jordan. We do have a lot of questions, except that almost all of them are all on the same topic. So we'll get started.

Did the commission explore other alternatives to the identification system? What were those, and what was the driving force to include the identification system?

MS. JORDAN: I'm going to ask the vice chair, Larry Fuchs, to comment on that, please.

MR. FUCHS (*Vice Chairman, U.S. Commission on Immigration Reform*): The question is, how do you make employer sanctions work? You know, it was 1952 that Senator—

MS. JORDAN: They did explore other ways to do it.

MR. FUCHS: Yeah, I know—*(laughter)*—and the other ways of doing it. But the question is how to make it work. And so, when you look at the alternatives that we explored, we wind up with this as the most promising. What are the alternatives? Present system? Status quo? Abuse and fraud. Some discrimination attributable to the system. Burden on the employer at the work site. Modify the present system? Reduce the number of documents that have to be shown? You still have the same problem. You may improve it a little bit.

When you look at the alternatives, abandon every effort, abandon employer sanctions—what you do then is you go back to where we were when Paul Douglas and all those other people tried to get something done to make the employer responsible for hiring in a knowing way, as employers have done now for a long, long time, hiring illegal aliens and thereby creating an exploitable underclass and doing all the other bad things that grow out of that.

So we said we've got to have one that's credible in the sense that it's reliable, in the sense that it's secure. Let's figure out the best way to get the most secure system of employee eligibility linked to the sanctions against employers who knowingly hire and evade the law. And this is the alternative of the various things considered that looks clearly the most promising, most likely to reduce fraud, burden on the workplace, and be consistent with civil rights and civil liberties.

MS. JORDAN: All right. You had another question?

MR. KLEIN: Oh, yes. *(Laughter.)* What was the commission's demographic source to estimate if an immigration problem really exists? Some 3.5 million undocumented aliens are said to live in the United States. Does that justify imposing an ID system on 250 million people?

MS. JORDAN: I have up here our executive director, Susan Martin, and when they talk about our demographic source, that sounds like something the executive director should respond to directly. I don't know. *(Laughter.)*

SUSAN MARTIN (*Executive Director, U.S. Commission on Immigration Reform*): The commission for the most part in determining—in looking at the numbers of illegal aliens used the data that the Immigration and Naturalization Service has done. They actually now have quite a good statistics department. Robert Warren is heading it and he has done some very, very good estimation of the numbers. So we feel that those right now are the most credible figures on the scale of illegal immigration, and that somewhere in the 3.5 to 4 million base illegal population in the country, about 300,000 people being added each year on a permanent basis, but far more people coming in and out over time, and that we have much less data about.

Now, it's certainly a very small part of the overall labor force, and yet in certain cities, certain counties, it's quite a sizeable proportion. About 75 to 85 percent of all of the illegal aliens are actually in five states, and within those five states they're in only a few counties. So, it's a concentrated problem, but a very serious one for those particular communities.

MR. KLEIN: Is there a state, or states, which is most promising as the pilot of this Social Security number test?

MS. JORDAN: Well, I think Texas is. *(Laughter.)* But it's not my decision to make, and of course the five states that we're going to look at first will be Texas, California, Illinois, New York, Florida, and then the determination will be made.

Now, we're also going to look at states where immigration has a lesser impact, but I think that most people are going to focus on what is found in Texas and California, because we've got about 80 percent of the problem, once you get that one cleared up, and Florida.

MR. KLEIN: As you pointed out, this is not your decision to make. What is the process here? How much does Congress have to do to implement your recommendations, and how much can be done by executive decision?

MS. JORDAN: You know, the good news is the Congress doesn't need to do anything—*(laughter)*—but provide money. That's what we need from Congress is money, because the law already has the authorization for the president to act today, if he wants to, to say, "We like these recommendations, and let's start the pilots," and he could start it tomorrow. And I don't know whether the president has read our report. I do know that the president has had detailed to the commission administration workers who have worked with us every step of the way, and yesterday I did brief the president's chief of staff, Leon Panetta, on it, and the commissioner of INS, Doris Meissner, has been on it, so if they want to do something about this report they can do it without delay.

MR. KLEIN: What guarantees can you give that your proposal will not lead to a national ID card?

MS. JORDAN: I know that that is the fear, that a national data bank will lead to a national ID card. It is not proposed by the commission. It is not thought desirable by the commission. We don't want anybody to think we are proposing an ID card because we are not.

Barbara Jordan, Gil Klein and Lawrence Fuchs, Vice Chairman of the U.S. Commission on Immigration Reform. September 30, 1994.

We've got Jewish input into the decisions of this commission, and for a Jewish person, a card is the most abhorrent prospect to ever contemplate. We don't think it will lead to a proposal for every citizen to carry a card. What if it looks like it's headed in that direction? I don't know, throw ourselves on the Capitol steps and say hold it, don't let it happen. We will certainly voice our concern about—if this indeed becomes an unintended consequence of what we've recommended.

MR. KLEIN: Given the allegations of widespread inefficiency and even corruption at INS recently described in a series of reports in the New York Times, what step does the commission propose to make INS data a reliable base for the proposed identification system?

MS. JORDAN: The point is, as I said, Doris Meissner, the commissioner of the INS, has been working with us lock-step and she was with me yesterday as I briefed Leon Panetta on our commission's recommendations, and she understands the problem with INS data, and she has a determination, which, if you look in her eyes when she talks about it, you would say a fierce determination to clean it up. And what you have got to do in this is trust somebody to do what they say they're going to do, and that's the only thing I can say, is trust this INS commissioner to do what she says she's going to do. And beyond that, there is no guarantee.

MR. KLEIN: In the press conference this morning, some of the groups that oppose this, it seemed like their main concern was that a worker will go in, want to apply for something, have a foreign-sounding or looking name, and the employer runs this through a computer, it pops up no good, and so that person's out the door, even if—but there's no assurance of quality control in that data. And they see this as discrimination, potentially highly discriminatory. How do you respond to those concerns?

MS. JORDAN: What we have recommended with regards to the Office of Special Council addresses that directly, and I would like for Susan Martin, our executive director to please comment on that.

MS. MARTIN: Yes, there are two aspects to the commission's recommendations on that. First of all, in the pilot programs themselves, the commission is recommending that they be phased in with an ongoing evaluation, and certainly, if those types of problems are arising, then it wouldn't go to the next level of implementation. We would want to be able to document if there were people who were in employment problems because of faulty data.

The second thing is that we would build on the provisions of a current pilot program that the Immigration Service is doing which has a secondary verification process. Employers would be told that they can only do the verification after hire, which is the current law, and that they must maintain someone until a secondary verification is done in order to be able to ensure that people don't lose a job because of this process. And then they could figure out why the Social Security number doesn't show up as it's supposed to. I certainly would want to know that; if my number wasn't showing up, I'd want to know why it wasn't showing up in the records. I'd be kind of worried about my own Social Security earnings records as well.

The third thing, as Professor Jordan mentioned, we are making recommendations that the Office of Special Counsel for Unfair Immigration-Related Practices be much more proactive in identifying where there may be discriminatory practices taking place.

MS. JORDAN: That's proactive.

MR. KLEIN: This questioner says the report is vague on how privacy rights and civil liberties will be protected under this verification system. How can you possibly guarantee that when we've seen an increasing abuse on other computerized systems by the government and other parties?

MS. JORDAN: We either are going to test something to see whether it works and whether these horror stories happen or don't happen. And what I have said, and this is all I can say on this point, is that if we do get the kinds of horrible consequences which are being predicted, I, once presented with the evidence, will be the first one to denounce the report, call the commission back into session and tell them we need to go back to the drawing board. And I don't think there is one member of that commission who would say that they would not be willing to do that. Now, if you would not be willing to do that, hold up your hand. *(Laughter.)*

MR. KLEIN: Let the record reflect, no hands.

MS. JORDAN: No hands. No hands.

MR. KLEIN: As a constitutional scholar yourself, do you think that the proposals to deny certain benefits to U.S.-born children of illegal immigrants, even to deny welfare benefits to legal immigrants, are constitutional?

MS. JORDAN: To deny benefits to legal—

MR. KLEIN: To U.S.-born children of illegal residents.

MS. JORDAN: Born in the United States?

MR. KLEIN: Yes. The children of illegal residents who come in here and have a child in the United States who then obviously becomes a United States resident.

MS. JORDAN: The Fourteenth Amendment to the Constitution of the United States reads, "All persons born or naturalized in the United States are citizens of the United States." I am not about to advocate changing the Fourteenth Amendment to the Constitution of the United States. Those parents who have that baby, they are not citizens. But that child is a citizen, and as a citizen of this country that child is entitled to benefits and they are not to be taken away.

MR. KLEIN: Could you comment, please, on Proposition 187 in California?

MS. JORDAN: Why should I? *(Laughter.)*

MR. KLEIN: It's related to immigration. *(Laughter.)* Are you taking lessons from Ted Turner, or what? *(Laughter.)*

MS. JORDAN: The major problem I see with Proposition 187 is that it goes too far, and why is it that you would want to correct a problem through violating the law? And to deny and deprive the children who are entitled under constitutional decision to education benefits violates our law and will land the school system or whomever in court as they try to test Prop. 187. And I just regret that the political atmosphere and environment in the state of California has yielded an ill—what I term an ill-considered proposition.

MR. KLEIN: You characterized your proposal as a pilot in five states, but people move from state to state. How can you implement your pilot without first collecting data on every person in the country?

MS. JORDAN: Oh, I don't think every person in the country would need data collected on him or her in order to get at least fairly reliable data from the five states. We're not going to have to measure everybody. Yes, people move from state to state but we're not that mobile. I mean, people are going to stay in place just long enough to state their name, residence and date of birth. They're not going to escape to another state before you're able to ask them a question—*(laughter)*—and so I think that the rule of reason is going to prevail here. *(Laughter.)*

MR. KLEIN: One of your recommendations is to make families that bring in immigrants take more responsibility so that they don't end up on SSI benefits. Can you explain how this is a problem and what you would expect from the families?

MS. JORDAN: The persons who—Susan, maybe you had better comment on that. Under the law now, you know, citizens who are going to become a public charge are not supposed to come into this country. Aliens, immigrants who are going to be a public charge, under the law as it is now, are not supposed to receive any benefits. And so, what we are giving the enforcers is another source to try to get those benefits.

If you have sponsored a person to come to the country, and you have said this person is responsible and will not become a public charge, then we are saying that you should have a legal obligation to, if this person comes upon hard times or whatever, honor your commitment under law. And "under law" means that you can be contractually sued.

MR. KLEIN: This questioner asks, "Won't some of the objectives you have to be achieved through the North American Free Trade Agreement"—to summarize this thing: Will the North American Free Trade Agreement change the pressure of illegal immigration on the United States from Mexico, since it was designed to improve the economy there? Have you seen any indication that that design has come true?

MS. JORDAN: Well, it hasn't been law for a year yet, and the early returns are that it will have that exact effect, that it will relieve the immigration pressures between the United States and Mexico. Now that was the promise, and early returns so reflect that it is having that kind of an outcome, and the longer it stays in place we will know more. But just think about the dire consequence we were warned of before NAFTA became law, and they didn't happen. Ask Ross. *(Laughter.)*

MR. KLEIN: Okay. That's an invitation to Ross Perot in case he'd like to have equal time.

We are, unfortunately, about out of time. This has been excellent and we have learned quite a bit here.

I would like, of course, to present you with a—before asking the last question—with a certification of appreciation for appearing here.

MS. JORDAN: Can I sell it?

MR. KLEIN: You can sell it. *(Laughter.)*

And a National Press Club mug, which is worth maybe 50 cents more than the certificate! *(Laughter.)*

MS. JORDAN: Thank you. Thank you.

MR. KLEIN: And the last question is: Given your track record of speaking, being the keynote speaker at winning Democratic conventions, have you been booked into the party's 1996 program yet? *(Laughter.)*

MS. JORDAN: That decision really comes from the president and—the incumbent president and the Democratic National Committee. And as soon as we know who the chair is of the committee and they get around to consider this, I don't know whether that call will come, and it depends on who appears to be viable as a prospect at that time, I suppose, as to who would be the speaker. But right now we're concentrating on November 8. That's a little shorter time frame than 1996. And so the only notes I'm sounding right now for the Democratic Party are Democratic notes to try to save at least a modicum of our strength and support in the Congress and throughout the country and in the governorships, particularly in Texas. *(Applause.)*

Thank you very much.

NATIONAL PRESS CLUB

LUNCHEON
September 27, 1994

PEAKER

TED TURNER
Chairman of the Board of
Turner Broadcasting System Incorporated

MODERATED BY: Gil Klein

HEAD TABLE GUESTS

⁂

LEW PERLMAN
Author and Contributor to Forbes and ASAP

HIDETOSHI FUJASAWA
Washington Bureau Chief of NHK Japan Broadcasting

DEBORAH HOWELL
Washington Bureau Chief for Newhouse Newspapers

WILLIAM HEADLINE
Washington Bureau Chief for CNN

GARY CLIFFORD
Washington Bureau Chief for People Magazine

DANIEL SCHORR
Columnist

JANE FONDA
Wife of our Speaker

CHRISTY WISE
Freelance Journalist and Chairwoman of the National Press Club Speakers Committee

ROSEMARY GOUDREAU
*Assistant News Editor of Knight-Ridder Newspapers and the member of the
National Press Club Speakers Committee who arranged today's luncheon*

ANDREW GLASS
Washington Bureau Chief for Cox Newspapers

BERT CARP
Vice President of Government Affairs for Turner Broadcasting System

BETTY COLE DUKERT
Senior Producer for NBC News "Meet the Press"

CHARLES THOMPSON
Producer of CBS News "60 Minutes"

MARK GUNTHER
TV Columnist for the Detroit Free Press

GIL KLEIN

MODERATOR

ood afternoon. Welcome to the National Press Club. My name is Gil Klein. I'm the club's president and a national correspondent with Media General Newspapers, writing for the Richmond Times-Dispatch, the Tampa Tribune and the Winston-Salem Journal.

I'd like to welcome my fellow club members in the audience today, as well as those of you who are watching us on C-SPAN or listening to us on National Public Radio or the Internet global computer network.

Now, what can one say about Ted Turner? That he transformed the television industry, that he's a world-class sailor who won the America's Cup, that he took a losing baseball team and made it World Series contenders, that he's an environmentalist, a moviemaker, a humanist, Jane Fonda's husband. *(Laughter.)* His biographer, Porter Bibb, once said, "He's a man who has literally done everything." At 55 years old, he recently said of himself, "I've got the mileage of a 150-year-old man."

He began his rise to what the New York Times called a "broadcasting visionary" in 1970 by buying a small UHF station in Atlanta that specialized in showing old movies and reruns of Mr. Ed. Based on the conviction that what people want are sports, movies and news, Mr. Turner built that single station into a media empire that took advantage of satellite transmission technology and cable distribution. I remember seeing a poster many years ago with his picture on it, and underneath were these words: "I was cable when cable wasn't cool." *(Laughter.)*

They laughed in New York when he founded the nation's first 24-hour news channel, CNN, in 1980. They called it "chicken noodle news." They don't call it that anymore. CNN has become the world's news source, used by heads of state to figure out what's going on. In New York they call him "Mr. Turner" as they fight off his network take-over bids while courting cooperative arrangements with CNN to cover international news. Just today the New York Times reported that Mr. Turner is interested in purchasing NBC News from General Electric—but would face financial and regulatory obstacles.

Apart from these business deals, Mr. Turner also is committed to such social issues as environmentalism and population control. He and Jane Fonda serve as special ambassadors to the United Nations. And although he was not able to be there, she was at the world population conference in Cairo recently.

As the owner of the Atlanta Braves, he must be immersed in the baseball strike. And apart from all that, one of his key goals is purchasing or starting a major motion picture studio. Indeed, in the making of the movie "Gettysburg," which Mr. Turner financed for his TNT movie network, he had a cameo appearance as a confederate general. And what did he do? He unsheathed his sword and shouted, "Charge!"

And, ladies and gentlemen, that pretty much sums up Mr. Turner. So please join me in a warm press club welcome for Mr. Ted Turner. *(Applause.)*

PHOTO, GEORGE BENNETT

Ted Turner

hank you. You've got to like that introduction. Thank you very much. But it doesn't feel like I've done all that much, I want you to know.

Well, what are we going to talk about today? The lady sitting beside me said, "Where's your speech?" You know, I said, "It's in my head." But there's a lot of things in my head. I've got to say, though, that one thing Mr. Klein failed to say, that right after I said "Charge!"—and I didn't say "Charge!" I said, "Let's go, boys." My line was, "Let's go, men," but I got it wrong because, when I saw what I had there, they looked more like boys to me. I was too old.

If there was anything wrong with "Gettsyburg"—and there was one thing that was wrong —the average soldier that fought there was 19 years old and nearly starving to death, whereas the re-enactors and the movie stars, the average age was probably more like 40 and there were a lot of fellas with comfortable midsections there. But, you know, they weren't back there during the Civil War. The army on both sides ate notoriously poorly, and they didn't have canteens with candy bars and that kind of stuff in those days. And also, right after I said that, I got shot—*(laughter)*—shot and killed, which is, you know, somehow I barely managed to avoid in my previous life.

I think everybody knows—I'm going to give you a little bit of information that you don't have. And that's always good, particularly when you're dealing with members of the press. But, you know, this is the press club. How many people here are really members of the working press? Would you raise your hand? I just want to see how many. Probably one out of 10. Yeah, about that. That's right. How many are not? Yeah, I mean, what the hell are you all doing here? I mean, this is supposed to be the press. You know, that's what was really impressing me about this.

I've been at this podium upon several other occasions, but I don't see—my picture doesn't seem to be on the wall outside. And there's a lot less luminary folks than me out there. How come my picture isn't out there? *(Laughter.)* I mean, I'm really serious. I ain't coming back unless my picture gets up there. *(Laughter.)* You know, I mean, you've got a bunch of bozos up there who haven't done near as much. *(Laughter.)* You know, they represent more mainstream. When did we become mainstream is what I want to know? Actually, I think we probably are. At what point? I mean, I don't know.

Anyway, the thing I'm going to talk about just for a few minutes is my network take-over attempt and how it's being blocked by one of my major shareholders, Time-Warner. While they go out and try and get a network of their own, they're holding me back from doing so. And it just isn't right. I mean, yes, 10 years ago when I bought MGM, I nearly bankrupted the company, that's true. And I needed some investment money because I didn't have enough capital, like most start-up businesses.

Unfortunately, I haven't been around as long as Time-Warner, and I don't go back 75 years and had lots of time in previous generations to build up a huge amount of capital for me to inherit and move forward with. I had to do almost all of it myself. And those of you who have had any experience with business know how hard it is to accumulate billions of dollars in one lifetime, yet less in a couple of decades.

So I had three choices, oddly enough, for investors. One was Rupert Murdoch, and I appreciated his offer very much. The other was General Electric and the other was from the cable operators. Well, it wasn't hard to decide who I wanted to go with. But the cable operators wanted some restrictions on me because they were investing in my company and they thought I was, you know, a little bit looney because I had just started CNN a little before and nearly went bankrupt there, and I nearly went bankrupt when my father died, and I nearly went bankrupt when I bought MGM. Of course, subsequent time showed all of the deals that I made were excellent deals. They were risky only because I was under-capitalized to do them. But I wouldn't be here today if I hadn't done them.

And particularly when you're younger and you are entrepreneurial, that means you have to take a certain amount of risk. That's what makes business and, really, life exciting. When you come right down to it, when you're getting married, when you go out and date, when you have children, when you buy a house, we all take certain risks. Particularly when you become a journalist you take certain risks. And we have journalists—I get asked about it all the time, about Christiane being out there and Peter Arnett being behind enemy lines. I mean, you journalists are kind of like soldiers. I mean they have to be willing, at times, some of us, to risk our lives to get the story.

And a lot of journalists get killed, and a lot of journalists get imprisoned. And you know, we don't have the First Amendment. You know, there's the Committee to Protect Journalists; we've got all these journalistic organizations. I like it because, you know, I'm kind of a quasi-journalist myself. You know, I mean, I'm sort of a journalist. I like being a journalist. And I was in journalism when I was ten years old. I used to sell newspapers at the streetcar stop in Cincinnati. I mean, I started in the newspaper business. This is before there was any television. You know, it was great. I mean, "Get your paper and read all about it."

You know, I'm not kidding you. I made people buy those papers, and they were only a nickel too, if you'll recall. Most of you can remember those days. But you know, so we know about risks, and they have to be taken.

So anyway, they told me they had to have financial controls over me, so I wouldn't make a big mistake and imperil the company—like I wanted to imperil the company. Remember, every move I've made, not one of them turned out to be a wrong move. I mean, I'm not talking about how I ran the Braves for the 10 years I ran it; that was a disaster. *(Laughter.)*

But buying the Braves was a good move. And as soon as I relinquished control of the Braves and gave someone else the responsibility for running the Braves, they did well. And the Braves were just about to turn around, because you know, you have to have the players in the minor league system. It all starts with scouting. I mean, it's a very complicated thing, running a major league baseball team, and those that are successful doing it, I take my hat off to, because I was unable to do it myself.

So I had these controls. But then after that, I mean, at the time I did it, Time—and listen, I like the people at Time. I mean, I've known Jerry Levin for over 20 years. He was the one that came up with the idea to put Home Box Office on the satellite, and I borrowed that idea for TBS, which was TCG at the time, and I came up with the idea of the Super Station. But basically, it was Broadcasting Magazine and the other communications magazines that wrote about the satellite and Jerry's move that gave me the idea.

But I think it was my idea that I had the idea to get a network before he did, because in 1984, '85, after trying to merge unsuccessfully with all three of the ownerships of the then networks, I felt like I had to mount a hostile takeover bid for CBS, not as a greenmailer—I didn't buy one dime's worth of stock beforehand to sell out or anything—I just wanted to buy a network. It was a public company, and there was nothing wrong with that. It's not illegal to make an offer for something, even if it's not for sale, particularly a public company, because a public company is for sale. The stock's traded every day. You can buy as much as you want to or all.

And usually entrenched managements that don't own very much of the stock want to fight you, because basically, they're trying to protect their jobs. They don't own the company themselves, they just run it. And in the case of somebody like Steve Ross, who was a good friend of mine—I knew him—I mean, he pulled $80 million—I don't know how much it was—but a whole lot of money out of the company, lived like a potentate on the corporate dole. But that was Warner.

Warner bought some stock in our company. They didn't really compete with us; they were a movie company. And Time didn't compete with us, because Time had Home Box Office and the magazines and the cable systems, which were complementary. Then after we merged, after I sold them that stock, then Time and Warner merged. Time went from two board seats and Warner with one, to where they had three board seats and they had the governor's clauses. And once they were in the television programming business, which Warner was, and the cable businesses, then they became a competitor. And they've been an increasing competitor as the years have gone by.

And I want to tell you something that nobody has known up until now. I had a basic deal worked out to acquire NBC, a little over a year ago, for about $5 billion. A billion was going to be equity that they were going to take, and a billion dollars in a preferred and $3 billion debt, which would have been no problem to finance. And I went to Time-Warner with that, and they said, "No." So, the networks weren't all in a—you know, the whole industry wasn't in a state of turmoil. And I tried to be a good partner. I mean, when they told me not to buy Home Shopping Network, I said, "Okay." When they wouldn't let me buy FNN years ago, before NBC ended up buying it, I said, "Okay."

But when I wanted to get New Line and Castle Rock, I had to literally go almost to war with them. I had to threaten going public so that we could get the movie business. They did not want us to get into the movie business. They did everything short of voting for it. In the end, they abstained and let us do it, but under the greatest amount of pressure. They said it's not a good business to be in, the movie business. I said, "Wait a minute, you're in it. I mean, how can you"—*(laughter)*—you know, and now—and they said the network business is a lousy business. You don't want to be in the network business.

But now they're trying to get a network. And they said, "We've got to have a network." And I said, "Hey, there's three of them. Go buy one. You know, I'm pulling for you. There's three. Go get one, I'll cheer you on, but let me go too. And I've been negotiating with NBC for a number of years. And I want to be free to negotiate with them too, like you're doing right at the present time." And they won't let me do it. And it's not right. Those restrictions were put in to keep me from making errors, and they're using them—they're using them to hold our company back, and that is wrong, and to keep their control, keep their hard and firm control over us. And that is a little bit of news.

And I haven't leveled anything. I haven't made any charges. I haven't filed any lawsuits. I haven't filed any complaints at the FCC or the Justice Department—yet. *(Laughter.)* And I hope I won't have to. I hope that Jerry Levin, God bless his sweet soul—I mean, I was one of the people that honored him last week at the Cates Dinner, the cable dinner. And he's a wonderful guy, and he's brilliant, and he was cum laude, and he's got more college degrees than you can shake a stick at, and you know, he's a great guy. But we need to be able to move forward.

Why do we need to move forward? Because the industry is consolidating. I don't like it. I mean, I don't like the communications industry consolidating the way it is. You just had—Sumner Redstone bought Paramount. I think I really believe that all three of the networks will be realigned with other companies. A combination of the cable regulations and the threat of the telephones getting in the business is forcing the entire cable industry to consolidate. That's not in anyone's best interest.

I'm on the board of NCTA, and I'm slated to be chairman in two years. We had a board meeting the other day. There are 40 members of the board, and 10 of those members are being merged out of their jobs right now, they're just waiting—Times Mirror—I mean big companies—Newhouse. It is an absolute tragedy. And we're going to end with four or five mega-companies that control just about everything that we see, certainly on radio and television, particularly television—and it is very distressing to me, and I think it should be to all of us in this business.

Now GE, with the turnaround, they were willing to get out a year ago, now they're not. They want to control anything. That's the reason that the talks broke off with Disney. They want to stay in and acquire, rather than be acquired. So that window of opportunity that existed a year ago, which was blocked by Time-Warner, isn't open to us at the current time. I mean, in fact, I can't even talk to GE. They won't talk to me until I've got clearances from my handlers to—(laughter)—be able to talk to them. I had a meeting tomorrow, but it was cancelled, as of yesterday. So I am upset about it. I'm upset about it. But I want to be a survivor and I think we've made a contribution.

Let me tell you about sports. We carried the World Cup four years ago. We were the only ones that were really interested—paid them a fair price. This time, when the World Cup came up, we were the incumbents, but ABC and ESPN came in, and ESPN said we'll put a number of the games on our network that reaches everybody. And the soccer people said, "Look Ted, it's not even a question of dollars, we need that exposure. You can't even bid. You can't even bid on the soccer." So we lost it.

I mean the combination of a network and cable network—let me tell you what else happened.

Remember the retransmission consent that our government put in, which—the idea was good—let the broadcasters be able to get paid if they can negotiate a fee from the cable systems. But that isn't what happened. All three of them, Fox, NBC with America's Talking, Fox with the Fox Network, and ESPN with ESPN2—they got new cable networks. So the government mandate created competitors for me, you know, like I didn't have enough competition. In the cable universe, there's 60 networks. I mean, it's not like I'm hollering about I can't stand competition, but it's unfair competition when you don't have a piece of the puzzle that your competitors have. And since they all have broadcast networks and cable networks now, with the exception of CBS, who never could seem to get it right, now CBS will, I promise you, CBS will be gone within a year from current ownership. Its ownership will change hands. Larry Tisch's program was not a successful one, even though his profits will be up this year because he doesn't have the NFL and doesn't have baseball, but his position is dramatically deteriorated for the long haul.

And now I have got to compete with Rupert Murdoch, who has his own studio, who has his own broadcast network and who has now his own cable network. And so I am having to play with one hand tied behind my back. It's like fighting a war without an air force. And all you've got to do is look what happened to Poland to see what happened to that, you know? And what happened to Iraq, and what would have happened to Haiti, you know? I mean, that's—you know, you just can't win if you're—if the people you're fighting with have got an air force. You've got to have one. If they've got a navy, you've got to have one. If they've got tanks, you've got to have them. You know? I mean we fought the Cold War. We know about that. You've got to be able to meet them everywhere. You've got to have all the elements.

A newspaper can't win a competitive battle—there are no more, or hardly any more newspaper competitions, but there's one here in Washington. And both of them got sports departments, and both of them got feature departments, and both of them got editorial pages and front pages and classifieds. You take one of those pieces out, one of the other guys.

And I'll tell you who else is going to get networks. Disney will get one of those networks—probably—uuh! *(Laughter.)* And Sumner Redstone is going to get one—probably. And Time-Warner is going to try to figure out how to get one, even though they, by the rules of the game, they can't have one. They're trying to figure out how to do it. And Rupert's already got one. So, hey, if all three of them get networks, I don't have a network. So I'm sitting on the outside.

It could mean that I have to sell out. That's what it could mean. I'd put my company up for sale. That's the only way to resolve this thing if I can't resolve it peacefully with Time-Warner. I've repeatedly begged them on bended knee to please let us go out and compete. And so far they've said no.

And you know who would be the buyer of our company? Anybody got a—I'll ask you a question. *(Laughter.)* Who do you think would outbid everybody else for our company? Rupert Murdoch. Rupert Murdoch would. I mean, he outbid everybody for the NFL. Rupert Murdoch is the only one that can do it. The rest of them are astute businessmen. You can't match a madman—*(laughter)*—and he's not really mad! You know, he's kind of like a mad genius. You know? There's a thin line between madness and brilliance. And, in fact, the most dangerous kind of competitor is one who is a little mad. You know?

And that's why Rupert is really driving the other networks crazy. He has raised NBC's costs on network compensation. I mean, they start—when they bought the network, it was $200 million a year. They cut it down to $100 million a year. Now it's back up to $200 million a year, and that comes right off the top. And he's done the same thing for CBS, and, to a lesser extent, ABC. And God knows where he will strike next. You know, God knows. I mean, when baseball comes up—and it could be up—I mean, I'll bet you he goes after that. And, I mean, I've only got one piece of the—I've got the cable piece of the NBA—he's going to be able now to go out and bid for both the cable and the broadcast.

I have to be able to compete, because I—and he's got his own studio with Fox. Time-Warner has got their own studio. Disney has got their own studio. Universal and Paramount not only have the USA network, but Paramount has got MTV and Nickelodeon, and Nick at Night and Showtime. And the only guys that are out there with no electronic delivery system of their own are Sony. And I had dinner with Peter Gueber a year ago, and he said any studio without its own electronic network distribution system is a dead pigeon. He's got it figured right. I mean, Sony is the odd man out. They will get out of the business. They'll merge with somebody else, too, because they've got no place in the sea. They've got no place—they're at a dead end. You cannot paint yourself into a corner in this business. You have to be able to move forward and have the necessary flexibility.

Now there are some other things I would like to talk about. But so, at any rate, one of them is the population conference in Cairo. I mean, I am so glad that conference worked out well. We're having dinner with Tim Wirth, who spoke here just a little while ago before the conference, and his wife. My wife was over there. I had to cancel because I had skin cancer and had to have it removed, and couldn't talk because it was on my lip. And it's a real tough thing to be Ted Turner with your lip sewed up. *(Laughter.)* Believe me. I could mumble—I could mumble a little bit through a straw.

I'll tell you one thing—we ran a story on clitorectomies. I don't know—it's not a funny matter. I mean, it's something I've been against for a long time, even before I met my ex-wife, and most people don't know about it, but millions of women have their clitorises cut off when they are 10 or 12 years old, so they can't have fun in sex. And we got a photograph of it—not a photograph, a video of it, and we ran it.

And now the Egyptian government, which is one of the countries—Egypt—between 50 and 80 percent of Egyptian girls had their clits cut off. I mean, how about that? You talk about equal rights. You talk about a barbaric mutilation. Well, I'm in an angry mood. I'm angry at that, too. I'm being clitorized by Time-Warner, and the women are being clitorized by—(Laughter.) That's exactly right, and I don't like it any more than they do. You know, that's exactly it. And they want to do it right. If they think it's bad for women to want sex, then why don't they cut the heads off of the little whackers of the 10-year-old boys over there too, you know—(laughter)—and make it an even-steven deal.

Who's got the first question? *(Laughter, applause.)*

MR. KLEIN: Well, there goes our G rating. *(Laughter.)*

Okay, the first question is—I can't top that. Even if you had clearance from your handlers to buy NBC, wouldn't you face federal regulations blocking the purchase?

MR. TURNER: No. *(Laughter.)* We have it structured in such a way that that's not a problem. Meet all the rules, like Rupert does, by the skin on our teeth. *(Laughter.)*

MR. KLEIN: If you do end up buying part or all of NBC, what would you plan to do with the news division? Given your ownership of CNN, would NBC News be redundant?

MR. TURNER: No. *(Laughter.)*

MR. KLEIN: You're as bad as Margaret Truman. *(Laughter.)*

MR. TURNER: Hey, I mean, you know, NBC is just one of the three. I want to be able to negotiate with all three of them, you know, I mean, get the best deal. Comparison shopping— you know what I'm talking about? Check in—what is it? What's that guide that you can get that doesn't take any advertising? Consumer magazine—Consumer Reports, I'm going to check that out.

MR. KLEIN: George Gilder predicts that the age of television will soon come to an end as the personal computer becomes the major information appliance. How seriously do you take this threat and what are you planning to do about it?

MR. TURNER: Phooey. *(Laughter.)*

MR. KLEIN: You warned me about this, didn't you? *(Laughter.)* Fortunately I've got a lot of questions. *(Laughter.)*

Do you agree with the opinion held by many that Time-Warner is a hodgepodge of companies which should be broken up so as to achieve greatest refund to shareholders—or greatest return to shareholders?

MR. TURNER: No comment. *(Laughter.)*

MR. KLEIN: Ah, you're going real fast now. *(Laughter.)*

Will CNN have to do away—move away further from a 24-hour news channel to stay in business?

MR. TURNER: Absolutely not. The ratings at CNN are through the roof. We had a bad first quarter, and boy, I mean, everybody made a big deal about it. I tell you, we don't have a lot of friends in the media, but I'll tell you what, that's okay. When you've beaten everybody as badly as we have in the news business, you've got to expect that when you do have a down time that everybody is going to jump on you.

Obviously an all-news network is going to do better, whether it's a radio—radio stations are the same way—all-news radio—their ratings spike up and down depending on whether there's a big fire or whatever it is. And on top of that is that we made that clearly because of re-regulation. Over half of our channels that we were on, we were moved to another channel, usually almost invariably up the dial to make way for this new must-carry rule that was put in, where even the home shopping channels have preference over CNN, and ABC has precedence over us, and any lousy little independent station has precedence over us. I mean, I think those must-carry rules are discriminatory and they're wrong, and I predict that they're going to be struck down by the Supreme Court. They waffled on it the last time. I mean, they don't have a lot of courage, and the Supreme Court should have courage. My God, if they don't, who does? *(Laughter.)*

MR. KLEIN: A question coming in from an Asian viewer.

MR. TURNER: Oh, good.

MR. KLEIN: Does the introduction of TNT's Cartoon Channel in Asia next month signal the intensification of the rivalry between TBS and Murdoch's Star TV in Asia?

MR. TURNER: Well, yes, but we're competing with everybody out there, you know, not just one, because there's a lot of people going to Asia, and there's going to be a lot of money lost out there because there's way too much of it and the market is not that big, because of incomes and everything and language problems. But we have such a low cost in the programming for the cartoons and the movies, since we own over 3,000 motion pictures and, I don't know, 8,000 cartoons, that basically all it costs us is a few million dollars to get out there and stake our claim to the video highway that will someday cover the world, just about the time the air becomes unbreatheable. We are going to really make it big—*(laughter)*—just as people are expiring from over-population and pollution. What else can we do? You know you've got to keep moving. *(Laughter.)*

MR. KLEIN: This questioner says: Please discuss the role of bluff in entrepreneurial success. *(Laughter.)*

MR. TURNER: Well, I remember when Kenny Rogers came out with that song "The Gambler." I remember my little cute daughter was six years old and I drove her to school every morning. She sang it every day. "You've got to know when to hold them, know when to fold them, know when to run away and know when to stay. You know you've got to never count your money while you're sitting at the table. There'll be time enough for counting when the dealing's done."

Business is very much like any other kind of competitive conflict. You have to use all tools at your disposal. And I guess bluff would be one, but bluffing means you are not really holding the cards, and I think I'm holding enough cards to be able to play at a certain level. And I want to be able to play at the big game. All my life I've been on the outside. You know, I don't know how many of you all came from some small town in the South. I think one reason that Bill Clinton and Jimmy Carter got beat on so much is because they are from small southern states. I really do—I know there's prejudice—I've had it against me all my life.

I've got to tell you one story. I was born in Cincinnati, Ohio and my father moved to Georgia when I was nine years old, and he sent me right away to Georgia Military Academy, which was a school for—it was like a prison school, I mean military school. And the kids— some of the kids had been there since the first grade—boarding students at military school. And they were so mean, and I was a Yankee and they were still fighting the Civil War. So they said, "Turner's a Yankee, kill the Yankee." They used to pile on. I remember hiding in a locker for six hours. They had a lynch mob with a rope. You know, they were just playing like they were the Ku Klux Klan, see.

So I became—I learned the southern accent. I mean it took me a couple of years. I finally got integrated in. *(Laughter.)* I became a southerner. I was getting killed, all right—it was awful—beat up all the time, pounded on, gangs. I wasn't sodomized, thank God. *(Laughter.)* We were too young for that. But everything else.

Then my father decided I had to go to college in the East. So now I'm a southerner, and guess what, it's 1956, Emmett Till has just been murdered. It's the beginning of the Civil Rights Movement. So everybody up there thinks I must be some racist, you know—God-damned southerner Turner. *(Laughter.)* So now I'm back in the North, I couldn't shake the southern, couldn't get in the right fraternities or anything, nobody wanted to be my friend. And then the New York Yacht Club and then starting CNN, a bumpkin from Georgia. I'm sick of it.

I want to be able to stand at the first class table. You know, I want the whole gamut. I don't want people pushing me around anymore.

Remember the Charles Atlas stories with the sand in the face. I mean, I need a network. I want to be able to—look, I'm in Atlanta. In 1996 the Olympics are coming to Atlanta. I helped get the Olympics there because CNN was from there. The people voted for it. I couldn't even bid for the Olympics—not allowed to be a bidder. NBC, ABC, CBS, yes. Once one of the three big networks got the Olympics they could put as much of it on cable as they wanted to, but only an over-the-air network could be a bidder.

And then NBC, to make it even better, they said there will be no cable involvement—not one thing. And the local people in Atlanta want to know why I'm not more enthusiastic about the Olympics. I don't even have a smidgen. I'm able to buy tickets in the 50th row back, you know. I'm tired of it. You would be too, wouldn't you? That's right, I'm mad. We own the movie "Network." Remember, the guy stuck his head out—Peter Finch stuck his head out the window and said, "I'm mad as hell and I'm not going to take it anymore." And that's the way I feel. *(Applause.)*

MR. KLEIN: Do you think the film industry can ever truly be decentralized out of Los Angeles? This questioner says: I understand your documentaries are based in Atlanta, but Turner Films will be based out of Los Angeles.

MR. TURNER: "Ever" is a long time; I mean people make films all over the place. But you're smart to have your—films mostly are now shot on location; they're not made in the studio like they used to be. Television programs, on the other hand, are mostly made in studios. But you need to have your headquarters there because that's where all the agents and stars are. Individual people now live outside, a lot of stars don't live in Los Angeles, but they have their business affairs conducted there, they travel there a lot. I mean I'm in the film business but I don't live there, but Alan Horne and Bob Shay and the guys running the film companies are.

MR. KLEIN: What do you believe is the comfortable balance between network access versus pay cable? *(Laughter.)*

MR. TURNER: Network access versus pay cable? I don't know; I mean that's—you could go on with that for a long time. You know, what's better, round or square? *(Laughter.)*

MR. KLEIN: Well, more specifically, then, on this question: If TBS did get the Olympics, anyone who doesn't have cable because they can't afford it won't be able to see it.

MR. TURNER: Not if I had a network, too. We'd put part of it on the network and part of it on the cable, you know, spread it around a little bit. You know, like the Democratic administration does—take a little from the rich, give it to the less wealthy. Nothing wrong with that. It's the American way.

MR. KLEIN: Yours and Jane's commitment to population issues, including your being the U.N. Goodwill Ambassador on this issue, is founded on what beliefs?

MR. TURNER: On population issues, the issue is founded on what beliefs? I mean I think the world's too crowded, that's simple, you know. *(Laughter.)* It's getting more crowded all the time. We live in a finite world with an infinitely increasing number of people. I mean, you know, it's easy to see. And one out of five of those people lives in abject poverty, and 80 percent of them live below the U.S. official designated poverty level. I mean, you know, come on. And it's getting worse all the time.

Incomes in the United States—the average income is going down as engineers and scientists that have been let go from military contractors have to go to work at McDonald's for the minimum wage. I mean, there's too many people, you bet.

MR. KLEIN: This questioner says Richard Rodriquez wrote recently that he would like to ask Ted Turner why, in CNN's reports on overpopulation, the screen is filled with images of black and brown people. Why not images of Norwegians filling restaurants, consuming more than their share of the world's resources?

MR. TURNER: Good, well, I mean hey, that's a good point. And that's why they call this conference the Population Development Conference because we in the rich world consume, I don't know, 50 times as much as somebody from the poor world. And I personally do— Norway actually is a great place. They have zero population growth and they give away a higher percentage of the gross national product to charity in the world than any other country. They give over 10 times as much per person in Norway as we do, like 2 percent of GNP, and we give one tenth of one percent of GNP to help out in the world. And yet the average per capita income in Norway is about a third what it is in the United States, so they end up using a lot less.

I mean, I personally try and use as little as I can. I mean, I live on the roof of my office so I don't have to drive a car to work. You know, I walk to work every morning, I walk downstairs, and actually I don't even take the elevator. I walk up 14 floors to get a little workout in the morning so I don't have to use that energy. And I breathe as little as I possibly can and— *(laughter)*—I don't even have to buy food because I go to banquets all the time and eat this garbage up, but it doesn't cost anything. *(Laughter.)*

MR. KLEIN: You now have a world network; what does American cultural imperialism mean to you?

MR. TURNER: I hate it. I do hate it, but I'm part of it. You know we're part of it. I don't know, I mean it's—American culture. I mean there are good things about our culture and bad things about our culture, just like everything else. And then, once again, they are in the eyes of the beholder. I am sure that Sumner Redstone loves Beavis and Butthead and the Grunt Brothers. I don't like them, I like Captain Planet better. I mean, you know, you can judge us by what our—but they both came from here.

We live in a world that's becoming more and more global, whether we like it or not, and I think it's almost imperative that we get to understand and know more about each other in order to foster the cooperation that is going to be necessary for human survival as there become more and more of us on this planet and the world.

I mean, 100 years ago you could fight a war and you didn't have anything but cannon and guns. It was limited to that area. But if we had fought a nuclear war—and we're going to do a 30 to 40 hour series like "The World at War," on the Cold War; I want to announce that. We are going to do the most in-depth—and I'm reading this new book that the New York bureau chief of the Guardian is writing. It's fascinating.

The Cold War was by far the most expensive war that ever occurred, and the casualties were greater than any war. The two major protagonists hardly ever fired a shot at each other, but it was fought in surrogates in the Third World all over the place. And we were very, very fortunate to conclude without it turning into a nuclear exchange which would have destroyed life on Earth. That's how close we were, and it's happened in our lifetime. It's only been over a couple of years.

I'm happily going to the Russian Embassy tonight. You know, Yeltsin's in town. He's the one that's proposing let's cut back on nuclear weapons. Why don't we get rid of nuclear weapons? Instead of telling North Korea that they can't have nuclear weapons and we'll come bomb them if they make them—what a dumb thing. We, the big rich guys, can have them but they can't. I mean that is a double standard that just doesn't cut it. It doesn't cut it.

If we want the world to get rid of nuclear weapons or not have nuclear proliferation, then we should propose at the U.N. that every country sign a non-nuclear treaty where we all get rid of our nuclear weapons and nobody makes them anymore. That's the answer to the problem.

But, you know, we ain't going to do that, we're sitting around—we don't even know what to do with them. You can't use them. Why don't we get rid of them? That's just too common sense, I guess. That's too common sense.

MR. KLEIN: Realistically, aren't there more cable companies today than can be profitable?

MR. TURNER: No. *(Laughter.)*

MR. KLEIN: Are there any ways to stem the violence shown on TV, bearing in mind that this would affect the ratings?

MR. TURNER: Don't watch it. And it'll go away if enough people don't watch it.

MR. KLEIN: On to baseball. Why shouldn't Congress revoke baseball's antitrust exemption?

MR. TURNER: I can't think of any good reason. It doesn't make any difference to me. We have more trouble than any other sport, and we've got the exemption and others don't. I never thought it meant diddly-squat. *(Laughter.)*

MR. KLEIN: Do you think the baseball strike will break the players' union?

MR. TURNER: It could, but that doesn't necessarily mean that it will. I mean, it could. It seriously can weaken it, let's say, but, I mean, the players' union gambled that the owners would cave in rather than lose the World Series, and they've used up most of their leverage. But then the government may step in, there's no telling.

The owners do want peace, I'm sure of that, and the players do too, so maybe there's some room for compromise. It's just too bad that this happened. I mean, it bothers me tremendously, but there are other things that bother me worse. I mean, clitorectomies bother me worse. That's more of a permanent problem, if you had it done to you.

MR. KLEIN: Do you believe there is little respect for the journalism profession, and why would that be?

MR. TURNER: You added that yourself. You're not even reading it right. *(Laughter.)* "Why would that be," is not on there.

(Laughter, applause.) It says, "Little respect for the journalism profession anymore."

MR. KLEIN: Okay. Well, why is there—

MR. TURNER: You're just adding that? You're not even reading the damned questions. You're editing them! That's the reason why journalism is held in such—*(laughter, applause)*—such low regard.

If certain elements of the press are held in low regard, it's probably because they deserve it. *(Laughter.)*

MR. KLEIN: Some people are saying if there were no troubles around the world, there would be no CNN. Would you agree?

MR. TURNER: Who said that?

MR. KLEIN: I don't know. *(Laughter.)* Some people. I'm just reading the questions.

MR. TURNER: Some people! I mean, you know, my father always said, "someone's" the biggest liar in the world. *(Laughter.)*

I don't agree with that. The honest truth, our ratings are higher whenever there's a disaster. The bigger the disaster, the higher the ratings, and that's true of all the newscasts and whatever else for the most part. But I would far rather have lower ratings and lower profits and live in a prosperous, happy, kind and loving world and have low ratings—we'd still have some ratings because there'd be so much good news that, you know, people get sick of it, I guess, but I'd rather live in that world and be a lot poorer. I mean, I gave $200 million away last year. It was 10 percent of what I had, not of what I made, and I'm planning, if, under the right circumstances—I'm giving it all away later, when I die. It's going to a foundation for population and environmental stuff. Seventy-five million dollars of that went to three educational institutions.

You know, you can't take it with you anyway. I mean, it's money. You know, when you're eating this kind of food that's free anyhow, what do you need money for? I mean—*(laughter)*—so I might as well give it away and—let's deal with some of the problems that we have in the world.

MR. KLEIN: In a recent "New Republic" article, they mentioned that CNN had undermined the news business by—

MR. TURNER: Nah. *(Laughter.)* That isn't even a question. It's your own question!

MR. KLEIN: I can ask a question, I'm allowed.

MR. TURNER: But you're palming this off as somebody else's question!

MR. KLEIN: No, I'm not, I'm holding it down like this. *(Laughter.)*

MR. TURNER: Okay. All right. What's the question?

MR. KLEIN: Okay.

MR. TURNER: What's the question?

MR. KLEIN: The question is.

MR. TURNER: "The New Republic" article.

MR. KLEIN: "The New Republic" article. I'm sure you're familiar with it.

MR. TURNER: Yeah. Yeah.

MR. KLEIN: Yeah. *(Laughter.)*

MR. TURNER: It was derogatory to CNN. It said we were giving people too much information too quickly, right?

MR. KLEIN: That's right, and undermining the power and the role of the—

MR. TURNER: *(Gives a Bronx cheer.)* I mean, what a jerk! What a jerk! Too much information and getting it too quickly. That'd be like the—remember in the old days when they had extra editions, you know, a special edition when there was war or something like that? I mean, they'd be criticizing the newspapers for getting it out too fast. The trouble is they get it out too slow. *(Laughs.)*

It used to be fast. You know, a hundred years ago, yesterday—having yesterday's news tomorrow—and, besides, they didn't even have—all they had was local news then, because there was no wire services and you couldn't get the news around. It took months to find anything out. I mean, you got it, I mean, but we're in a world—we're in a world now, an electronic world of speed and accuracy—well, it's not even accuracy, because sometimes you report it and you don't even know till later, but people want to know what's happening right now, and we give it to them.

MR. KLEIN: Some people.

MR. TURNER: Some people. *(Laughter.)* Some people don't care. *(Laughs.)*

MR. KLEIN: How do you maintain integrity in your station's programs to avoid stooping to entertainment and stimulate the public with a view to selling advertising to your sponsors?

"Quiz Show" demonstrates the beginning of the attitude that entertainment is all that counts.

Ted Turner, Chairman of the Board, Turner Broadcasting System and Gil Klein, NPC President.

MR. TURNER: Well, there are certainly elements of television journalism that go that way, and if you've seen "Natural Born Killers," it's supposedly a parody. It's awfully violent, but the Geraldo Rivera character that's there—he ends up joining the killers in killing the police. He gets so caught up in the story that he becomes part of it, and he gets blown away at the end, too.

And, you know, "Inside Edition" and that sort of thing—you know, we're not immune to it. We're not perfect, but I think we're better than most. I mean, we put less show biz into our news. I think, of the major television operations, we're the most credible and the most newsworthy, but we still—we tend to sensationalize a bit from time to time, so we're not perfect, but I think we're better than most.

MR. KLEIN: If you could reinvent Major League Baseball in 1994, how would you make it different from what we have had?

MR. TURNER: No strike. *(Laughter.)*

MR. KLEIN: Would you like to be Commissioner of Baseball, too?

MR. TURNER: No! That's not—that's another one of your questions. What's missing in your life?

MR. KLEIN: Okay. If you had more time, what would you do? Hobbies?

MR. TURNER: I'd fish more.

MR. KLEIN: You'd fish more?

MR. TURNER: Yes.

But I don't really feel like I have anything missing in my life except that network. Let's not forget that. *(Laughter.)*

MR. KLEIN: Where does religious broadcasting fit into the scheme of the future for communications when—what you've outlined?

MR. TURNER: Whatever. *(Laughter.)*

Well, I know a lot—there are some people that watch it, and I used to televise it. I mean, I was the first station to affiliate with Pat Robertson's "700 Club" and later on, when I learned more about him and threw him off the station, we put Jim and Tammy Bakker in business in Charlotte, North Carolina. *(Laughter.)* And I also used to carry Jerry Falwell's programming and Oral Roberts and Jimmy Swaggart. And I don't carry any of them anymore. I got sick when I learned out what was really going on.

But that's not all religious broadcasters. Those are just some of the more famous ones. I'm sure there are some that are legit, but, you know, I'm not much of a religious person, to tell you the truth. I don't like "isms." I mean, I don't like communism or capitalism. "Isms" have caused most of the problems in the world, and I think religion's response—it's religion that—under the guise of religion they've murdered tens of thousands of women as witches only a hundred years ago, burned them at the stake, you know. They blame it on religion in Egypt, even though Islam says it's not true, but the clitorectomies are said it's a religious thing, you know.

I mean, I'd like to see a religion where everybody was good, you know? I mean, not just the members of that sect. I mean, I'm sick of it. Heaven's going to be a mighty slender place, and most of the people I know and like aren't going to be there. There are a few notable exceptions, and I'll miss them. *(Laughter.)* But remember, heaven is going to be perfect, and I don't really want to be there. Those of us that go to hell—it'll be most of us in this room—most of the journalists are certainly going there. *(Laughter.)* Anyway, they're not that religious, because they know too much. But when we get there, we'll have a chance to make things better, because hell's supposed to be a mess and heaven's perfect. Who wants to go to a place that's perfect? I mean, boring, boring. *(Laughter.)*

MR. KLEIN: When do you plan to have CNN and TNT in Arabic and/or other foreign or international languages like the BBC and other television outfits?

MR. TURNER: Well, we already are basically doing it in Germany, and we've got some Spanish-language programming on CNN and TNT in South America, and we're looking at other languages, and we'll be going into more languages as there's enough viewers in any area to—of a specific language to make it economically justifiable.

It's not a problem broadcasting in multiple languages on a satellite, because you have—you can send one picture out on a number of audio tracks to the same thing, and we are doing it and will be increasing it more.

MR. KLEIN: I hate to tell you this.

MR. TURNER: You're out of questions.

MR. KLEIN: No, I've got plenty of questions.

MR. TURNER: Out of time? Thank God.

MR. KLEIN: We're out of time.

MR. TURNER: Hey, all right!

MR. KLEIN: Before asking the last question—

MR. TURNER: Oh, I get a plaque? No, just a piece of paper. Hey, look, it's not—I wish it was a check, but—*(laughter)*—this'll do.

MR. KLEIN: We were asking you for a check.

MR. TURNER: Oh, a free cup!

MR. KLEIN: Hey!

MR. TURNER: Hey, hey! Terrific! Thanks. This is, you know, real generosity.

MR. KLEIN: Yeah, it's the least we could do for you. *(Laughter, applause.)* And the final question is: Tell us about Jane. How has she changed your life?

MR. TURNER: That makes me smile just thinking about it. She's changed my life in a lot of wonderful and pleasant ways. And, Jeri, I really love you. Thanks for a lot.

MR. KLEIN: Thank you very much. That was a memorable, memorable performance. And we look forward to you coming back here real soon, and maybe for Jane Fonda to come back soon, too. *(Applause.)*

NATIONAL PRESS CLUB

LUNCHEON
December 7, 1994

SPEAKER

SARAH FERGUSON
Duchess of York

MODERATED BY: Gil Klein

HEAD TABLE GUESTS

꙳꙳꙳

EDGAR ALAN POE
New Orleans Times Picayune

CARL MOLLINS
Washington Editor of Macleans Magazine

SANDRA MCELWAINE
Independent Journalist

MARTIN FLETCHER
U.S. Editor of the Times of London

STEVE SELMAN
Washington Bureau Chief of the BBC

JOHN HOLLIMAN
CNN

CHRISTY WISE
Freelance Journalist and Chairwoman of the National Press Club Speakers Committee

ALMA VIATOR
Viator Associates

SUSAN SPAULDING
*Daily Oklahoman and the member of the National Press Club Speakers Committee
who arranged today's luncheon*

ED VIULLIAMY
Washington Bureau Chief of the London Observer

PETER PRICHARD
Editor of USA Today

BARBARA REHM
American Banker

WINSTON S. WOOD
Deputy Bureau Chief of Ottoway News Service

GIL KLEIN

MODERATOR

*g*ood afternoon. Welcome to the National Press Club. My name is Gil Klein. I'm the club's president and a national correspondent with Media General Newspapers, writing for the Richmond Times-Dispatch, the Tampa Tribune and the Winston-Salem Journal.

I'd like to welcome my fellow club members in the audience today as well as those of you who are watching us on C-SPAN or listening to us on National Public Radio or the Internet global computer network.

Now today we are honored to have with us Her Royal Highness the Duchess of York. It is only fitting that she would be with us at this time on this the 180th anniversary of the British burning Washington. *(Laughter.)* A poll of the American people taken after the last election found that 85 percent approved of the action and would like to invite British Admiral Cockburn back for another try. *(Laughter.)*

Born Sarah Margaret Ferguson, Her Royal Highness traces her lineage through her paternal grandmother to the Royal House of Stuart. She married Prince Andrew, the second son of Queen Elizabeth and Prince Philip, at Westminster Abbey on the 23rd of July 1986, at which time the Prince was created the Duke of York. Prince Andrew was a helicopter pilot in the Royal Navy so the Duchess decided that she, too, would learn how to fly a helicopter, which I understand is no mean feat for anyone. She nicknamed her helicopter "Budgie" which is British slang for parakeet. Out of that has come a new career for the Duchess and a new icon for preschoolers, Budgie, the Helicopter, the hero of a line of children's books that Her Royal Highness has written. The New York Times wrote that there was something of the Duchess in Budgie, "a cheery sort, given to rescue missions and a bit of mischief." And that has allowed the Duchess to pursue what she says is her real passion in life—helping children.

Among the charities she supports is one she helped create, Children in Crisis. Aided by profits from the Budgie books and the Duchess's energy, Children in Crisis has helped relieve the suffering of dystrophic babies in Albania, develop a refugee center in the former Yugoslavia and the Clean Air Recuperation Center in Poland that is helping at least 700 children each year fight the pollution that is killing them.

Building on the success of Children in Crisis, she is launching a new charity in the United States called Chances for Children. Its objective is to support those small projects that larger charities may overlook, and she is here today to highlight which particular charities will be pinpointed in the first year of activity.

Ladies and gentlemen, please join me in a warm press club welcome for Her Royal Highness the Duchess of York. *(Applause.)*

SARAH FERGUSON

SPEAKER

*W*ell, Gil, do you really want me to talk, because I think you've said it all. *(Laughs.)*

No, I'm really, really, really honored to be here today. I must say, it was a pretty brave step, and it's very nice that some of the journalists are actually applauding me out there today, too.

By the time that I had actually accepted this invitation to speak before the National Press Club, I had become as cynical as some journalists assembled here are widely said to be, faced with yet another earnest figure attaching herself to charitable causes in an apparent attempt to improve one's public image. *(Laughter.)*

So with this in mind, I decided to broaden the scope of my remarks this afternoon to include more than just a litany of good causes of which I'm affiliated, and to tell you a bit about my life. This way, my affiliation with charitable causes can be understood in the context of a much more general picture. Of course, I realize that I have had special advantages in doing these projects, but while my charitable activities form a very gratifying and fulfilling part of my life, they are by no means my entire life.

Her Majesty graciously allowed me access to the private Royal Archives for the work on my history books. This helped me to piece together the romantic adventures of Queen Victoria and her beloved husband, Prince Albert, through Europe. I was so excited. I drifted into the library and was lost in the romance they had for 21 years. He died very early at 41, and she mourned for him for 32 years. It's one of the saddest love stories of our time. And to be allowed to jump into the diaries and delve into her life was a real treat.

Since my separation, I have written and published a history book and overseen the transformation of my children's books into an animated cartoon. But my business career is not without problems and conflicts, as I'm sure a lot of you will agree. I try vigilantly to battle with the conflicts of interest that arise from my position and the necessity of providing for my family. I find myself in unchartered territory. The facts are that I am a separated mother of two children, and as an independent woman, I am now largely responsible for the finances of my family. Therefore, a great deal of my time has to be—has to be—occupied with commercial work. Believe it or not, that is the truth.

The world of women has changed, very much so, and this, I believe, has increased the options, but also the confusion of any woman who finds herself in a public position and tries to reconcile traditional values with modern demands.

I have become aware of other demands, too. Some of these were externally imposed and came to be true dictates of my heart, the heart. I find myself in hospitals, going from ward to ward. I've received letters that were just extraordinary expressions of suffering, hope and pain. And I came to understand what—really, to paraphrase what President Franklin Roosevelt said at his inaugural address, to those who much is given, much is expected.

There I was at the palace. At first I was wandering around with no compass, no fixed sense of what to do. It wasn't that I lacked the will or the ability. I simply did not know what was expected of me back in '86 as a member of the Royal Family.

This has been a time of real soul-searching, striving to achieve the reality which comes from understanding yourself. It is a long and a very arduous path, and certainly the path I have followed has not been as straight and narrow as it might have been. *(Laughter, applause.)*

However—*(laughter)*—I've been given a second chance in my life, and I want to do everything I can to give inspiration to those who need a second chance in their lives.

In the United Kingdom, I only became involved with causes that I can relate to and feel really passionate about, and now you're going to get a few more details on what those things are.

When I was 18, 19, 20, I had a lot of friends who became heroin addicts, or drug addicts, or alcoholics, and so I decided the thing to do was to sit in on a few therapy sessions to see how perhaps I could talk to them. Rather like learning to fly a helicopter, I wanted to know what my husband was talking about in the evening when he came back from work.

So what I did was I went on to therapy sessions and I went to the Chemical Dependency Center and I said, "Come on, what's all this about the 12 steps, the Minnesota method? Let's really get to grips with it." So I asked, actually rather rudely, if I could join the Chemical Dependency Center and they very kindly made me patron, and so I do a lot of work with drug abuse and addictions.

Teenagers—it's a big topic of mine, both in the general development as people, but more specifically those with cancer. I had a very difficult time at that age. Not only was I tall and even fatter than I am now, but I was also a redhead and a teenager. *(Laughter.)*

I think the most important thing, which is what was so good on yesterday, I think it was, when I went to the Monte Fiore Medical Center in the Bronx in New York, and it was so good, because I walked in and I saw that they actually have a special unit for teenagers so that teenagers can walk in and they can get over their cancer a lot better because they don't have granny on the right or a toddler on the left. And we are starting those units over in the UK, probably thanks to your direction. And it's very exciting, although they're 500,000 pounds—not dollars—per unit. We have already got two going, and so teenagers now do have a chance in Great Britain to get over the cancer, which with adolescents as well is a very difficult thing for them.

And I certainly just look at my two babies, who just are dreams—real dreams—and they are furious that I'm here today, actually, because they want me to pick them up from school. But I certainly realize that the more I can do to help children—so easily, one of my daughters or both daughters could be a teenager with cancer, so that's why I do it. And every day I thank the Lord that I have two such beautiful little girls—*(points to photo)*—there they are.

Whether it is fighting for the rights of mentally disabled or encouraging funding for fetal research, another two of my little hobby horses, these are projects which I really do personally believe in and see there is so much to do. Perhaps my greatest exposure has been to ALS, Amyotrophic Lateral Sclerosis, Lou Gehrig's Disease in this country. In Great Britain it's called Motor Neuron Disease.

Stephen Hawking has it and writes all his books from this muscle in his top of his thumb. He can't move any other part of his body, which shows you the intellect remains absolutely sharp as ever the day you die, but your body wastes away. David Niven died of it, and when he came off an interview he said, "Please, don't anyone get this awful disease. I am not drunk; I simply can't talk."

Before I was married, I worked in a publishing house and I was editing a book with Sir Robert Cook. It was called the "Palace of Westminster." When he started to write that book, he would sprint up the stairs to my office, six floors up. Eight months later, he had died of ALS. But on the day he died, he finished the last chapter of that book, dictating it into a machine, proving that his intellect was as sharp as ever but the body just wouldn't perform.

Now for all those sufferers out there who, perhaps, I hope, are listening today, it's really important that you hear my cheers shouting out for you because some of them, they obviously can't speak, they can't move a muscle. Douglas last week could only move this eye, and he still told me that he wanted to go bungee-jumping, with that eye.

But I really want you to realize that I am out here fighting for you because I used to say to them, "Don't worry, I'll be your voice, and whenever I have an opportunity in a public place to speak for you, I will speak for you." So I've taken that opportunity today, because nothing, nothing could be worse for me than being trapped in my own body. Nothing worse. Nothing worse. I could sit there next door to Christie and say, Okay, Christie, what am I going to say? I couldn't say it. I couldn't ask Christie for a glass of water. I just couldn't. I would be completely suffocated in my own body and unable to do anything. And that, I think, well, basically you go to jail, you're imprisoned in yourself. And the frustration is immense. So that's why I'm passionate about that.

I vowed to join the fight against the disease and I joined Motor Neuron Disease in Great Britain. Today, I'm president of the International Alliance for ALS, which is very exciting, because what I decided to do was the most important for all the sufferers out there, was to gather all of the professors together, so instead of them just sitting in their research laboratories talking about the successes they've found, that once a year they all meet together in one place and we really crack on and find a cure for this most debilitating tragic disease, of which there is none.

Last week I was in Australia, and I don't know if you remember "The Seekers," but I met the most wonderful lady called Judith Durham. She's fantastic, and she said, would I mind popping in to see her husband Ron Edgeworth? Well, I did, and Ron Edgeworth used to play the piano when Judith was singing for "The Seekers." He is the most incredible man, and she has still got a beautiful voice and sings very well. She's patron of the Motor Neuron Disease branch in Australia. The reason why is because Ron Edgeworth is lying in his bed, unable to move any part of his body and play any songs that he knows that Judith would love to hear.

And when I walked into his room, I said, "Ron, you know, it's great to see you," and you know, let's talk about the spiritual things that he likes to talk about. And he made a movement to his nurse and just turned on the television, and well, we remained speechless for the next 10 minutes, because I was so taken with emotion because he put on himself playing the piano and there he was, just watching it, knowing what he wanted to say to me, and he just—he couldn't say it.

So, all of you out there with ALS, we're fighting for you, and we'll find a cure one day. We've got to raise the awareness.

Where am I up to? Photographs. Through these works, I saw the needs which led to the creation of three organizations to attract financial backing and support for children and those in need. Children in Crisis helps children in forgotten war zones. We all know of the terror and anguish in former Yugoslavia. Last year, we opened a camp for 600 refugees. We sent in $4,000 a month of fresh fruit and vegetables, little things like that which are so easily forgotten. We recently saw the birth of a little boy called Zelimir, which means peace.

We provide candle-making machines, light, you see. We provide survival candles which will burn for 36 hours at a time and take 30 seconds to make and no electricity is needed. It may be small, but it is so important. It provides dignity for the men over there in the camps so they have a job to do so that at least they can make a candle so they can take it back to their family and say, "Well, at least I've brought you a candle." That gentlemen there, and there's one of the candles.

We also supply Doc Martens for teenagers because we mustn't forget the teenagers over there. *(Laughter.)*

I was here in April, and I talked to some of you about the fact that Children in Crisis goes in where perhaps other charities have moved on, because there are so many charities that are doing a great job, but they go into huge war zones or areas of great need like Rwanda or Afghanistan, and then they move on. And what we do is we back up, and we go in and we try and restore dignity, we try to give respect back and we do it through counseling and various other ways. But we basically try and give them their dignity back.

The fighting in Afghanistan. The fighting in Afghanistan has been continuous since the arrival of the Soviet forces in 1979, and the 15 years of war have resulted in widespread devastation with almost every family having been affected. Over 1.5 million Afghans have been killed, of which an estimated 300,000 were children. The situation for children in Afghanistan is among the worst in the world. They are poorly nourished, as you can see, and have no access to medical services. Three million to four million children have died from malnutrition and disease, mostly preventable with simple health care. More than 50,000 women have probably died during this period from causes related to childbirth alone.

Children in Crisis is in the United Kingdom. It's in Eastern Europe, Bulgaria, Romania and the Ukraine. Together with larger organizations like AmeriCares, who have been fantastic, Bob Macauley has been such a supporter. He's been fantastic. And he's one of the main reasons why I'm standing up here today.

And Peace Links, Betty Bumpers, well, there was a great dinner last night and, quite frankly, Peace Links and I hopefully are going to join together to do—well, Children in Crisis, sorry—to join together to ensure that the children of Belarus, the victims of the Chernobyl disaster, are given adequate drugs and equipment.

That photograph there, those little children there, they actually need iodine pills to get their thyroid working, and it's as simple as that. And if they don't get it, well, then they're going to die very soon.

We've set up a German foundation, Menschen im Not, which concentrates on the needs of those in Germany and Eastern Europe.

But more significantly, we have established Chances for Children. This is based here in America, raising awareness and funds to help the people of America to focus on the needs of our future, which is our children. They have so much to teach us.

One of the most unforgettable moments of my life was when I accompanied a climb to the Himalayas. This is this one here. Charming in that hat, don't you think? *(Laughter.)* We were a group of 38 people. Eight of them were mentally disabled. We climbed to 20,000 feet, just below the peak of Everest, and there we were looking down on Everest base camp, which is a bit of an achievement. And next to me a young man named Paul, my friend Paul, who called me the "Duchess of Crisps" because all the way up the climb, three weeks of the climb, he kept saying, "All I want is a bag of crisps," so—*(laughter)*—and obviously in Nepal up in the mountains there aren't such things as crisps, and so he named me the "Duchess of Crisps." And, in fact, he still calls me the "Duchess of Crisps," which is very nice. *(Laughter.)* When we got to the top, he was up on the top, and I was puffing and panting behind and eventually got there. And as we got there, he turned to me with a huge, big smile, big as the sun, and he said with tears in his eyes, "Crisps, this is the closest to God that I'm ever going to get while alive." He's mentally disabled. And he was meant to be in an institution? I don't think so. He's a wonderful boy.

So this is what we do. We're aiming to help children collectively and individually, one child at a time. Thalassemia, sickle cell disease, in Albania—there is no pediatric blood transfusion. We send it in. We get hold of Claudio, a little chap, age six. We hear he's got an enlarged spleen. We take him over to London, and we whip his spleen out, and we send him back, and he has a life. That is what Children in Crisis is about. We hear of situations, we try and do something about it.

It is the generosity of others that helped to pierce the darkness in Bosnia really seriously—a needy group of young people to a higher place, physically and spiritually, than they'd ever been before.

And you know why I want to start in America? I'll tell you why. Because, let me tell you, it was thanks to American medical centers here that this little girl, Cody, pictured with my two daughters here, has now—her face is much better. She had, when she came to Children in Crisis, a huge melanoma of the face. It was absolutely huge. And her mom and dad said, "We can't afford to have it treated. Could you help?" So we had a little dinner, we kicked everybody in the shins, we told them that you had to pay up, and sure enough—(laughter)—we sent her to America for her treatment. And now, little Cody now is 2½ years old, and she's a delight. And she's coming to tea next week with my children because they love her.

So that is an example. We're not trying to do huge, big things. We're not trying to be anything. We're not trying to be, you know, egomaniacs, here. We're simply doing regular, on-the-street boys and girls and their needs. And thanks to America, Cody's got a face. But also, I'd like to say that I like the American people because they're nice to me, which makes a big difference. (Laughter.) I think probably I could have been an American in my last life. Not sure. (Laughter.)

There actually has never been a time during the great trials of this century when Great Britain could not count on America to stand by her side. There would be no free world today were it not for the willingness of the American people to pay the ultimate price to preserve peace with freedom across the world.

In my own family, my wonderful stepfather, with whom I was very close, was a victim of cancer. He waged a long, brave battle before he succumbed. And part of the reason why he lived so long so we could all love him so much was because of the superb treatment he received at Sloan Kettering Memorial Hospital in New York. For that, I will always be grateful. So I want to give back, you see. So most of the things I'm saying is because I want to give back. I want to say, "Yeah, thank you. Thank you, Americans. You've done a great job. You really have." Plus, most of our historical monuments are funded by your kindness in Great Britain. (Laughter.)

And so, Chances for Children has now opened its principal office in New York City, soon. (Laughs.) No, it has opened, and we're going to start right now. We're ready to move, we're ready for action. In fact, I'm going to make a pledge to the American people today: that every dollar you give will go straight to helping those that need it. Initially, the administrative costs have been sponsored. (Applause.)

Already in the last two weeks, we have donated an initial check of $25,000, thanks to Joseph Sutton of Happiness Express, who, in fact, is the licensing agency for Budgie. See what I mean? See how Budgie—we can work it. We can work it. (Laughter.) And we're getting—we actually are going to give that straight to the New York Cornell Medical Center's Pediatric Emergency Fund because they were the kind people that—thanks to Schwartz as well—who entertained me there, so I thought I'd give it straight on so no one could accuse me of taking that money. So I gave it straight when it was given to me, straight to Dr. Skinner. And there we go.

But, one thing, since we've only been going a week—although this is an extraordinary story, actually. It's just an extraordinary story. And it was yesterday, and I'll be very quick because you're all probably getting bored, but yesterday, I was really lucky because I met Rhonda, Rhonda Armstrong. She's great. Fourteen years old. She's a young Guyanan girl who, thanks to the Monte Fiore Medical Center, had a brain tumor removed. But we were asked eventually; Allison Stone, Allison Stone to the Dr. Goodrich, to the mom, to the dad, to everybody, eventually got to us at a desperate, desperate stage, could we fund $15,000 to get Rhonda over from Guyana and have her operation. She was operated on on Friday. I saw her yesterday. I mean that's what Chances for Children's about, because we've only been going a week, and it was a very moving moment because Rhonda was lying in intensive care, and I just leant over and I spoke to her mom, and I said, "Mom, ask Rhonda what," because I didn't want to disturb her, I said, "Rhonda—I just wonder what—how she is and what she'd like," you know, "What would she like? What can we get her?" It's her birthday on Saturday. And so Rhonda—so mom turned to Rhonda and said, "Rhonda, what do you want Rhonda? What would you like?" And she just opened her eyes, which is extraordinary because the brain tumor actually had pressed down on the optic nerve so she'd lost her sight. But she opened her eyes very slightly and looked me in the eyes and she said, "I just want to thank God." That really got me. But it was just incredible. And I'm so pleased that I was able just to see and touch with such a special, special little girl.

We are small, and we intend to remain so. A supporting and funding arm, that's what we're about. We don't want any projects, we don't want any praise, we simply want to fund and support already existing, up-and-running organizations or any individuals. But our spirits are very great. Our energies are boundless—I don't think Christine will agree with me, but never mind—*(laughs)*—and our potential unlimited to provide assistance irrespective of race, color, creed or political persuasion, pitching in for children in serious need from coast to coast, underprivileged inner-city children, teenagers with AIDS, children trying to break free from drug addiction and children with juvenile diabetes, to name but a few.

Our potential for doing good is limited only by the limits we place on our own imagination and our will. One thing we do know: the need is there.

But let me end on a really special project. On a recent visit to the states, I visited Children's Mercy Hospital in Kansas City, Missouri. I met the mother and father of a young girl named Lisa Jones, just 14 years old. There she is, pretty as a picture, that one. *(Motions to displayed photograph.)* Ten minutes before I got there, Lisa died of cystic fibrosis. Look at how pretty she is. Anyway, I said to her mom and dad that, at the NPC speech, I was going to say that it's dedicated to Lisa Jones, because her dad turned to me and said, "Do you know what? Lisa really wanted to become a doctor because she was so bored with everybody coming up to her and saying, "There, there. We really understand how awful it is for you to have cystic fibrosis. We know you must be in pain." And she said, "But, Dad, they don't. They really don't understand. They really don't know what it's like. And I'm going to become a doctor. And I'm really going to go up to those patients and little people with cystic fibrosis, and I'm going to say, 'But I do know what it's like, because I've had cystic fibrosis.'" That was her dream. So I said, "Well, the least I can do is tell everybody today about cystic fibrosis and Lisa Jones."

Anyway, Chances for Children. Harambi, that's a word I learned in Kenya. It means teamwork, and that's what it's about. Teamwork commercially, teamwork charitably. Just teamwork. We must all get on together. That's how wars are started, from lack of communication. Let's all get together now and let's really make it happen, and, together, we can really make dreams turn into reality.

Thank you, Gilbert, for allowing me this opportunity. *(Applause.)*

MR. KLEIN: That was truly a moving speech. Thank you very much.

The first question is, with so many needy children in the world, so many places where there is so much suffering, how do you go about choosing what causes you are going to support?

DUCHESS OF YORK: It depends on the resources we have in the kitty at the time. And what I thought of yesterday was that if we hear of a really, really—a quick case which needs, like, a brain tumor being removed, well, perhaps we can have a very quick fundraising event and raise the money to do it. That's a simple answer to that. Depends whether we've got enough in the kitty to do it, really. We'll try as hard as we can.

MR. KLEIN: We already have people up here suggesting charities that you might support here. How would somebody go about requesting your support?

DUCHESS OF YORK: Where would they like to—where would they like to know which? In America? In Eastern Europe?

MR. KLEIN: This one is in Haiti. This one is an AIDS—families affected by AIDS.

DUCHESS OF YORK: Oh, yeah. Great. Well, all they have to do is write to Chances for Children, and Christine, have you got the details? Yeah.

There's a press release going around with the name and the address and where to get hold of us. Just write to us and we'll soon have a fundraising event and see if we can't raise some money for you. It's the only way to do it, because we haven't got that much yet. We've only been going a week. *(Laughter.)*

President Klein gives 2 bears for Duchess of York's 2 children saying, "Can't Bear Not to be a member of the NPC."

MR. KLEIN: Are you getting good support from Her Majesty in pursuing your charitable causes?

DUCHESS OF YORK: Her Majesty has been quite extraordinary with her support to me.

MR. KLEIN: This questioner says: People perceive a crumbling of the monarchy tradition. To what extent is this a matter of generation, that the institution is outdated for people of your age? *(Laughter.)*

DUCHESS OF YORK: Somebody asked me in Australia last week, "So what do you think"— and it was on radio, too—"So what do you think, do you think that Australia should become a republic?" And I just smiled and I said, "I'm just going to go out and keep on trucking about my charitable causes and see how they go." *(Laughter, applause.)*

MR. KLEIN: There go all my questions about Ireland. *(Laughter.)*
How have your charity, your refugee center in Yugoslavia, fared in the recent turn of events there? Are they out of the way of what is happening in Bosnia?

DUCHESS OF YORK: Well, luckily, it is a little bit out of the way. But also—*(chuckles)*— we're rather sneaky, because we have great fiends in the nuns and the Roman Catholic priests and they have very good boots which we put lots of things in, so we can quickly get across lots of different places where perhaps other people can't get. And they've been fantastic. But we make sure—we have two trucks now for Children in Crisis, and there is no question about it. We never let anything get in the way of getting the aid to where it was meant to go.

MR. KLEIN: What advice about men would you give single girls? *(Laughter.)*

DUCHESS OF YORK: Let me think. *(Laughter.)* Get to know them. Perhaps live with them for a bit. Contrary to what mom and dad will tell you to do, they'll tell you not to, but I think it's probably a good idea. Really get to know what's going on really, I suppose. *(Scattered laughter.)* Difficult question, though.

MR. KLEIN: Oh, yes.
What are the largest problems facing children in the United Kingdom today?

DUCHESS OF YORK: Love. I think Mother Teresa said that, didn't she, the greatest disease of all is the lack of love.

MR. KLEIN: Is there much that you can do through a charity to do that, to help that?

DUCHESS OF YORK: No, that's just gone. Was that a question or was that you, Gil? *(Laughter.)*

MR. KLEIN: Well, let's see. How and when did you begin your charity work?

DUCHESS OF YORK: They weren't listening to my speech, were they? *(Laughter.)* Well, I'm not going to read it again, but actually—*(laughter)*—in 1985 Sir Robert Cook, Motor Neuron Disease—remember that one? *(Laughter.)* Yeah. *(Applause.)*

MR. KLEIN: We're going to get back to Northern Ireland here in a minute. *(Laughter.)*
What means will be used to raise funds for Chances for Children? This questioner says all charities are stressed and they're having trouble getting—that the contributors are tapped out at this point.

DUCHESS OF YORK: Well, we'll just have to find very different ways of tapping the already tapped out distributors, but I think there are ways. And I think food chains, actually, is a good way and, I think, supermarkets. And, I think, if we get to the people, you know. I mean, we'll just have a go. You know, we can but try. Where there's a will, there's a way. I've got the will, you've got the way. *(Laughter.)*

MR. KLEIN: What do you think of monarchy as it is practiced in Sweden or Holland, where the royals ride around on bicycles and wear jeans? *(Laughter.)* Could you ever buy into that? And would the British public buy into that?

DUCHESS OF YORK: Well, funny enough, actually, I can ride a bicycle and I do wear jeans. But I think it's a free world. Anyone can do what they want really, can't they? *(To Mr. Klein)* Sorry, you're up and down like a yo-yo.

MR. KLEIN: I know. *(Laughter.)* You're pretty fast here.

DUCHESS OF YORK: I know.

MR. KLEIN: If you were a reporter assigned to cover the Royal Family, how would you go about it? *(Laughter.)*

DUCHESS OF YORK: I bet that came from you, Charles. *(Laughter.)*

I'd probably do exactly what they do out there anyway. It's my job, isn't it? They've got a job to do; I've got a job to do. And actually, we're all very keen to criticize the media, but if it wasn't for the media, I couldn't be standing here, could I, and be telling you about plights and raising awareness over the world. So, thank you to the National Press Club. *(Applause.)*

MR. KLEIN: This questioner says that in the British press all the royals are lumped together. What do you see as the difference in your role and that of Princess Diana?

DUCHESS OF YORK: As long as we bring awareness to the plights of charitable causes, then Diana and I, we're going to keep on that path. *(Applause.)*

MR. KLEIN: There's a questioner—this picture over here, is that the Afghanistan picture? They wanted a better explanation of that picture, it's such a moving picture.

DUCHESS OF YORK: Well, there really isn't a better explanation. It's a little boy that was photographed by a very brave journalist that went in to bring the photographs back out so that we could all talk about Afghanistan and remember the children there that are suffering. And this little boy, who's since died of malnutrition. It's as simple as that.

MR. KLEIN: This questioner would like to know, do you view the British class system as a continuing obstacle to social and economic mobility—*(laughter)*—and do you think that change is inevitable regarding the abolition of the House of Lords or the monarchy?

DUCHESS OF YORK: You have to just read that again, because—no, I think we'll leave that one. *(Laughter.)*

MR. KLEIN: You're going to leave that?

DUCHESS OF YORK: I didn't actually understand the question. No, no. We'll leave it anyway. *(Laughter.)*

MR. KLEIN: Okay. Where is the natural loyalty to the monarchy in Great Britain, among the Labour Party or the Conservatives? Or is it a complex mixture between the two?

DUCHESS OF YORK: Not in politics.

MR. KLEIN: No? No. No politics. *(Laughter.)* Anybody have any questions, please pass them forward. *(Laughter.)* Well, let's see. If you could set the record straight about any of the nasty rumors concerning the Royal Family, what would you say?

DUCHESS OF YORK: Now, I'd like to set one record straight. Anyone thinks that I make $3 million a year from Budgie, well, do you think honestly I'd be asking you for money for Chances for Children? Okay? So, I would really like to set that record straight, wherever you are out there, whoever says that, because that really is rubbish.

What you all must understand is that the Budgie books were produced in 1987. That's when I gave a large percentage to charity. Since then, the rights to the animation were sold to another company, of which I get a very, very small percentage of it. And maybe after costs, after the animation is made, after everything else and the popcorn and everything else, then perhaps in five to 10 years, maybe I might receive a little bit of my percentage, and that, I hope, will be at that time going back into Chances for Children.

So, I really want to say that because it really bugs me—*(laughter)*—that every day, every day, I have to read that I'm a millionairess three times over. I tell you! *(Laughter.)* I mean, I'm in a rented house, which actually has just been practically whipped from under my feet and I've got a month to get out. I mean, I think if I had $3 million I'd buy my own house, don't you? *(Laughter.)* Can we be a bit logical on that? *(Laughter, applause.)*

MR. KLEIN: What would you like the headlines in tomorrow's British papers to be out of this appearance, and what do you expect it will be? *(Laughter.)*

DUCHESS OF YORK: I know what it will be, yeah. "Fergie Flops in Washington." *(Laughter.)* No, actually—no, sorry, it will be, "Freeloading, Fun-loving Fergie Flops in Washington." *(Laughter, applause.)*

MR. KLEIN: Well you are kind of fun-loving! I don't see nothing wrong with that! *(Laughter.)*

Is there a special skill one should have to write children's books?

DUCHESS OF YORK: Well, someone asked me that just this morning and I said, well, Budgie was written because when I flew Budgie I was very mischievous, because when we walked into the hangar all the big airplanes and all the big helicopters were huge because it was the Queen's flight and they were all frightfully grand and smart and stood up there. And there in the corner was this really wicked little single-engine Jet Ranger—tiny wee at the back of the hangar. And so of course I called him Budgie, and I got in him and you could imagine his socks were rolled down, his cap was on wrong, and I flew around in him and I called him Budgie. I put on my talking hat and I behaved like a child, really. That's the reason I wrote it down because I was behaving so like a child. And so I think if you're going to write children's stories, think like a child. *(Laughter.)*

MR. KLEIN: I'm pretty sure I know the answer to this, but you're researching Victoria and Albert. Is Queen Victoria your favorite member of the Royal Family, I would assume, and if so, why?

DUCHESS OF YORK: Apart from my husband, you mean? *(Laughter.)* He's my most favorite. But Queen Victoria is somebody that I really look up to. I think she did incredibly well. I mean, what a woman. I mean, can you imagine, you know, she married the man she loved. At the top of the stairs she saw him down at the bottom and she said, "I'm in love with that man with the moustachioed face, the small waist and the large shoulders and I'm going to marry him." And three days later she proposed to him, which we like a lot. *(Laughter.)* And then they were married 21 years, had nine children and had an incredible life. He died at 41 and she mourned for 35 years. And I just—just an incredible story, that's why I wrote it down.

MR. KLEIN: This questioner finds it hard to believe that the Royal Family doesn't support you and your children. If not, why on Earth, why not?

DUCHESS OF YORK: That's a really good point, whoever asked that. *(Laughter.)* No, my husband pays the school fees. *(Laughter.)*

MR. KLEIN: Okay. What sort of role models are important for your children?

DUCHESS OF YORK: Role models. Well, I think it's really important. I have table manners A, B and C. Okay? I'm C. Granny is A, very much so. *(Laughter.)* And table manners

B are when you go out to a restaurant, so you can be a little bit wicked if it's a hamburger joint, you know. And so that's what I keep to. When you're with mommy, you just can have fun and relax, because there's so many disciplines out there. You can't do this. You can't do that. And the education system in Great Britain is very strict, you know, and Beatrice and Eugenie, they like to just be able to be themselves. I think confidence boosting, I think creativity, I think all those good things are really good, too, for the development of children.

MR. KLEIN: This questioner says that, "As a parent of a disabled child, I want to thank you for making the public aware of their many gifts. How do you handle the prejudice against these children, and how do you overcome your own as you lobby for them?"

DUCHESS OF YORK: That's really good. I'm really glad I've got that opportunity, that you asked, because I believe that we shouldn't judge anybody until we get to know them. I think we should look into the windows of their soul, which is their eyes. The eyes are the windows to the soul. And I think we ought to treat everybody with the respect and dignity that we expect to be treated ourselves. *(Applause.)*

MR. KLEIN: This questioner wants to know, any other projects in the future from materials or the archival collection at Buckingham Palace?

DUCHESS OF YORK: Maybe. *(Laughter.)* Yeah, there is, actually. I'm very interested in Queen Mary now. I've gone from Queen Victoria. I thought that I'd tie in the two and see how Queen Mary relates to Queen Victoria. But that's for me, because I'm fascinated in the history of how these ladies managed. Because in fact, she was due to marry the first prince who—and she didn't. And she loved him, and he died. So she had to marry the second one. Because she was so suitable to be queen, she was told to marry the second one. So she actually married without love, which is very sad.

MR. KLEIN: Okay. What do you most like and dislike about the British way of life and the American way of life?

DUCHESS OF YORK: Oh, that'd take me hours. Everybody wants to go home. *(Laughter.)* I just love the way you're all sort of saying—you're really positive people. You give me the impression that you want to say, "Okay, come on. Let's do it. Let's try it. Let's see what we can do about it." And I find that in Great Britain someone like me, who's very spontaneous as you know, extremely opinionated and very pushy, they find me a bit too much, you know. And I walk, you know, waddling in with my red hair flowing, and they think, "Oh, not her again." You know? *(Laughter.)* "Princess Pushy is back." You know? And I think here in America that you sort of take it—you take people as human beings. You don't judge them. They walk in the door—some of you might, but if I walked in here, you'd sort of say, "Okay, well, she's got a smile and she's pleased to see us. Let's go for it." That's nice.

(Applause.)
How much longer have I got?

MR. KLEIN: Only a couple more minutes here, don't worry. *(Laughter.)*
There was an article in the newspaper yesterday, in the Washington Post, saying that members of the Labour Party were talking about cutting off members of the Royal Family, cutting about maybe in half the number of people who should be considered royals. Where would you make the cut? *(Laughter.)*

DUCHESS OF YORK: Well, I really like that question because guess what? As soon as I separated I was—I'm not on the royal payroll. So, very much married to my husband and I'm a separated women now with two children, but living apart and so I'm now on my own really, anyway, so that's great. I'm all right, Jack, because I've got to work hard, as I said in my speech, to continue. So I will. So that's the answer, really.

MR. KLEIN: Of course many people have asked, is there a chance of reconciliation there? *(Laughter.)*

DUCHESS OF YORK: I knew that question was going to come.

MR. KLEIN: You had to.

DUCHESS OF YORK: We take every day as we play it, and that's very, very private between me and my husband, and that's the way it'll stay. *(Applause.)*

MR. KLEIN: There are many things that you're fighting for. Which ones of them touch you the most?

DUCHESS OF YORK: Well, I've sort of answered that in my speech, haven't I really? I mean, I think you know, don't you? *(Laugher.)* Otherwise we'll be here all day. I'm sorry Gil.

MR. KLEIN: I'm going as fast as I can here. *(Laughter.)*
   Now I do understand that they have discovered oil—it was announced yesterday—they've discovered oil under Windsor Castle. What change will this bring to the Royal family? *(Laughter.)*

DUCHESS OF YORK: Nodding donkeys at the bottom of the long walk—I don't know. *(Laughter.)* Do you call them nodding donkeys here? You know, those oil things. I don't know. I hadn't even heard of that, so that's a good one.

MR. KLEIN: You haven't heard of that one?

DUCHESS OF YORK: No, I haven't. Pity it's not under my rented house. *(Laughter.)*

MR. KLEIN: If the United States had a royal family, do you think the American media would be kinder to it than the British media is to the British Royal Family?

DUCHESS OF YORK: Loaded question, loaded question.

MR. KLEIN: Loaded question.

DUCHESS OF YORK: Cut.

MR. KLEIN: Okay. Well, you wouldn't like this one, this is—*(laughter)*—this is Senator Robert Dole and Margaret Thatcher and Yugoslavia—

DUCHESS OF YORK: Nah, nah—

MR. KLEIN: Nah, nah—let's see. You wouldn't want to talk about Great Britain being a model for U.S. health care? *(Laughter.)*

DUCHESS OF YORK: No.

MR. KLEIN: How can one volunteer for Children in Crisis? Is there a location in Washington?

DUCHESS OF YORK: Yes, there is, actually. It's through Alma. Whoops! Is that all right, Alma? I just made that up. *(Laughter.)*

MR. KLEIN: Well I've just got the signal that we are unfortunately out of time. This has been a wonderful, wonderful event. *(Laughter, applause.)*
   Before your departure I would like to present you with this certificate of appreciation for appearing here.

DUCHESS OF YORK: Thank you very much.

MR. KLEIN: Plus this book, "Eye on Washington." These are the photographs by George Tames. They appear in the back of our ballroom, and they are—he was the New York Times photographer who took pictures from the Roosevelt administration to George Bush.

DUCHESS OF YORK: Thank you very much. Did you sign it?

MR. KLEIN: Yes, I did.

DUCHESS OF YORK: Thank you very much, Gil.

MR. KLEIN: And finally for your two children—*(chorus of "ooooooo's")*—Beatrice and Eugenie, I'd like to present you with these two bears, one each, which says, "I can't bear not being a member of the National Press Club." *(Laughter.)* And we'd be glad to take your application.

DUCHESS OF YORK: Thank you very much. Gilbert, thank you very much indeed.

MR. KLEIN: Thank you very much.

DUCHESS OF YORK: No, no. I'm very pleased because I had to—I think I might have to slip into a shopping mall and buy them something, so I've got two bears now, so it'll save a shopping trip. Thank you very much.

MR. KLEIN: Thank you. *(Applause.)*

NATIONAL PRESS CLUB

LUNCHEON
May 12, 1994

SPEAKER

KIM DAE-JUNG
Republic of Korea Elder Statesman and
Peace Activist

MODERATED BY: Gil Klein

Head Table Guests

❦

Lee Sang-Seok
Washington Bureau Chief of Hankook Ilbo

Mike Putzel
Columnist for the Boston Globe

Melinda Liu
Newsweek Magazine

Youn Hauk
Member of the Korean National Assembly

Nak-Cheon Baek
Washington Bureau Chief of the Seoul Broadcasting System

Lee Hee Ho
Spouse of our Speaker

Christy Wise
Freelance Journalist and Chairwoman of the National Press Club Speakers Committee

Jack Reynolds
*Jack Reynolds Communications and the member of the National Press Club
Speakers Committee who organized today's luncheon*

Young-Sup Chang
Washington Bureau Chief of Yon Hap News Agency

John Sodergreen
Defense Weekly

GIL KLEIN

MODERATOR

Our guest today, Dr. Kim Dae-Jung, is one of Asia's human rights pioneers. I first heard of Dr. Kim in 1987 when I was the club Speakers Committee chairman. At that time he was in the middle of what proved to be South Korea's first truly democratic election and we scheduled him to speak, but he decided not to come to the United States; he wasn't sure if he would be allowed back into the country.

South Korea has made a lot of progress since then, and much of it can be attributed to the stubborn tenacity of Dr. Kim. In 1973, during the military rule of General Park Chung Hee, he survived a kidnapping and attempted assassination by the Korean central intelligence agency. Later, under another military dictator, General Chun Doo Hwan, he was sentenced to death by a military tribunal, his life spared only because outgoing President Carter and incoming President Reagan told authorities in Seoul that U.S.-Korea relations would be jeopardized if Dr. Kim were executed.

After launching a career that combined business and journalism, Dr. Kim entered politics and became leader of the Opposition Democratic Party and their presidential candidate in 1971, running against General Park. Despite a blatantly rigged election, Dr. Kim received 46 percent of the vote and General Park suspended the country's constitution.

Over the years, Dr. Kim has been imprisoned a number of times and spent more than 15 years under house arrest. After escaping his death sentence, he came to the United States and founded the Korean Institute for Human Rights. He returned to Korea in 1985 and led the non-violent, pro-democracy struggle that finally forced the military regime to agree to democratic reforms. He then ran for president two more times, losing to General Roh Tae Woo in a hotly contested three-way race in 1987, and in 1992 to former fellow dissident Kim Yong-sam.

Dr. Kim comes to us in a crucial moment in Korean history. While the Cold War has ended just about everywhere else, on the Korean peninsula sabers are still rattling. Just this morning in the Washington Post, international columnist Jim Hoagland warned that North Korea may be willing to plunge the country into war rather than allow international inspectors to examine its nuclear production capability. Within the next few weeks, it should be clear whether North Korea has begun to stash away enough plutonium to build five or six new bombs. That would trigger an American push for international sanctions against North Korea, and the North Korean government has said that would be tantamount to a declaration of war. Secretary of Defense William Perry was quoted as saying, "When that happens, we will have to take seriously the risk of war."

The thought of another war on the Korean peninsula just seems absurd in this day when the tensions of the Cold War are about gone. Dr. Kim, we hope you can enlighten us on what is happening in Korea.

Ladies and gentlemen, please join me in a warm press club welcome for Dr. Kim Dae-Jung. (*Applause.*)

KIM DAE-JUNG

Thank you, Chairman Klein, for your kind introduction. And ladies and gentlemen, I am very much pleased to be here with you today. I have come here with my cane because I have an injury in my hip joints because of military government assassination. But I have never used this cane and will never use for the purpose of caning to anybody else.

I will now share my ideas on the three problems confronting the United States today in Asia. They are: the North Korean nuclear program; desirable relations between the U.S. and East Asian nations; and those between the U.S. and Korea. It is possible to resolve the North Korean nuclear problem that has been confounding us and taxing our patience. I am convinced it is. That is because North Korea's goal in this adventure is not to develop nuclear weapons, but to realize its number one foreign policy objective: normalization of diplomatic relations with the United States.

Kim Il Sung desperately hopes, through diplomatic relations and economic cooperation with the West, to escape from the hopeless economic situation and the extreme international isolation so that he can pass a stable regime on to his son. Needless to say, it is impossible for the North to improve its relations with the West unless it gives up the development of nuclear weapons. These two are mutually incompatible.

Until the 1953 armistice, Kim Il Sung attempted to unify the Korean peninsula using military force. After that attempt failed, he tried repeatedly to instigate communist revolution from within South Korea. But, following the collapse of the Soviet Union and the disintegration of the communist governments in East Europe, Pyongyang began to experience international isolation and rapid deterioration of its economy. As a result, the North made a series of policy shifts.

In 1991, North Korea made three major concessions to the West. The first was the joint entry, together with South Korea, into the United Nations, which the North Korea had opposed for more than three decades. The second was the acceptance of cross recognition of two Koreas by the world community, especially the U.S., Japan, Russia and China, which South Korea and the West had advocated since 1973. The third was its mutual recognition of the South and the North Korean governments as legitimate entities by signing a North-South agreement in December 1991. Through this series of concessions advocated by the moderates, Kim Il Sung expected a quid pro quo in the form of diplomatic and economic cooperation from the West. He also anticipated the cancellation of the annual "Team Spirit" exercise. But such expectations have not been fulfilled.

Consequently, the hardliners gained the upper hand, and the result was the North Korean declaration of its intention to pull out of the NPT and a series of belligerent statements. The hardliners think, "if we are given no way out but to ruin, we might as well go down fighting to the end." North Korea doesn't have military capability to win a full-scale war, but has enough power to inflict casualties to millions of South Koreans and Americans.

When North Korea announced its decision to abrogate the NPT on March 12th last year, I was at Cambridge University as a visiting fellow. Upon hearing the news, I immediately proposed a two-pronged approach to this problem: a package of simultaneous give and take, together with cooperation from China.

What should each side give and take? Two things should be given from each side simultaneously. North Korea must give up its nuclear ambition and guarantee South Korea's security. At the same time, the United States must reciprocate with diplomatic normalization leading to economic cooperation and North Korea's security assurance, including cancellation of the annual "Team Spirit" exercise.

However, it is important for the United States to consult with China and seek its cooperation on the North Korea's nuclear weapon program. China would no doubt cooperate in this matter because the nuclear issue is not only Korea's and the United States' problem, but also China's problem, and because China, too, does not want North Korea to possess nuclear weapons. This is fool-proof approach. If the North accepts this package deal, so much the better. If, on the other hand, Kim Il Sung rejects this package, China will have no choice but to support economic sanctions, unless, of course, it is willing to endure international criticism and lose face. There is nothing for us to lose with this one-shot package deal. We do not need to waste time any longer. I am not saying we should trust North Korea, but simply test its real intention.

We are now entering the era of the Asia-Pacific region. If the United States really believes itself to be an Asia-Pacific country, as declared by President Clinton, the U.S. must understand the sensibility of Asians.

To the Asian, face-saving is as important as saving his life. Instead of the give-and-take method of the West, an East Asian, if he feels he is treated with dignity, may cheerfully give two for one. On the other hand, if he is displeased, he might reject the deal altogether, no matter how advantageous to him. To formulate policies based on accurate understanding of these characteristics of the Asian sensibility is to assure the success of American foreign policy and gaining friends in the Asia-Pacific region. Face-saving is reciprocal. I save your face, then you will save my face.

The United States is the only country that bases its foreign policies on human rights, and it is important for the U.S. to stay the course. And I give high marks to the U.S. But the U.S. must respect the Asian way of thinking, especially face-saving, to get good results.

I do not have right to meddle in the international affairs of the United States. However, since U.S. actions in Asia will profoundly affect us, and as a friend of America, I am compelled to ask you to respect face-saving as an Asian way, while insisting on human rights progress and improvement in trade practices. This is how you ensure success in the long run. We feel very strongly about the tactics America has used in opposing Beijing's bid for the Olympics, pressing China on MFN, and advancing its trade interests with Japan, South Korea and other Asian countries—Asian nations.

Face-saving is even more important in dealing with North Korea, a country ruled for five decades by one man with absolute authority. Kim Il Sung's face cannot be compromised no matter what might be offered in return. We must make good use of this point in dealing with the North Korean nuclear program. Concerning this issue, President Clinton has recently made a magnanimous gesture to sending the Reverend Billy Graham to Pyongyang with his own message to Kim Il Sung. By receiving an emissary and message from the leader of the most powerful nation in the world, Kim Il Sung's stature has been greatly enhanced. Not long after that, North Korea accepted IAEA inspections to a considerable degree. I believe that the Reverend Graham's Pyongyang visit played a considerable role in North Korea's change of attitude.

And I heard today that there is a good development, you know, about nuclear inspection between North Korea and IAEA, you know, with effort of American go-between role.

I propose to President Clinton that he send to China and North Korea an elder statesman, respected internationally, trusted by the Chinese and North Koreans and sharing the views of President Clinton. Mr. Clinton's emissary can play an important role there.

In recent interviews with the American press, Kim Il Sung showed a gesture of conciliation and willingness to make concessions. He even expressed his wish to visit the United States. I urge Washington not to miss this opportunity. Kim Il Sung's visit here, by itself, will signal the end of a 50-year-old war-like situation on the Korean peninsula. His American visit may take the form of attending the U.N. General Assembly as the leader of a member nation. A National Press Club invitation may be suited to Kim Il Sung's visit very well.

I must stress that the U.S. should consult closely with the South Korean government before sending the emissary to the North, lest the North Korea should believe it can divide the U.S. and South Korea. Furthermore, the emissary's mission may fail without the South Korean cooperation.

Last, but not least, is the U.S.-Korean relationship. There are several points to be made about this.

First, the U.S. must keep its troops in Korea. U.S. forces are needed not only to keep the North from attacking the South, but also to prevent an upset in the balance of the power in the region.

Second, the U.S. should exercise leadership in creating a "two plus four" Northeast Asia cooperative security system. These six countries are North and South Korea, plus the U.S., China, Russia and Japan. This Northeast Asian security system may resemble a scaled-down version of CSCE. But I am not proposing that this multilateral system replace the existing security treaty between the U.S. and Korea.

Third, Korea is the eighth-largest trading partner of the U.S., and I hope the two countries remain good economic partners for mutual long-term benefit. I might add that the trade conflict between our two nations should be resolved harmoniously and with patience instead of the excessive unilateral pressure.

Fourth, some in the U.S. have raised fears of war and created excessive tension about the present nuclear problem. Koreans are worried about such attitudes in the U.S. Authorities of the U.S. and South Korea must maintain their cool and solve the problems patiently and peacefully.

Ladies and gentleman, I have been concerned about the rocky relations between the United States and North Korea and East Asian nations. I hope my brief remarks here today will help shed new light on desirable American approaches toward Asia and promote better understanding and cooperation between our two countries.

Thank you for your listening to me with patience. *(Applause.)*

MR. KLEIN: Thank you very much, Dr. Kim. It is part of National Press Club history that the Korean War was actually caused by a National Press Club speech when Secretary of State Acheson spoke here in 1950 and outlined the United States' security perimeter and left off South Korea. If we could have a role in ending the conflict on the Korean peninsula by having Mr. Kim Il Sung speak here, as you suggest, that would be—we would certainly be pleased to do that. And I'll ask Speakers Committee Chairwoman Christy Wise to get an invitation off to him as soon as possible.

Dr. Kim, the first question is: Why do you believe that Kim Il Sung would accept an invitation to visit the United States? With conditions so tense today on the Korean peninsula, wouldn't he prefer to remain in North Korea?

Dr. Kim is having an interpreter go through the question for him so that he can make sure he understands the—whatever nuances are in there, and then he can speak at his leisure.

MR. KIM: Thank you very much for your agreement to send an invitation to Kim Il Sung. And after you are sending an invitation, if Kim Il Sung accepts, so much the better. But if not, Kim Il Sung must be criticized by world opinion, because he has—he expressed his strong desire to come to the U.S. and going hunting and fishing here and getting friends here. So no loss for you in this effort to send an invitation to Kim Il Sung. Thank you.

MR. KLEIN: But do you really believe that he can leave North Korea at this time? He's 82 years old, I believe, and in ill health. Do you think that he could really leave North Korea at this time and make this trip to the United States?

MR. KIM: The problem of his visit we have not raised, but he raised. He was willing to come. So, as he says it is so, we send an invitation. So, whether his health is good or not or the Korean—situation in Korean peninsula, that's his own business, because he proposed his, you know, willingness—he expressed his willingness to come to the U.S. And I think there must be, you know, some discussion in the North when Kim Il Sung expressed such a desire. So it is, you know, good for you to test him, sending an invitation to come to the U.S.

MR. KLEIN: You have said two things that are somewhat at discrepancy with each other. One is that we should be respecting the internal rights of Asian nations, such as China. The other is that we should be pushing for human rights. Now, in the matter of Most Favored Nation status for China, do you think it is best for the United States to push for human rights in China by cutting off Most Favored Nation status for that country? Or would that be counterproductive to getting China to agree to help with North Korea?

MR. KIM: I am not saying we should force the China to persuade North Korea to accept nuclear, you know, transparency because of MFN. I am saying China is sharing the same interest with North Korean issue—North Korean nuclear issue. If North Korea does have nuclear, South Korea may follow—and Japan. There's a possibility Japan goes nuclear way. If Japan wants, you know, to accept that way, as we know, you know, Japan can become easily a nuclear superpower concerning its, you know, economic and technical power. So this is absolutely a serious problem for Chinese, you know, national interest. That's why China is opposing any possibility of North Korean nuclear position. So that's why I told—I said in my speech this is not only an American problem, but also China's problem. So there's no relation of MFN issue.

MR. KLEIN: You proposed that President Clinton send an elder statesman to China and North Korea. Can you give us an example of a specific person who you think would have the stature to carry out such a mission?

MR. KIM: I hope such a remark should not be taken as my intervention in your domestic politics. *(Laughter.)* So I am hesitating. But, you know, the chairman of this National Press Club is so, you know, dignitarious *(sic)*, so I can't resist to his question, not giving answer. So I will try. So I think one of the most suitable leaders—elder statesmen must be President Carter. And President Carter was a president who opened diplomatic relations with China. So he's so suitable. And also he is widely respected, trusted by international society.

So, in fact, yesterday I had a telephone discussion with President Carter about the East Asian problem, including North Korean nuclear issue. And also, as far as I know, North Korea has long admired President Carter, so they want to see President Carter visit North Korea. So, if the U.S. sent such an elder statesman to North Korea, that will greatly, you know, compel Kim Il Sung to make some decisive concession toward the U.S. As you know, in North Korea Kim Il Sung is the only man to make concessions. So I think whether President Carter goes to China and North Korea or should he not, that's not my business, but he must be one of the most suitable elder statesman to visit China and North Korea. I think so. Thank you.

MR. KLEIN: The South Korean President Kim Yong-sam, is he aware of your proposals here today, and do you know if he supports what you are proposing?

Translator-interpreter gets the ear of Dr. Kim Dae-Jung. May 12, 1994.

MR. KIM: Well, I have not discussed with President Kim Yong-sam about this emissary, so there is no reason for me to have that discussion because this is, you know, American business. But I have, you know, long proposed President Kim Yong-sam to have a summit meeting with Kim Il Sung as soon as possible. That is very necessary to reduce mutual hatred and misunderstanding between both countries, both governments, and to restore the consideration and good cooperation between both sides. After my such proposal, President Kim Yong-sam responded proposing North Korean Kim Il Sung, I am ready to meet with Kim Il Sung anytime, anyplace, if he agrees.

I really want to see his meeting with Kim Il Sung to solve our problem. We must realize reconciliation, mutual cooperation, must develop peaceful, you know, reunification stage by stage. So I really want, you know, such a meeting.

And I have been long invited by North Korea. So I openly declared before my people, unless President Kim Yong-sam meets with Kim Il Sung, I'll not go to the North. So I am waiting for his meeting with Kim Il Sung. Then I'll consider my visit to the North.

MR. KLEIN: Dr. Kim, you mentioned that Koreans fear certain U.S. attitudes that raise the specter of war. What would Korean opinion be if the United States ignored the North Korean nuclear inspection stalling tactics?

MR. KIM: Our absolute condition with North must be North Korea's agreement of complete transparency of nuclear ambition and nuclear program, and without the realization of such a thing, you know, the U.S. or South Korea shouldn't give any tolerance to North Korea.

So the transparency of the nuclear issue comes first, but only to achieve successful negotiation I am proposing, simultaneous negotiated package deal. So dealing between the U.S. and North Korea must be achieved concurrently. So I don't think there is any worry that we lose our, you know, position. And, as I mentioned earlier, we should propose negotiated package deal to North Korea, as North Korea many times said such a thing by Kim Il Sung and top-ranking leaders.

They said, "We have no intention, no ability, to produce nuclear weapons; our first goal is to have diplomatic relations with the U.S." They repeated such, you know, advocacy. So now we should say, "Yes, now, we will allow the participation, so you should prove your, you know, remarks were true, accepting nuclear transparency." We are in such a position.

So if North Korea accept this, that's good. If not, we should ask China to persuade North Korea. And if North Korea doesn't agree to such Chinese pursuit, then with China we should bring North Korea to the U.N. economic sanction. If Chinese is cooperative, economic sanctions will be very effective. This is our way. Nothing to lose. We don't need much time to solve this problem.

Yesterday when I met with, you know, State Department leaders, including Assistant Secretary Gallucci, I told them it is time for us to put an end to this problem. We have consumed too much time. If we continue such a thing, it's not good for us. The longer we, you know, continue such nuclear negotiations with North Korea, the more the U.S. and South Korea must lose its, you know, prestige. Nothing to gain by such a thing. This is my, you know, analysis and suggestion. Thank you.

MR. KLEIN: As I said before, Kim Il Sung himself is 82 years old, and his son, who is the heir apparent, has been described in the American media as unstable. Do you think that there is a pressure to get some kind of resolution to this thing while Kim Il Sung is still alive?

MR. KIM: There has been a long saying in Korea and abroad, as long as Kim Il Sung is alive, there will be no change. But the reality is not true, is not so. In 1991, after collapse of Soviet Union, Kim Il Sung made three major concessions as mentioned in this—in my speech: simultaneous entry to the U.N.; cross-recognition; and, you know, mutual recognition as legitimate entities between both Koreas. So Kim Il Sung made such significant concessions toward us. Only Kim Il Sung makes such things because, about these three of our proposals, North Korea has long advocated—even more than 30 years—this kind of American imperialist plot to divide our nation forever, so we shouldn't accept such plot. But Kim Il Sung did this without the servants in the North.

Kim Il Sung is like the almighty man in the North, whether it is good or not. We don't support such system. No doubt, without Kim Il Sung—even if Kim Jong Il succeeds his father's position safely, but Kim Jong Il couldn't be—he couldn't exercise same authority and couldn't be strong like Kim Il Sung.

I suggest in another speech, which was delivered yesterday before the American Enterprise Institute—in that speech I also suggested we should solve the problem before Kim Il Sung's death. And let me tell you, this is not my own judgment, but American experts' judgment, such as former—the U.S. ambassador to Korea. I know two such ambassadors whom I met. They told me same there last year, we should solve this problem before Kim Il Sung's death. And, as far as I know, China's government also thinks that, before Kim Il Sung's death, the problem in the Korean peninsula should be solved. And if you allow me about different relations with the North, this not—you know, our—the giving, allowing of no privilege, in a sense, this is our promise with two reasons.

One is, in 1991, North Korea became regular U.N. member with the blessing of the U.S. government. So diplomacy doesn't mean ally or a friendly country, but means, you know, relations with an existing country. It is contradictory for us not to have a regular U.N. member—not to have diplomatic relations with other U.N. member.

And in addition, when, in 1973, South Korea then-president Park Chung Hee proposed this, you know, cross-recognition. Since that time, including the U.S., the West has long supported this. But now cross-recognition is only working on our side not North Korean side. North Korea feels kind of breach of promise. And also, diplomacy is not, you know, advantageous only for North Korea but for us. Imagine if we have, you know, our embassy building in the North with hundreds of our diplomats from Western society and South Korea, and naturally there would be our businessmen to invest there with North Korean businessmen, tourists—tourism will be there, many tourists go to North Korea, then such things will greatly change the atmosphere in North Korea, you know, pushing North Korea to become another China.

So let me tell you, as my conclusion, let's make North Korea, you know, too involved in economic development, then the North Korean economy will become better. You know, it is natural, when we feel hungry we get angry, but we feel full of stomach, we laugh. China is good example. During cultural revolution, how much China was hostile, but now with, you know, a prosperous economy, how much Chinese people is laughing. In their mind there is no Mao Zedong or cultural revolution or socialism, there is a little, you know, but in their minds there is, you know, business and making money. So we should make North Korea another China. This is what we should take to solve our problem peacefully, I think.

MR. KLEIN: You mentioned often in your speech the need to make face-saving overtures to Asian leaders. Do you believe the United States government at times has acted arrogantly in its dealings with East Asia?

MR. KIM: A difficult question. But unfortunately, I feel many of American people—Asian people feel that. So they—when there is a problem about trade issue, other things, America has been at time to time, too much suppressive—even, we feel, somewhat too strong. So, as I already mentioned, Asian people take face-saving most important. So with some moderate attitude to save Asian peoples, then that will be good for the U.S. not losing friend, but to achieve, you know, its goal with, you know, voluntary cooperation expressed by East Asian governments. Sometimes it may need time, but such a patient attitude very much desire to take. If America has, you know, a strong attitude, subversive attitude, it may be helpful in some times to get short-sight interest; but I am afraid it will lose, you know, friends, and in long term, it will be harmful to American, you know, interests.

As far as I know, in East Asian countries, basically speaking, they want to be cooperative with the U.S. If only the U.S. can understand their situation, if only U.S. can take, you know, such a face-saving attitude, then I think they would be much more willing to be cooperative with the U.S. I say this as one Asian people. I have long supported American democracy and I have owed much to America in the course of my struggle against dictatorship, because it saved my life two times, so I am saying I have always feel some, you know, bond to America.

So I am saying this as a real friend of America. So I have a worry that such recent American, you know, somewhat strong attitude is gradually losing Asian people friendship. I am afraid this.

MR. KLEIN: Following up on what you just said, one questioner asked, can you tell us whether it is true, as has been reported over the years, that the American CIA intervened to stop the Korean CIA from killing you after you were kidnapped from Japan?

MR. KIM: Yes, that was nearly true, near true. Without such American intervention, my life would not be saved. In 1973, that time I was in exile in the U.S. and Japan. And in August I was in—I was abducted in a—some Tokyo hotel. Abductors, Korean CIA men, first had plan to kill me in the bathtub, hotel bathtub, dismembering my body. So they prepared three rucksacks, a heap of tissue paper, strings.

But they gave up killing me at the bathtub because I shouted "help" so they afraid of my voice was known by others. They brought me to the, you know, sea, leaving all these things—rucksack, papers. And also they left their North Korean cigarette, disguising North Korean activity. And in the ship, military ship, I was about to be thrown into the sea. My whole body was, you know, tightly tightened. That very moment, as far as I know, a Japanese plane came there over the ship and, you know, threw a warning bomb. So I was narrowly escaped from death. That time, American CIA visited Korean president warning not to kill me, and provided this information to the Japanese government. As far as I confirm at present. So I am—I was able to be saved with such American CIA activity at that time.

And also in 1980, when I was sentenced to death, without the American, you know, effort to save my life, together with world opinion, my life would not be saved. At that time President Carter and President-elect Reagan—it was in 1980—made their best effort to save my life. So I don't know, at this time, in 1980, whether CIA was involved in this case or not. But it is true that the American government saved—much contributed to save my life. Thank you.

MR. KLEIN: Thank you very much. (*Applause.*) That was excellent. I'm afraid we are out of time. In honor of your appearing here, and to save face, we would like to present you with a certificate of appreciation for appearing here, and with our traditional National Press Club mug, which we certainly appreciate your coming here.

MR. KIM: My honor. Thank you very much.

MR. KLEIN: Thank you, sir. That concludes our program for today. (*Applause.*)

NATIONAL PRESS CLUB

LUNCHEON
October 18, 1994

PEAKER

CHARLES OSGOOD
Commentator for CBS Radio & TV

MODERATED BY: Gil Klein

HEAD TABLE GUESTS

✦

DANIEL ROSHA
WILC Radio

DAVE McCONNELL
WTOP Radio

JACK REYNOLDS
Jack Reynolds Communications

LINDA KRAMER
People Magazine

DARREN GERSH
WPBT-TV "Nightly Business Report"

EDMUND SILK
Anchor of Standard News Radio Network

NANCY WIDMANN
President of CBS Radio

CHRISTY WISE
Freelance Journalist and Chairwoman of the National Press Club Speakers Committee

BOB KIPPERMAN
Vice President for CBS Radio

ED LEWIS
American Automobile Manufacturers Association and the member of the National Press Club Speakers Committee who arranged today's luncheon

TAMARA LYTLE
New Haven Register

WILLIAM GORMLY
NBC Radio News

CHARLES THOMPSON
Producer for CBS News "60 Minutes"

GIL KLEIN

Today we are pleased to have with us CBS Radio commentator and "Sunday Morning" television anchor, Mr. Charles Osgood.

A man known for his wit and wisdom, Mr. Osgood wakes up America on its day of rest with his special take on national and international news. He is considered in some households the Letterman of Sunday morning television.

(Laughter.)

Mr. Osgood is best known as a daily CBS Radio commentator for the inimitable "Osgood File" with the tag line, "See you on the radio." He shares his sense of wonder, dismay and amusement on current events. More often than not, as he comments on the vicissitudes of everyday life, he will burst into Osgoodian verse. In fact, friends say he is known as the CBS News poet in residence.

Not bad for a fellow who started his career right here in Washington as the announcer for the U.S. Army Band.

Born in the Bronx, Mr. Osgood was drawn to radio at Fordham University, where he worked at the college station with colleagues Alan Alda and Jack Haley, Jr. He joined CBS in 1967 and learned his style from the greats of the business, Walter Cronkite, Douglas Edwards, Lowell Thomas and Charles Kuralt.

Asked how he evolved his own special style, he told the New York Times that on one particular story, he incorporated a little rhyme. Management came back and said, "Very nice, Charlie. Don't do it again." *(Laughter.)* But he did. And he found, as he has said, that there is poetic justice after all. And on April 1st, April Fool's Day, CBS announced that Mr. Osgood would replace the retiring Charles Kuralt as the anchor of "CBS Sunday Morning."

He perhaps is known as much for his bow tie, which has become his trademark, as for his wit. In his latest book he offers us this verse on the art of wearing a bow tie:

> "For those who have lusted to be honored and trusted,
> A bow tie, I say, doesn't hurt;
> It isn't your tie that most people eye,
> It's the soup stain there on your shirt." *(Laughter.)*

With that, I'd like to get into the spirit of things and introduce

> A man known for his unusual wit,
> Whose gift for gab is always a hit,
> Who looks dapper in bow tie when few others could,
> None other than today's speaker, Charlie Os-good. *(Applause.)*

CHARLES OSGOOD

Thank you, Gil. What is it old Jimmy Durante used to say? Everybody wants to get into the act! *(Laughter.)*

Let me explain about the bow tie before we proceed with other things. I want you to understand that that poem was a reference to the fact, that it is thought in some circles, that if you wear a bow tie that this attacks your credibility. And Mr. John Malloy, who has written these books "Dressed for Success," suggests that if you are a stockbroker, or a banker, or a lawyer, or someone else for whom credibility is important, that you should never wear a bow tie.

So, since I was in the news business, I thought credibility has little to do with—*(laughter)*—I guess I would wear it anyway.

Malloy goes so far as to say that if you are going to wear a bow tie, then you really should wear the rest of the ensemble, which is a beanie with a propeller. *(Laughter.)*

So, I don't go along with that whole thing, although I did try to see whether I could find a beanie with a propeller to bring along just as an illustration.

I have further added to this image of unreliability in various ways, one of which I will now demonstrate.

You do have to understand that the first newspeople, the first Dan Rathers and Connie Chungs of the world, were minstrels who would travel around from village to village, from country to country, and talk about the activities of the king, or the prince, or the duke in the town that he had just left, and do so not only in rhyme, but he usually carried with him an instrument of some kind, a musical instrument, a lute perhaps, or a lyre to accompany his little verses.

The word "lyre" is still very often used in connection with the news—*(laughter)*—business to this day.

(Mr. Osgood begins to play the banjo.) This is "Occasional Song," as, like, occasional verse. *(Mr. Osgood sings the following to the tune of "On Top of Old Smoky.")*

> The National Press Club is known far and wide
> for all the insiders that you'll find inside.
> Perhaps you don't realize how lucky you are
> to sit at these tables or to drink at that bar
> and hear the reporters while having a drink
> reveal to each other the things that they think.
> There's nothing to fear there if they talk to you.
> The stuff that you hear there might even be true.
>
> But while they're relating how much they all know,
> it's so damn fascinating, who cares if it's so.
> But the drinking and noshing sets up deja vu
> when you're watching the "Washington Week in Review"
> because I'll bet you Ken Bode or some other star
> is having a sody right now at the bar.

Though the fate of the nation may hang by a string,
unless it's discussed here, it won't mean a thing.

For the matters they take up and the things that they say
tomorrow will make up the news of the day.
These are powerful forces, of that there's no doubt.
They're the Washington sources we've heard so much about.

(Laughter, applause.)

Thank you. Well, I did want to get that out of the way. *(Laughter.)* But I'm going to do it again before we're finished here, and then I understand after 20 minutes or so that you have questions, that I'm to answer them. I'll, therefore, try to talk as long as possible to leave as little room as possible for questions. *(Laughter.)*

Well, as Gil has told you, I am not a total stranger to Washington. I have been here before. And I have—and some of you I know from way back then. Actually the person who's here today that I've known longest is Jack Reynolds, who went to school with me at Fordham in about 1907, 1908, something like that. *(Laughter.)* And then I worked in Washington at WGMS, the good music station, where I met Pat Hayes and Evelyn Swartout. That was just about 1923, 1924 or something like that, that we did that. *(Laughter.)* And it's amazing how time passes. And some of you I know from New York. There is a delegation of people, some of whom you've met, who came down from New York to act—from CBS—to act as a sort of a truth squad. *(Laughter.)* They followed me here so that whatever I happened to say about the business or the company, they would have an opportunity to rebut.

In addition to those you've already met at the head table there are others. My producer for the "Osgood File" is Phil Chin, who is here. I don't know where anybody is, but I'll just mention them, and Gail Lee, who is a writer on the "Osgood File"; Missy Rennie who is the executive producer of "Sunday Morning"; and senior producer, Marquita Poole also are here, and I appreciate their coming down. And I can explain later to them—and also Tom Goodman, one of our CBS corporate vice presidents. CBS has more vice presidents by far than the United States of America. *(Laughter.)* For example, the United States only has one.

Now, in a way I feel like an imposter here speaking to the National Press Club. To me it's incredible, that someone with as little background as I have, should be invited to speak here. At Fordham, when I was there with Jack Reynolds, I did not major in communication arts, I never took a course in journalism, I never took a course in writing, none of that stuff. I majored in economics, and my only earned degree is this old BS in economics that I have from 1954.

Now, I've had a couple of honorary degrees since then. You know, when you do a commencement address they give you an honorary doctorate. That's the quo that goes with the quid. *(Laughter.)* But as I said, the only legitimate earned degree I have is this BS in economics. But I have discovered in my line of work, I have to tell you that a little BS goes a long way. *(Laughter.)*

I wanted to be taken seriously as a journalist all this time, but none too successfully, I must say. I've operated pretty much from the fringe. I've been at CBS now for 27 years. It's hard for me to believe that it can have been that long, but it is true. And when I started there and I saw my name on the list of CBS news correspondents, along with the ones that Gil has mentioned, Cronkite and Severeid and Bill Moyers and Mike Wallace and Charles Kuralt and some of these other giants in the business, I was somewhat taken aback to realize, and this was quite some time ago, that I was the only one on that list that I never heard of. *(Laughter.)*

And now all these years later I can say that I've heard of myself, but not always in the context that I would like to have heard of myself.

The only time that I can think of that I actually was asked by the CBS News bureau here to come down to Washington and do a piece, and this is a fantasy that I had for a long time, to do what Dan Rather had done and Lesley Stahl had done and Bill Plante and Rita Braver and others, to stand out in front of the White House and to speak with that background to the audience of the "CBS Evening News," and here was an opportunity to do this. I was told that this was going to be an "Evening News" piece and I was going to get to do it and that the White House was going to be the location that I should report to.

Well, it turned out when I got here that the story they wanted me to do was this: A census was being taken of the squirrel population in Lafayette Park. *(Laughter.)* The Park Service had enlisted volunteers to stand there with clipboards and to record the point of entry of each squirrel that came into the park—*(laughter)*—to record the squirrel's activities while in the park—*(laughter)*—to time the length of his stay there and then to record the time and point of exit when he left the park. All of this information was going to be used for some purpose, I'm not sure what. But in any even, that was the story, and I actually did it, and I actually got to stand in front of the White House.

But the only reason that I got the story, I thought it was because this would be something that they felt that I would have some special ability to cover. But it was just that nobody in the Washington bureau would do it. *(Laughter.)* So that was the first opportunity that I had.

Come to think of it, over the years my friend Charles Kuralt and I, I think, have shared just about all the animal stories on the "CBS Evening News." *(Laughter.)* He got to do the swimming pig. I remember that one. I, however, got to do the piano-playing duck. *(Laughter.)*

The piano-playing duck was a story that was the end piece on a broadcast that was done the night of the Camp David Accords—Sadat and Begin and Jimmy Carter, a memorable picture that began that broadcast of the three of them standing and shaking hands in the historic moment. And the broadcast ended that night with me at this little animal training camp in Hot Springs, Arkansas, where they trained animals for small circuses and carnivals and that sort of thing. They did have a piano-playing duck, but my principal encounter was with a tic-tac-toe playing chicken. *(Laughter.)* That's how that broadcast ended that night, was with me playing tic-tac-toe with a chicken. *(Laughter.)* And I lost. *(Laughter.)* The most—the most embarrassing moments.

Since I mentioned Kuralt, I'm now doing "Sunday Morning" on CBS. But long before I started doing that broadcast, people would say to me, on the street or in airport terminals or hotel lobbies, they would say, "Charles, is that you?" And I'd say, "Yes." And they would say, "We think you're wonderful." And I'd say, "Well, thank you very much." "Our whole family is a big fan of yours." And I'd say, "Well, that's very nice to hear, thank you." "And we think your work is terrific and we wanted you to know it." And I'd say, "Thank you very much." And then they'd say, "And we watch you every Sunday morning." *(Laughter.)* Mind you, this is two or three years before I started doing "Sunday Morning." Now, either these people had tremendous foresight or they were confusing me with Kuralt. Obviously, that's what they were doing.

And over the years, not only because he had the same first name as I do and did end pieces for the evening news, but also because my hairline and waistline have approached his and finally caught up and gone past, I think, his own, this confusion existed. I think maybe the time that was the most striking about this was when I spoke to the Chamber of Commerce, the North Dallas Chamber of Commerce, awhile back, and the fellow who stood up to give the invocation asked the Lord to bless the president of the United States and members of Congress and the governor of Texas and the members of the Texas State Legislature and the members of the North Dallas Chamber of Commerce, and "Today Lord," he said, "we especially ask your blessing on Charles Kuralt."

So, when I—I told him when I stood up that when I got back to New York I'd probably be seeing Kuralt and—(laughter)—you know, and how touched I was sure he would be—(laughter)—to know that they had prayed for him in Dallas that day for no apparent reason. (Laughter.)

Anyway, I did see Charles and I mentioned this to him and he said that I shouldn't feel bad about this because this happens to him all the time. And I said, "You mean, people say, aren't you Charles Osgood?" And he said, "Well, not exactly." (Laughter.) He said, "They say, aren't you the guy that does those silly little poems on the radio?" So—actually he didn't really say that, Charles is too kind and sweet a gentlemen to do that. But I told him that what I would do is that the next time somebody said to me, "Aren't you Charles Kuralt?" I was going to say, "Yes I am. And buzz off." (Laughter.) That that ought to do it.

Actually, I didn't—buzz was not exactly the word that I used but—(laughter)—you know, now that I'm mentioning Kuralt, there's something about him that I want to say, and it applies to the main serious subject that I want to talk about.

Somehow, you know, I felt talking to the National Press Club, I really ought to be saying something about the national press, the situation of the press today and the role that it's playing, and its future and the role of the various media. But I'm not a student of any of this. I'm a practitioner of my own little fringe in this business, but I have no particular expertise about that. But as I said to the American Periodontal Society in a keynote address which I delivered to their convention this year—(laughter), just because a person—if I hesitated to speak to a subject simply because I didn't know a damn thing about it, what sort of a broadcast newsman would I be? (Laughter.) So I did deliver that keynote address to the periodontists, and I do have some thoughts that I would like to pass along, that have to do with the press, and let me start by using Mr. Kuralt as a touchstone.

He won the Paul White award of the Radio and Television News Directors Association in Los Angeles the other night, and that is a prestigious award named for the first president of CBS News. And he certainly deserves it if anyone ever did. And it fell on me to introduce him. I had to do it on tape, however, since I had to be back in New York to do "Sunday Morning" the next day. And in putting together my thoughts about Kuralt—which was not easy to do because I've had such respect for him for such a long time that to try to put into a short introduction what those feelings were is difficult—I did mention in passing that it had been said at the time that Kuralt announced his retirement—the man is two years younger than I am, he is—that if ever he wanted to come back, CBS News would welcome him with open arms. And this was said by Howard Stringer, the president of the broadcast group, and reiterated by others, including Eric Ober, who is president of CBS News. When I heard this, I could not have agreed with it more. Since then, of course, I have been named as his successor on "Sunday Morning," and now—(laughter)—I'm not so sure this is a good idea. No. I'm probably the only person in captivity that feels this way, but I'm against it. (Laughter.)

In any event, to express the other, serious thing that I wanted to say about him, what is it that I admire so much about Kuralt? It seems to me that it is that he is himself an admirer. And what we see on "Sunday Morning" and what we have seen in "On the Road" pieces over the years is Kuralt very often doing a story that would not find its way onto the evening news or to the morning news or any of the other broadcasts that we do because those programs are occupied with not always very pleasant or positive things that are going on in the world, often things going wrong, often reflecting the most negative side of human nature.

There are stories that are full of greed and violence and other not so admirable qualities. And here would be Kuralt, saying—not staying with the pack at all, maybe trailing the pack some, and then calling us back and saying "Here, I want you to see this person. I want you to meet this artist. This singer, this poet. This collector of a ball of string. Whoever it is and whatever he or she does. Because there is something I want to tell you about them. This is what this person does and this is why they are to be admired. And then you'd say yes, that's true, isn't it? And calling attention to the fact that although the news tells the truth— and I would not—I'd be the last one in the world to say that we should go looking for good news to report—it does seem to me that while we are reporting all of the unfortunate events—catastrophes that are—some natural but some man-made, that we like to think that we're telling the whole story. But—and this is something that I want my own children to know, because I think it's very important.

Yes, they have to know about the traps and pitfalls that there are. They have to know that there is selfishness and greed and that there are people out there willing to take advantage of them if they let themselves be taken advantage of. But that's not the whole story. There's also love and kindness and laughter and challenge and opportunity and beauty and joy; and all of these things have no lesser reality than the composition of the evening news on a given evening.

And so, I'm happy to say that on Sunday Morning we have an a opportunity to point to people who do wonderful things and express the creative, the beautiful, the positive side.

You know, if you go out and ask people these questions and ask them whether this is true or false: Business people will do anything for a buck. Politicians will do anything for a vote. Journalists will do anything for a story and don't care who gets hurt in the process. Broadcasters only care about ratings and will do anything—put anything on the air for a ratings point.

And ask people if those statements are true or false, most people in this country will tell you that they are true. And they're not. They're wrong about that. Somehow they got the idea that everybody is out to get them, that everything is a scam or a ripoff, and it's not. Where do they get these ideas? Is it possible that somehow in the reporting of the news, we've crossed the line between skepticism—which is a healthy thing—and cynicism, which is very unhealthy? There's not an accusation built into that question that I just asked, but there is a suggestion that we might—you can't eliminate the negative and you can't always accentuate the positive, but it does seem to me that there are things that we can do and stories that we can look for which are more positive than the ones we use.

Associated with this is another thought that I had which is that in dealing with one another, there's been a terrible—it seems to me—decline in civility over the last several years. We're not as nice to each other it seems to me, or as polite or—nor do we approach one another with the respect that we ought. When I do deal with news stories that are of major consequence, sometimes I will try to find some aspect of it that ties into this thought.

And recently I had the occasion when, for the second time in a matter of a few months, former President Jimmy Carter was called in and managed to achieve what had not appeared to be achievable. How does Jimmy Carter do it? What's the secret of how he can find in the impossible some possibility? He hacks his way through jungles so impenetrably dense that nothing anybody says is making any sense. How does Jimmy Carter deal with these most difficult of cases? With things so dark men cannot see their hands before their faces, with people yelling epithets and waving guns and bombs, he somehow quiets down the waves, the wind he somehow calms. What is it that he says to them? What is it that he does to make them see some daylight where before no daylight was? He did it in Korea, now in Haiti, too. I wonder what the Jimmy Carter secret is? Don't you?

Kim Il Sung of North Korea was a source of global worry.
To comply with nuclear agreements he was in no hurry.
Seemed to many experts North Korea was a threat,
that Kim had nuclear weapons—some were pretty sure, and yet
no matter how we yelled at him, how fiercely or how loud,
he remained completely stubborn, dictatorial and proud.
But when Jimmy Carter went there and the two met in Pyongyang,
it was a different song from then on North Korea sang.
We still don't know how that one will work out it should be said
or how the dust will settle now that Kim Il Sung is dead,
but from that meeting you remember, Carter came away
saying, "Everyone relax, please, because everything's okay."

And the former president has walked on water ever since.
Last month he led the three-man team that went to Port-au-Prince
with troops and mighty warships at the ready just off shore
prepared if General Cedras didn't yield to go to war.

And here was Jimmy Carter with the time all but run out.
He didn't run in circles, and he didn't scream or shout.
He smiled that little smile of his and down with them he sat
as once he did at Camp David with Begin and Sadat.
And somehow he got them all to see they had nothing to gain
from a battle that they could not win, but would cause grief and pain.
No chip upon his shoulder, no line drawn in the sand,
but something you or I or anyone could understand.
It was another element applying to each side;
he had to find a way for everyone to save his pride.
Some of Jimmy Carter's secret we could all use, I suspect,
and that is to treat everyone we deal with with respect.

That's not a profound or original thought, by any means, but it seemed an opportunity out of the news to find something that one could say to a national audience that might have some meaning that goes beyond the immediate story of the day.

Let's see what time it is here. Whenever you want to stop this and start answering questions, just grab the hook.

If I were a real newsman, I suppose I would be much more obsessed with the O.J. Simpson case than I am. *(Laughter.)* If I were a real newsman I suppose I would find it very interesting, this obsession we all seem to have now, the media seems to have and also the public, with Wayne Bobbitt cases and the Menendez brothers' case, and the Tonya Harding-Nancy Kerrigan case, and all of these stories which surely are not of great importance historically. It's understandable our interest in them; these are stories of human nature, and so on. But if I had the power—maybe I do—I would declare the "Osgood File" and "Sunday Morning" O.J. Simpson-free zones! *(Laughter.)* Obviously, if there's some major development, you will hear it here first!

But aside from that, I think we—I'll tell you what my idea of a great story is. This just happened in the last week or so. You have to go back to the 10th of January, 1992. Storm in the North Pacific, and our freighter, carrying a cargo on its deck, the cargo spilled into the

North Pacific, so the cargo was lost. I'm happy to say that no one was killed in this terrible incident. However, lost were 29,000 rubber duckies and other bathtub toys that began then bobbing around in the North Pacific. *(Laughter.)* Well, they're still out there, 29,000 rubber duckies.

It turns out, we find from the National Marine Fisheries Service in Seattle and from oceanographers associated with them, that the migration of these rubber duckies can teach us a lot about the movement of the currents and the movement of the winds, especially when this data is used in association with what we have learned from the great Nike sneaker spill of 1990—*(laughter)*—when 61,000 sneakers were lost at sea and began bobbing around.

They show up in one place or another. Now, I'm not sure whether that's 61,000 pairs of sneakers—*(laughter)*—in which case we'd have 120,000 more—I mean, it would have been an outrageous number of sneakers out there. But anyway, together with these, we have actually been able to learn something about the currents and the wind. This in an age of satellites and radar and all kinds of wonderful technology. Now that's a story—*(laughter)*—I think.

I have one other little song I want to do for you before we take questions, if you don't mind. This has to do with another thing. I notice that if you go to Europe—I have occasion to go to France quite frequently, and you never encounter anybody, they don't say "bonjour," even the people at the toll booths on the auto route will say bonjour when you arrive and they'll say merci when you hand them the toll and then they'll say au revoir when you leave.

We don't do that any more. We—most of the time, the people that you deal with sort of avert their eyes and they pretend that they don't see you. And I think that's kind of unfortunate, I think you should at the very least say goodbye. And this is a goodbye song, this is why I choose it for last. It's also a Washington song.

> Mike Espy was having some trouble, I fear.
> He's leaving effective the end of the year.
> Though some allegations he stoutly denied,
> It was getting a little to stuffy inside.
>
> So long, it's been good to know ya,
> So long, it's been good to know ya,
> So long, it's been good to know ya,
> I know that you think that you did nothing wrong,
> But you better be rolling along.
>
> Bill's friend Roger Altman had get-up-and-go.
> On Whitewater he was real loyal although
> At no time did he ever mean to deceive
> But it seemed like a good time to get up and leave.
>
> Saying so long, it's been good to know ya,
> So long, it's been good to know ya,
> So long, it's been good to know ya,
> I know that you think that you've done nothing wrong,
> But you better be rolling along.
>
> Jean Hanson was also caught up in the spin,
> And found herself on the outside looking in,
> As did Art *(sic)* Nussbaum no doubt about that.
> No hurry, they told him but here is your hat.

Webb Hubbel had trouble,
They showed him the door.
Also David Watkins, not there anymore.
He once took a chopper to chase a golf ball,
And Bill said, "Thanks, David, but that will be all."
(Laughter.)

So long, it's been good to know ya,
So long, it's been good to know ya,
So long, it's been good to know ya,
I know that you think that you did nothing wrong,
But it's time to be rollin' along.
(Applause.)

Speaker Charles Osgood, host of CBS News "Sunday Morning" and CBS Radio the "Osgood File."

MR. KLEIN: That was even better than Garrison Keillor. *(Laughter.)*

First of all, I'd like to say that your song about the National Press Club was the best thing anyone has done for us since John Philip Sousa wrote the "National Press Club March," and we will get it printed and put it right up next to the "National Press Club March," and you will go down in National Press Club history for that.

So my first question is: What was it about the Fordham class that you were in that produced you and Alan Alda, Jack Reynolds and could you describe those times in your radio studio with Alan Alda?

MR. OSGOOD: Let me think while I talk, which is really a dangerous thing to do. But I want you to know that I may be one of the only people in captivity, after three years in the United States Army Band, who knows the "National Press Club March." *(Laughter.)* At least I have heard it played, anyway. I don't know if there was anything special about our class, but this thought does come to mind. That I'm not sure that, had I majored in journalism, or if I had found out what the technology of the day was—you know, when television was still using film, tape wasn't around yet, and we didn't have satellites, and the equipment was very different in radio and television than the equipment that we're using now, and so I think that maybe the one thing that we all did have in common there is that we all had courses in cosmology and epistemology, metaphysics of all kinds, and logic, and other kinds of scholastic philosophy which I think has stood me in pretty good stead. It certainly helped me to get that BS degree that I was talking about. *(Laughter.)*

And I really do believe that it's important, and one of the things that people are lacking today in this country, and this story has many angles to it, but I think there has been a decline in thinking. It's a very serious problem and, you know, intelligence levels are said to be declining and all of that, but I think it's not that people can't think, it's just that they don't. And I think the ability to be analytical, the ability to be critical, and even self-critical, is something that you can—that can be taught, and the Jesuits are real good at it. *(Laughter.)* If you don't criticize yourself, they will take care of that for you. *(Laughter.)* So I think all of us learned a little bit from the Jesuits.

I have a son who just started at Fordham. No coincidence that that's the case. I'm also now cycled completed. I just joined the board of trustees at Fordham as well. So time passes and we all play different roles.

MR. KLEIN: Anything about you and Alan Alda cooking up something in the radio studio, or do you want to pass on that?

MR. OSGOOD: I made a suggestion to him one time there. I remember we were just kids, but I said, "Alan, why don't you make a television series"—*(laughter)*—"about these doctors out in Korea"? And I didn't think he was even listening, but the rest is history. *(Laughter.)*

MR. KLEIN: If you could cover the White House on a full-time basis, rather than just the squirrel beat, how would you change broadcast journalism in that field?

MR. OSGOOD: The question is so preposterous. *(Laughter.)* That job has come open several times since I've been associated with CBS, and not once has anybody offered it to me, so I've never really had to cope with the idea as to how I would do it. But I don't know. I would think that it might be possible, and again this is criticism from the fringe and to be understand in that context, but it seems to me that in covering the news out of Washington, whether it's the White House or the Capitol or other places that are news sources, that there is a preoccupation here with process, with the horse race aspect of it—who gains and who loses politically.

And I can understand why that's a matter of great concern around here. But it seems to me that greater emphasis could have been placed, for example during the health care debates and discussion, on the content of all of those bills, or at least of a few of them. And I think all of that was given very short shrift in favor of the concentration on the process and who gains or who loses from the day's events.

MR. KLEIN: The questioner would like to know at what point did you develop your unique style? Was there one thing that triggered it?

MR. OSGOOD: No, there certainly was not one thing that triggered it, and I don't—I'm not aware of having any particular style. I can tell you that I sound almost exactly the way my father used to sound. When I was living at home and I would pick up the phone—and his name was Charles also—so people would say, "Charles?" And I'd say, "Yes." And then this conversation would start about textiles, which was the business that he was in, and I'd realize and say, "Wait a minute, wait a minute, let me go get my father."

So as far as speaking style is concerned, it certainly was nothing contrived or an attempt at some kind of style, that's just the way we talk in New Jersey. *(Laughter.)*

The other aspect of it is, I think that if I had majored in journalism, no doubt in my mind that along around sophomore year sometime somebody would take a look—if I did what I'm doing now, some professor would look at it and say, "Stop that!" And unlike my defiance to the management where I continue to do poems, I would have flunked out and I would have probably gotten out of journalism all together. So I think—I think I probably was better off focusing on other things and not trying to learn the—whatever the ABCs of Journalism 101 were at that time.

MR. KLEIN: Over the course of your broadcast career, how would you say the perspective of the American people has changed?

MR. OSGOOD: Whew!

MR. KLEIN: In 25 words or less. That's an easy one!

MR. OSGOOD: *(Laughing.)* Yes, well—in the 27 years—well no, not much has happened. I don't know. I don't know whether it's that the perspective of the people has changed. I know my own perspective has changed, and I guess that happens as you have experience and you have your own kids and you try to deal with the world around you. And I think the way that I have changed is that I'm much less sure of myself now than I used to be. I'm much less confident that an idea that I may have on a given subject is the only right one. So probably that would make me—I would be a very poor choice to sit in for Rush Limbaugh—*(laughter)*—or somebody on the other side. I would be a poor choice to sit in for anybody where a great deal of conviction was required because it seems to me it is possible to deal with one another—and this goes back to the subject of respect that we talked about. It seems to me that that's another thing that we really ought to try to get away from—not belittling the person who's opposed to us, or that person's position. Or at very least, it seems to me, we ought to accept the idea—and I believe at one time that it was accepted that a person who has an idea that's different from your own might be quite sincere about it and come at it from entirely noble motives and that he's not just trying to get elected or make a point or make a buck.

And I hear in the political discourse coming out of this city—and I'm not just talking about out of the media, but out of people who are politicians—a sense of not only distrust, but a distinct impression that the other side is in some way malevolent, and I think that is very unfortunate.

MR. KLEIN: You spent an entire career in radio, and radio has changed considerably over the past few years—the past several years. So, of course, that gets us to what do you attribute the surge of popularity of talk radio?

MR. OSGOOD: As far as I'm concerned radio never went away. I mean, when I was having my childhood fantasies, what I would do when I grew up, television didn't enter in because there wasn't any television. I thought about radio and I think I'm one of those sort of lucky people who got to do what he dreamed he would do. I didn't know that it would be in so-called journalism, but I knew I wanted to get into broadcasting because the whole idea of radio I thought was absolutely magic.

I still think that radio is the superior medium with all due respect to my colleagues in television, and paradoxically I think it is better because the pictures are better. It's a very visual medium because you supply the pictures yourself, and therefore they are—it involves a certain creativity on your part, an involvement on your part. I just think—I think television is wonderful, I really do, I think it has the potential for being more wonderful than it is. Don Hewitt, in a talk in Los Angeles last week—the producer of "60 Minutes"—said that he remembers when he was a kid that teachers sometimes would write on your paper, "You can do better work." And he said he thought that that's what somebody ought to say to television.

At the same time there are wonderful moments in television and the thought comes to my mind that some of those wonderful moments are on Sunday mornings. And maybe the most wonderful of all, the one that everyone talks about, when you mention that you're associated with this broadcast they say, "You know what I like?" It's always the same thing. They say "I like the part at the end, when the anchorman shuts up"—*(laughter)*—"and you go out to a mountaintop or out into the woods somewhere in a field, and watch the birds and butterflies and wild animals, and listen to the sounds that they make, and to the wind rustling through the trees and no commentary to go with that. No music." But there's something about—after seeing all these stories about people—and remember this is Sunday morning so that some of this is people doing wonderful things. It's almost as if—I gave a couple of talks in the last couple of weeks; one to the women's auxilliary at Temple Emmanuel, and another to a meeting of the Christophers. Somebody asked me—at each of these meetings somebody asked—why television seems to be so afraid of the subject of religion. Television is almost afraid to mention the Deity. And my response was quite spontaneous, because I hadn't really thought about it before.

But it seems to me that that last couple of minutes where we say, "Okay, you heard from the singers and the dancers and the statesmen, and now—a word from God"—that's a prayer. And I suppose we would never identify it as such on Sunday morning or on the CBS News broadcast, but inside me that's what that is.

MR. KLEIN: Tell us a little bit about your workday, how you go about what you do, how you come up with your ideas. I understand you start at 2:00 in the morning and—how do you do that and manage to stay so young-looking?

MR. OSGOOD: Well, thank you for that. Let me say that there's not a morning that the alarm goes off at 2:30 that it doesn't feel to me like some horrible mistake. *(Laughter.)* Because as you truly realize, 2:30 in the morning is not the morning at all, it's the middle of the night. But if you're going to do four network radio broadcasts—four different ones an hour apart, starting at 6:25 in the morning—you better get a jump on it. And so that's what—the time is spent in finding the stories and then putting them together with the help of Phil Chin and Gail Lee, and we always put four programs on.

You know, some people—a lot of people complain that they don't like their jobs because they don't have enough opportunity to express themselves. Well, I do like my job but I have no complaints about the opportunities to express my ideas. In fact, I have—I'll tell you this, just between you and me and however many people watch C-SPAN and listen to NPR—that I have more time to express ideas than I have ideas. *(Laughter.)*

MR. KLEIN: This questioner says, "You've been criticized for writing and delivering your own commercials. Doesn't this risk misleading the casual listener?"

MR. OSGOOD: Well, we try not to mislead in that department. I do commercials on radio. I don't do them on television, but it's sort of—it's the way network radio works. It's sort of the way that it's structured now and anybody whose name you know on network radio is likely to be somebody who does commercials. I have never had an ethical or a philosophical problem with it.

My father was a salesman. I thought he was a wonderful fellow. My sister and I used to—when he would come back from a sales trip, as I say he was in the textile business, and one of the things we used to do was to file his orders that he had gotten while he was out there. And you could see, sometimes there'd be a nice little stack and sometimes the stack wouldn't be so high, and we learned early on that the high stack was the good one. *(Laughter.)* We all learned to appreciate that very much. I have a lot of—I have always been aware—even before I started doing commercials on radio—that every dollar that was sent to me in a paycheck at the end of the week came from commercial money, and so I do not mind in the least being very up front about that. But we try to start the commercials by saying, "Now a word from Rembrandt Toothpaste" or whatever it is. And that's excellent toothpaste by the way. *(Laughter.)*

MR. KLEIN: All right. How much O.J. Simpson coverage is enough? Are you pleased with how TV is covering the story?

MR. OSGOOD: Well, I think that that question was probably written down before I made my passing reference to the "O.J. Simpson-free zone" that I would declare. I think there's curiosity about it, and I certainly think the story should be covered, and I don't—I would not want to wield any magic wand that would keep it off anybody else's broadcast, but it's just—I think that there's probably—we've had enough, more than enough. And—but I'm sure we'll have a whole lot more before it's all over.

MR. KLEIN: This questioner asks, can you please give us some examples of stories you won't or wouldn't do?

MR. OSGOOD: Well, I did declare "The Osgood File" a "Bobbitt-free zone" at the time of that story. *(Laughter.)* I mean, there are some things—It's not that I wouldn't do the story out of principle, although I can think of some things that maybe—there are certainly some things that I wouldn't do. I would not like to think that, in order for me to do my job as a journalist—and I'm afraid that some of this does go on, spawned as the journalists that came after Watergate, that seems to feel that you really haven't done your job unless you have your fangs bared and your claws unsheathed all the time and you have to leave somebody in a pool of blood or you haven't done it. I would hope that—and it seems to me that that's not true, that you can shed a lot of light on things and do a pretty good job as a journalist without hurting somebody in the process, and I would—I think that, if I thought that what I was doing was going to—really going to hurt somebody, that I wouldn't want to do it. And I've never really had to face that. If I—I may have inadvertently hurt somebody in the process, but I would never have done that on purpose.

MR. KLEIN: We are, unfortunately, about out of time, and I—before asking the last question, I'd like to present you, of course, with a certificate of appreciation for being here, something—and, of course, the ever popular National Press Club mug, which I hope you will use on "Sunday Morning."

MR. OSGOOD: Thank you.

MR. KLEIN: You can toast us all. *(Laughter.)* And I don't want to put you on the spot, but do you have a piece of verse or something you'd like to leave us with? Or would you like me to find another last question? *(Laughter.)* Perhaps a song?

MR. OSGOOD: No, I have not prepared either a verse or a song to leave you with, just—how about this one: I'll see you on the radio. *(Applause.)*

MR. KLEIN: Ladies and gentlemen, that was a memorable event here. We don't get great entertainment up here like that very often. Judy Collins once sang a campaign song, but this was even better than that. *(Laughter.)* I appreciate you all coming.

Thank you very much. Excellent stuff. *(Applause.)*

NATIONAL PRESS CLUB

LUNCHEON
March 17, 1994

$\mathscr{S}$PEAKER

RITA DOVE
Poet Laureate of the United States

MODERATED BY: Gil Klein

HEAD TABLE GUESTS

DEIRDRA DONOHUE
USA Today

DAVID STOREY
General News Editor of Reuters

MARY OTTO
Knight-Ridder Newspapers

JOHN McCOTTER SAWYER
Washington Bureau Chief of the St. Louis Post-Dispatch

TOM BRAZAITIS
Washington Bureau Chief of the Cleveland Plain Dealer

WALTER DELLINGER
Assistant Attorney General at the U.S. Department of Justice

CHRISTY WISE
Freelance Journalist and Chairwoman of the National Press Club Speakers Committee

JULIA SPICER
*Director of Public Affairs for GTE Washington and the member of the
National Press Club Speakers Committee who arranged today's luncheon*

LELAND SCHWARTZ
Editor and Publisher of the States News Service

ERICA GOODE
Senior Writer for U.S. News & World Report

ROGER ANDERSON
Arts, Entertainment and Literature Editor of Scripps Howard News Service

DAVID STREITFELD
Washington Post

GIL KLEIN

MODERATOR

*G*ood afternoon. Welcome to the National Press Club. My name is Gil Klein. I'm the president of the club and a national correspondent for Media General Newspapers, writing for the Richmond Times-Dispatch, the Tampa Tribune, and the Winston-Salem Journal.

I'd like to welcome my fellow club members in the audience today, as well as their guests, and those of you who are watching us on C-SPAN, or listening to us on National Public Radio, or the Internet global computer network.

Now, for those who love poetry, for those who enjoy a fresh and graceful approach to contemporary writing, for those who want the art of poetry to be widely enjoyed, today the National Press Club presents Rita Dove, the poet laureate of the United States. She follows notable predecessors, the likes of Robert Penn Warren, Richard Wilbur, Howard Nemerov, Joseph Brodsky and Mona Van Duyn. In her first months of her tenure at the Library of Congress, Ms. Dove has created not only a unique as well as ambitious schedule of poetry readings, but she also continues to achieve distinction with her own writings.

Born in Akron, Ohio in 1952, Ms. Dove was a 1970 Presidential Scholar, as one of the 100 best high school graduates in the United States. Your mother must have been very pleased. *(Laughter.)* She graduated from Miami University of Ohio summa cum laude, and studied on a Fulbright scholarship in Germany before earning a masters in fine arts at the University of Iowa. She has published four collections of poetry, including one entitled "Thomas and Beulah," in 1986, which was loosely based on the life of her grandparents. For that collection Ms. Dove won the Pulitzer Prize. She also published a book of short stories in 1985, entitled "Fifth Sunday." And last year she published her first novel, "Through the Ivory Gate." Scheduled for release later this month is a verse drama that she has written called "The Darker Face of the Earth." She is past president of the Associated Writing Program, which is the Association of Creative Writers in American Academia. And since 1989 she has been on the faculty of the University of Virginia in Charlottesville, where she is a Commonwealth Professor of English.

Ms. Dove has brought tremendous energy to her position as poet laureate at the Library of Congress. She presented one program that combined jazz music with poetry reading, and in another she brought eight Crow Indian schoolchildren and their teacher, who is a poet, from their Montana reservation to read their poems to a full house.

When reporting Ms. Dove's accolades, one must certainly recognize her true claim to fame. She is known around the Library of Congress as the singing laureate. An accomplished soprano, she enjoys classical voice training, and occasionally performs with the University of Virginia's Opera Workshop. Too much culture for one room. I don't know whether we can stand it. *(Laughter.)*

Ladies and gentlemen, please join me with a warm National Press Club welcome for Poet Laureate Rita Dove.

(Applause.)

Rita Dove, author of Through the Ivory Gate *and* Selected Poems *(Vintage Contemporaries, October 21, 1993).*

RITA DOVE

SPEAKER

Thank you. Thank you, Mr. Klein. Thank you all for coming, ladies and gentlemen, friends, guests and colleagues. It's a great pleasure for me to be here. I almost said a perverse pleasure to be here today—*(laughter)*—a poet standing before the distinguished members of the Fourth Estate. I've always wondered what the Fifth would be.

The media coverage since my appointment as poet laureate has been tremendous, and I find it exhilarating that poetry has become news once more.

As poet laureate, I am continually asked to clarify my position, to list my duties, to elaborate on my plans for promoting the arts, and occasionally I am asked to define poetry, as well. Rarely does a journalist ask about poems themselves. In fact, one television reporter confessed afterwards that he had been so nervous about our interview that he had solicited advice from his colleagues before venturing over to the poetry office at the Library of Congress. The consensus in his office was: Ask her how she started writing and who her favorite poets are, but don't ask her about poetry. *(Laughter.)*

So what I'd like to do today, in the manner of St. Patrick, who charmed the snakes out of Ireland, is to chase some of the bugaboos about poetry out of this room and hopefully from the hearts of those who are listening either on the radio or television and in America.

"Poetry. Merely whispering its name frightens it away," said Jean Cocteau. Today in our country, we could change that remark to: "Poetry. Merely whispering its name frightens everybody away." *(Laughter.)* It can send grown men scurrying to the other end of the reception hall or plunge a pleasant airplane conversation into thunderous silence.

There are 1,001 myths about artists in general and poets in particular—that poets are eccentric, not quite of this world, that poets are blessed with imagination that the rest of the population can never hope to approach, that poets lead wild or at least wildly disorganized lives and enjoy saying outrageous things in polite company. But these prevailing notions about artists in our society makes it very difficult for the creative arts, and especially poetry, to be taken seriously or even taken into account at all.

There was a time when I would hide behind less than the whole truth when asked what I did in life. As long as I was a student, it was easy. I could say that I was an English major and then a graduate student. After graduation, I satisfied the curiosity of casual acquaintances by timidly replying, "I'm working on a book." And later, after I began to teach at the university, I shied away from, I think, the easy, partial truth of my official designation, because although I was an English professor, it sounded fraudulent to me, for I had nothing to do with the brilliant second-guessing of dead writers that one associates with English professors. *(Laughter.)* Instead, I was a live writer, very much alive, thank you.

So I fudged by slurring all of my occupations together in one sentence: "I'm a writer and teach creative writing," usually said at that speed. *(Laughter.)*

Then about a few—well, actually about 12 years ago, a young woman started up a conversation at a bus stop and she posed the inevitable question. I hedged and said merely, "I write," to which she replied cheerfully, "Oh, I do calligraphy, too." *(Laughter.)* And that day I made a vow to tell the uncompromised truth. So now, when asked what I do for a living, I answer, "I'm a poet. I write poetry," and then I endure one of two reactions caused by my confession: Either they grab my sleeve and regale me with the story of their Great Aunt Maude whose delightful verses have brought joy to family festivities, and yet, hard as she tried, she could not get them published, and they might look at me, as the published poet, as if I were part of the conspiracy of the modern language Mafia who had deprived their great aunt of her chance to be a master wordsmith in the Mother Goose tradition. Or my confession might cause confusion, embarrassment, a kind of bumbling discomfort.

The more damaging of these two notions is, of course, that one that poetry is hermetic, cerebral stuff, impossible for mere mortals to comprehend.

So where does poetry reside and where does it begin? When the painter Edgar Degas claimed to be full of ideas for writing poems, his friend Mallarme replied, and this is a famous response, "My dear Degas, poems are not made out of ideas, they're made out of words."

Emerson qualifies this claim by saying, "Words are also actions, and actions are a kind of word."

And though I think that poetry turns upon the action of words, poetry roots itself in the acts of life. It springs from the inner sources that are at the very core of our humanness. It resides in the interstices between the world and the unarticulated emotions circumscribing our souls.

But instead of sliding deeper into philosophical discourse, I'd like to offer an example from my own work. My third poetry book, "Thomas and Beulah," as Mr. Klein has said, is based upon the lives of my maternal grandparents. It rapidly became, in the writing of it, an amalgam of biographical fact, imagination and creative scholarship, but "Thomas and Beulah" began with a real event, one that was insignificant in the grand context of history, but it was indispensable within the confines of personal biography.

My grandfather had died when I was 13 years old, and the family took turns keeping my grandmother company in the ensuing weeks. Since I wasn't old enough to date yet, I was the grandchild who was assigned to take over the weekend slot. It was wonderful actually, and I spent many hours with my grandmother just letting her reminisce. But one Saturday morning at breakfast, she fixed me my one allowed cup of sweetened coffee, and sat down and told me a story from my grandfather's life. It was a story from his life before he met her, and he must have told it to her countless times.

In his late teens, my grandfather worked the Mississippi River on a riverboat as part of a song-and-dance duo, and late one night on the boat, my grandfather had dared his partner, a mandolin player, to swim across the river to an island where a chestnut tree was growing. And the friend dove into the Mississippi and headed for the tree, when the island sunk and the maelstrom sucked him down.

This true story, as you can see, was pretty unbelievable. Chestnut trees in the middle of the Mississippi, okay, but islands that sink? As my daughter would say, "Come on. Get real."

My grandmother, however, stuck to her story with an obstinance that made the anecdote undeniable. And many years later, I recognized this as the crucial point in my grandfather's life, that moment when fate steps in and your life takes a sickening 90-degree turn and plops you down facing a wilderness. We've all had those moments, and the events surrounding those moments, recalled later, seem almost surreal, with that slow-motion over-magnification of anything that you worry over and obsess over time and time again.

Let me read you this poem: "The Event. Ever since they'd left the Tennessee ridge with nothing to boast of but good looks and a mandolin, the two Negroes leaning on the rail of a riverboat were inseparable. Lem plucked to Thomas's silver falsetto. But the night was hot, and they were drunk. They spat where the wheel churned mud and moonlight. They called to the tarantulas down among the bananas to come out and dance. 'You're so foreign and mighty, let's see what you can do,' said Thomas, pointing to a tree-capped island. Lem stripped, spoke easy, 'Them's chestnuts, I believe,' dove quick as a gasp. Thomas, dry on deck, saw the green crown shake as the island slipped under, dissolved in the thickening stream. At his feet, a stinking circle of rags, the half-shell mandolin. Where the wheel turned, the water gently shirred."

Now this story was my own. It haunted me, and it became my own. I wanted to know now how to go on after that sickening turn. I asked myself, "What are you going to do now, Rita? What would he do?" And the answer came like an echo, "Pick up the mandolin."

Now I don't know if my grandfather picked up his friend's mandolin or not. Actually, my mother corrected me years later when I interviewed her for more material for the book. My grandfather had played the guitar she said, when he was young, not the mandolin. I had remembered incorrectly. Or had I? Because as Stravinsky has said once, "One lives by memory . . . and not by truth."

Well my Thomas then picks up the mandolin and the scraps of his partner's life, and he learns the double stringed song. He gives up the river boat life, continues north and finally settles down in Akron, Ohio, which is a booming town, or used to be a booming town, the rubber-bearing city on the banks of the crooked Cuyahoga River, which was then forced underground in order to service the factories of man and man's dreams of industry and wealth. That river today, rich with chemicals and waste products, has burned more than once and inspired a Randy Newman song which goes, "Now the Lord can make you tumble, the Lord can make you turn, the Lord can make you overflow, but the Lord can't make you burn."

Thomas lands in Akron in 1921, however, and then it is still a city on the up and up, the American dream in full flower beneath the sickening stench of burning rubber and the ever present time clock. And at that point I got stuck, because what did I know about this town in 1921? How could I begin to follow Thomas through those streets if I didn't know what those streets looked like, how many black people he would see in passing, what a black working class man could or couldn't do in 1921, what is hoped for for the future and what they might have been grounded on? So, I went to the library and I began to amass notes on working conditions in factories, census reports, demographic charts—things that I thought I was done with after I left school. You're never through with school.

I learned how rubber is vulcanized, I learned what the times were for the factory shifts, how many white workers from West Virginia were recruited in proportion to black southerners. I learned that the Goodyear aerospace airdock was, around 1930, the largest structure of its time without interior support, and that it was so large that it had its own weather system. Occasionally fog would accumulate and lightning would flicker right under the ceiling. And how much of this material did I use? Next to nothing. *(Laughter)*.

The process is very much, I think, like writing a feature article. You ask probing questions, talk to the subject for as long as you can before you get thrown out. And then, since you've only got 750 words, say, you look for an angle. I call it the hinge, that which swings open the door into the world of the poem. And it can be a detail, the color of a scarf or the number of upholstery studs in a leather-backed office chair.

Well, frustrated, I interrupted this trying to write long enough to bake oatmeal cookies, and as usual, I burned the first tray. And that stench stopped me right in my tracks. Because

I knew this smell. It was the smell that I had grown up with, I had lived in it and walked in it. You see, Akron, Ohio was also governed by another scent, other than that burning rubber. It was the smell of burning oats from the Quaker Oats silos. And neither of these smells, of course, was pleasant, but they were so prevalent that they had become natural, a part of life, and they aroused the imagination of the children of Akron. The rubber brought to mind huge truck tires rolling anywhere as long as it was out of Akron. And later, in geography class, we dreamed of those massive rubber trees somewhere in India whose lashed sides streamed white latex.

But the Quaker Oats smell brought a feeling of security, the comfort of the kitchen and its warm oven. And the combination of these smells was a delicious push-pull that I had forgotten. So I found my hinge and entered my grandfather's Akron through smell, Quaker Oats.

"The grain elevators have stood empty for years. They used to feed an entire nation of children, hunched in red leatherette breakfast nooks, fingers dreaming, children let their spoons clack on the white sides of their bowls. They stare at the carton on the table, a miniature silo with a friendly face smiling under a stiff black hat. They eat their oats with milk and butter and sugar. They eat their oats in their sleep where horse-drawn carts jolt along miry roads, past cabins where other children wait, half frozen under tattered counter panes. The man with the black hat, a burlaped sack tucked under his arm, steps down from the wagon saying, 'Come out, don't be afraid.' And they come, the sick and the healthy, the red, the brown, the white, the ruddy and the sallow, the curly and the lank. They tumble from rafters and crawl out of trundles. He gives them to eat, he gives them prayers and a good start in the morning, he gives them free enterprise, he gives them the flag and p.a. systems and roller skates and citizenship. He gives them a tawny canoe to portage overland, through the woods, through the midwestern snow."

The first half of "Thomas and Beulah" is Thomas' story, and the second half is determined by his wife. Beulah is a self-taught hat maker who picks up the skill while working in a dress shop, so she is very aware of colors and textures. And it is Thomas' favorite color, which is blue, that becomes the memory trigger in one of her poems called "Winged Foot Lake." It's the perfect blue of a forbidden, because segregated, swimming pool. It's also the blue of redemption. It gives equal time to the blue sky, the Fourth of July picnics that her daughters have invited her to, as well as the blue sky over the heads of the Civil Rights demonstrators marching through Washington, D.C. in 1963.

Winged Foot Lake is a lake in Akron, Ohio actually. And it's—the winged foot of Apollo —is the logo of Goodyear Tire and Rubber Company.

Winged Foot Lake, Independence Day, 1964. "On her 36th birthday Thomas had shown her her first swimming pool. It had been his favorite color exactly, just so much of it. The swimmers' white arms jutting into the chevrons of high society. She had rolled up her window and told him to drive on, fast. Now this act of mercy, four daughters dragging her to their husband's company picnic, white families on one side and them on the other, unpacking the same squeeze bottles of Heinz, the same waxy beef patties and Salem potato chip bags. So he was dead for the first time on Fourth of July. Ten years ago had been harder waiting for something to happen, and ten years before that the girls like young horses eyeing the track.

"Last August she stood alone for hours in front of the TV set as a crow's wing moved slowly through the white streets of government. That brave swimming scared her. Like Joanna saying, 'Mother, we're Afro-Americans now.' What did she know about Africa? Were there lakes like this one with a rowboat pushed under the pier, or Thomas' great Mississippi with its sullen silks? There was the Nile, but the Nile belonged to God. Where she came from was the past, 12 miles into town where nobody had locked their back door and Goodyear hadn't begun to dream of a park under the company symbol, a white foot sprouting two small wings."

Although that poem revolves around recognizable historical events, the world arena is peripheral to the details of that picnic, because human beings do not live for history. They might live under its thrall, or in spite of it, or even in it, but not because of it.

Why does poetry affect us differently than, say, a newspaper feature or a documentary, or even a mini-series? Well, let me read to you one woman's explanation. This was a reaction from one of the—what is now well over a thousand—letters that I've received since assuming the laureateship. Her name is Dennie Moses, and she's from Putnam, Vermont, and she wrote: "I'm not a poet, formal or learned, and I certainly don't understand it intellectually. However, the musician in me, as a healer, are very drawn to it as a medicine of expression. Maybe because it can have a quality of intimacy that I feel comfortable with. And in the past three years I find myself, at times, flooding with words that demand to be put to paper, unbidden by me consciously. This outpouring is a kind of therapy, I suppose. I call it poetry."

I'm always astonished when people claim that poetry is intellectual or elitist, and that it has to do with books and flowers and stuff. To me, a poem is so firmly rooted in the world, or rather that juncture between the world and the individual spirit, that I find poems more useful for negotiating the terms of our identities, more effective in providing a stay against extinction than, for instance, the mass media.

The mass media can provide us with the news, but they can't tell us what to do with it. Of course, it's not the task of news media to crank out solutions, but with no instructions on how to incorporate what's happening close to home or far away, how to locate our private emotions in the public sentiment, we can't help but feel helpless and ultimately betrayed.

It's a pity that large segments of our society regard the creative arts with some degree of apprehension, even suspicion. And that they don't expect the arts, especially the arts by their contemporaries, to be assessable, nor do they see any reason to incorporate the arts into their everyday or professional lives.

Who's afraid of poetry? It's not as interesting a question as why one is afraid, or just apprehensive. Many of those of who profess an aversion to poetry have not read a poem since being forced to memorize Invictous in the eighth grade, which is hardly a fair sampling of the field. But one reason that keeps recurring in an infinite number of variations is, I don't understand it.

Other variations on this theme include, it's not about real life, it's old-fashioned, the language is weird, it's too serious, too self-indulgent, you need a Ph.D. to decipher the stuff or it makes me feel stupid. Well, many of us have suffered a classroom experience where our brave interpretation of a teacher's treasured poem was declared wrong. Poems then became coded texts, something you were supposed to decipher, not enjoy. And for many of us, unfortunately, that was the end of poetry.

In one of the most popular poems in the English language, a full one-fifth of its words cannot be found in the Webster dictionary—they can't be found in any dictionary, in fact, because they are nonsense words. That poem is, of course, The Jabberwocky by Lewis Carroll, which begins: "T'was brillig and the slithy toves did gyre and gimble in the wabe. All mimsy were the borogoves and the mome raths outgrabe."

The precocious seven-year-old Alice, reads this poem, and her tentative response shows that she's both befuddled and intrigued. It seems very pretty, she said, when she had finished it. But it's rather hard to understand. Somehow it seems to fill my head with ideas, only I don't exactly know what they are. Then Alice goes on, in spite of her reservations, to give a very accurate gloss of the poem, saying, however, somebody killed something, that's clear at any rate.

Well, that's exactly what happens in the poem. She got that part right. But the part that fills Alice's head with ideas, that, my friends, is poetry.

Thank you. *(Applause.)*

Rita Dove, Poet Laureate of the U.S., with Speakers Committee member Julia Spicer. March 17, 1994.

MR. KLEIN: Thank you very much, that was wonderful, just wonderful. If you all will pass up the questions here, I'll start with one of my own. I was fascinated by your academic background, how you became one of the top 100 students in the United States and all that, but tell me a little bit about how—when did you begin to think that you would make a career of poetry. Obviously, when you talked to your grandmother, were you thinking about it then? Is this something that came from within or is this something that you stumbled into career day, and the counselor said you ought to be a poet?

MS. DOVE: No career counselor tells you you ought to be a poet, unfortunately, I think. I grew up—I wrote poetry, and I wrote stories, and I wrote plays when I was a child. And I didn't think of it as anything odd. It seemed to me natural that if I was going to read, and I was a veracious reader, that sometimes I would also write stories, so that I could put myself in situations that I didn't find in the other books.

The difference was that I didn't think of myself as a writer. I didn't think that that was something real people did. I certainly didn't know that there were any black women who did it at that age, 10 or 11. And I wrote, but I didn't think about it as anything other than something you do when you are a child. And when you grow up, you put away childish things and get this career thing.

I was a pre-law major for the first 10 minutes of my undergraduate career, and then realized that I had absolutely no aptitude for that, and I didn't even like it, particularly. So I fudged for a couple of years, taking English and saying I was pre-law, and trying to figure out what I was going to do with my life until I realized that I was scheduling everything around my one creative writing class. And that's when I realized that not only that's what I wanted to do, but that I had absorbed, really, what society was telling me, that you couldn't be a poet and be a grown-up. And that's really when I decided to do it.

When my grandmother told me that story, I did not think of it in terms of a story. It haunted me for many years, until I think I realized that I had to write about it.

MR. KLEIN: When you go back—the poets—do you go back to Tennyson or—do these people you—Shakespeare? Or did you put all that aside and do it all from the modern context?

MS. DOVE: You can never put it all aside. I don't think of any poets—when I think of other poets, I don't think of them in terms of being my contemporaries or modern poets, or classical poets, they're all in one family. I think that's one of the things about poems that you love. They seem very actual, very real.

I kind of cut my teeth on Shakespeare in the best of circumstances, and I think that isn't my—there was a book of complete Shakespeare in the house, because you were supposed to have a complete Shakespeare, I think, in the house. But I read it without anyone telling me that I was too young to understand it. And I think that, very often, if you can read something knowing that no one's going to ask you about it later, you're much more relaxed and able to enjoy it. And so I was reading these plays when I was about 12, and I didn't understand a lot of words, but I got them, I mean I kept going. So I don't just stick with the contemporaries.

It's hard for me to talk about influences, because, I think, when I know my influences, and they cease to influence me anymore because I'm thinking about it? But I do know that I go back to Shakespeare, William Carlos Williams, that when I was about 16 or 17, to read— Langston Hughes was a real revelation—that there was someone who was actually writing about the kind of people that I knew in the language that I recognized, the language that had the music that I recognized in it, jazz and blues, and there's a whole host of people, and I'm not going to get myself into trouble by naming them all.

MR. KLEIN: A couple of people have asked about the lyrics of gangster rap, maybe considered poetry, but how do you assess it?

MS. DOVE: Like most things, there is a very small, I think, level of very good rap, and then the rest is popular. And they're like most things in our lives. What I find that most gangster rap is, for me, is irresponsible, and that what joys it can give in terms of language are certainly overridden by lots of other things. And I find that most of it has been, unfortunately, so commercialized that it's very difficult anymore to tell whether something is heartfelt or not.

In the very early days of rap music, there were some phenomenal, absolutely phenomenal, I guess you could call them lyrics. And these really sprang out of the oral tradition in black communities, where one had to be virtuoso, and it was part of survival, learning how to deal with one's situation by articulating one's concerns about it. And that is, in certain ways, the wellspring of poetry.

Much of today's gangster rap—I don't want to be absolutely carte blanche and say that all of it is horrible—but I find myself distressed by its lack of tolerance and the violence. And I find a lot of it a little too easy.

MR. KLEIN: What did you mean when you said that poetry can be a stay of extinction? If poetry were less broadly read, do you predict that some calamity would befall mankind?

MS. DOVE: Hmm. *(Laughter.)* When I said that poetry can be a stay against extinction, I think that what one of the things that poetry does is to allow us or to help us contemplate ourselves, both as individuals and as a larger group, in terms of the planet. I'm talking really broad terms. But in our day-to-day lives, we just—we get through them, and we don't— very often we don't think of the larger picture.

A poem can remind us in a very, very intimate way that we are stewards, I guess you could say, on this planet, and that, in a sense, can be a stay against extinction, because if we don't begin thinking about what we are doing on this earth and what we can do to make sure that it still is here when we individually leave this earth, then we will grow extinct or we'll blow the place up. So in that sense, I think it can be a stay against extinction.

I think that if poetry were not read, if people did not have the arts, that we do become atrophied in that we are heading for destruction. If you cannot, if we do not allow ourselves to think about the reasons why we are here and what it means to be here, then we are going to behave irresponsibly. So the arts in a way do remind us of that. They remind us of how alive we are. They remind us how important each individual is. They remind us not to look at the world in generalized terms, but to think about it in humane terms.

MR. KLEIN: I remember my wife telling me, and she's a teacher, that one day a poet came into her class and looked at the children's poetry and sniffed and said, "Ha! Poetry doesn't rhyme anymore. This stuff isn't any good." So this questioner asked how much do you think about rhyme and meter when you sit down to write?

MS. DOVE: Well, first of all, I'd like to say that it grieves me to hear this story, because I think that when poets or artists go into schools they have to recognize that they are—they may be there for a day or two, and they don't know what those students have been told that poetry is or not.

I pay a great deal of attention to—I wouldn't say meter, necessarily—but to the rhythms and the cadences of a poem. I believe that poems are, in a sense, our way of speaking musically and that they convince on levels deeper, let's say, than intellectual levels. They convince us, actually, in our bones that we know that someone who tells a good story or someone who can tell a good joke, that the same joke can be told by someone else and make no impact whatsoever because they don't have the right timing, they don't use the right words. How you say things does matter. How we say things and the words that we choose, help, I think, clarify what are actually very amorphous emotions. So I pay a great deal of attention to the meter because I feel that a poem has a sense of itself as sound and that sounds can also influence the way we think.

There are a thousand different words for saying "quiet," for instance, and being placed into the—choosing the right word will often give a hint, though it's a subliminal hint, of how to relate to quiet in a poem, whether you say silenced, or quiet, or hushed or, you know, still, they all have a different quality of silence, and that's very important to me.

MR. KLEIN: This writer says, and it's not me, "I'm a journalist by profession but a poet by vocation. What can be done to expand the avenues of recognition for poets who aren't part of academia?"

MS. DOVE: First of all, I think it is absolutely wonderful that there are poets who are not in academia. I happen to be in academia myself, but I do feel that today we are at a crisis in American letters because so often many of the arts, and literature in particular, have been kind of holed up in academia, and there is a great rift between the world of the people in the street and those in academia, so that poetry has been kind of—it's become, in a certain way, put into an ivory tower, and it should not reside exclusively in academia.

One of the things I think that can happen to bring poetry more out into the open, and for poets who are not in academia, is that you, many of you as journalists, it would be wonderful if you could prevail upon your newspapers to do more reviews of poetry books or even more coverage of events in literature. I think that it's appalling that many newspapers have ceased to produce or ceased to review poets, and if they do review poetry, they review them in groups— group reviews.

I think that what I'm trying to do at the Library of Congress is to expand the notion of the audience for poetry by combining poetry with other media, such as the jazz and poets, and next year I hope to do an environmental symposium which will have guests, not only poets but photographers and journalists and scientists to see if we can all actually talk together.

One thing that you can do individually, the people who are interested in poetry, is to actually bring it up and actually, when people ask you what you do, you can say, "Well, I'm a journalist, but I also write poetry," so that we can start to explode this notion that poets don't fit in or that poetry's something that can't fit in with life and that poetry is of no concern to those who are interested in math, or geography, or engineering or journalism.

MR. KLEIN: Tell us a little bit about your soon-to-be-published work. You call it a verse drama. What is that, and how does a novel tell a story differently than poetry?

MS. DOVE: Oh, two questions. The verse drama is a—a verse drama is a play that is written in verse. This is not—mine is blank verse, it's not rhymed, but it's written like poetry. In other words, it has lines. On stage, it's not intended—you're not intended to think that they're all reciting poems, but if you think of Shakespeare, these work very well as plays. The language is very—it's heightened, though, and taut. It's a play—it's a historical drama. It is a—tells the story of a slave rebellion in antebellum South Carolina. And I did it in verse because I wanted to get a sense of—it's a very—it's not surreal, but there's a lot of stuff in it about the sense of destiny and omen. And there's a lot of music in it, as well, and so I wanted that quality, again, of music and cadence to come into it.

How is a novel different from poetry?

MR. KLEIN: What skills do you bring into it that are different?

MS. DOVE: Well, when I wrote my novel, at first I told myself that while they're both made of words, one just has more—*(laughter)*—and that that's the way you approach it. I must admit that I had—really my respect for novelists, which was considerable already, really grew when I began writing the novel because it was a slightly different ballgame. Every word in a novel counts, too.

I think it really is a myth to say that novels just have a bunch of extra words. Words are used in different ways. You use words sometimes to buy time. You use words in a novel because you want to create a sense of the time of the novel, which is not real time, most of the time, but it's something in between. And that means that every word matters. Every "he said" or "she said" also has its purpose or not. And some words are transparent. They're not meant to be really read. I mean, you read them but you aren't really meant to register them. But you have to know that they are transparent, that they don't really matter.

So there was a great difference in my working habits between the two of them. The novel, because of all those words, I had to really go at it sometimes very, very much mechanically in that I sat down at 8:00 in the morning and worked till 2:00. With poems, I may sit down at 8:00 in the morning but I'll get up about 20 times in between, and I'm still working, but it's all in my head. I could not do that with the novel.

MR. KLEIN: What can be done to increase interest in poetry and literature in this electronic age? Following up on that, have you considered promoting the idea of a "poet of the week" show for TV or radio or the Internet?

MS. DOVE: *(Laughs.)* What a great idea. It's kind of nice, isn't it?

MR. KLEIN: Yeah.

MS. DOVE: Very good. You know, it's been really wonderful to get all these letters from people from all over the country who offer their ideas, and some of them are very good. One of the things—one of the ideas that was sent in to me by someone was—they said, "Why not just try to approach some of the major newspapers to simply publish a poem, a poem a week or a poem a day, without any commentary, really, but just like they used to have today's chuckle or today's—just to have it in the paper." And then they went on for another two pages trying to explain how one could do this.

And it is a bureaucratic nightmare, but I think that if one stops thinking about, "Well, we've got to understand this poem. There's a significance to choosing exactly this poem." If we simply said, "Well, today we'll do this one or today we'll do that one," that's a way to open the paper. If you run across a poem often enough, people will look through and see what this is that keeps appearing, this thing that doesn't look like an article. That's one of the things I think, you know, we could do.

I think also in the electronic age, this is a field that's wide open. I do know that there are all those bulletin boards out there in the computer world. There are sometimes fascinating conversations going on about classical music when I peek in all the time, that the art of letter-writing is being revived through the computer age, and in a certain way the art of using language precisely and conscientiously.

I think that to do a poet, and I've been approached to do, I guess you could say, a correspondence on computer as a poet. I just haven't been able to do it because I don't have time. I'm still answering all those other letters. But I think that the idea of having a poet for the week in the computer would be a wonderful idea, or even on television.

I've been exploring and I will do a couple of electronic classroom things, interactive video with classrooms, because I have gotten so many requests from librarians and from teachers to come to their class and I couldn't even do a tenth of them without being gone all year. I began to think, "How can you actually appear in a classroom without being there?" And that's when I thought about doing something, perhaps on the order of the town meetings that President Clinton had organized, but to actually work with telecommunications.

And I'll be doing one in April in Virginia with several sites within the state where I'm with one class and there are several other classes scattered across the state who are connected by video and they can see me, I can see them, and we can interact. And I'm hoping that these kind of—I'm doing another one in South Carolina in the fall which will have four or five classrooms all over the country. But what I'm hoping is that that will at least give other educators perhaps the idea that they can use this, because the technology is there.

The people that I've been working with have been incredibly helpful. I came to this saying, "I know nothing," and it took me a month to learn what uplink and downlink was without asking because I was afraid to ask what the difference was. But they've been very helpful and said, "Look, don't try to think like an engineer. Think like a poet. What do you want to do? And we'll tell you if we can do it." And so I've learned a lot in the process. And it's right there. It's nothing to be afraid of as an educator. I think we're afraid of a camera coming into our class, but it's a way of reaching lots of other people.

MR. KLEIN: I've just passed on to Tom Brazaitis of the Cleveland Plain Dealer this comment, that in the '30s and '40s the Cleveland Plain Dealer published a poem on its editorial page every Sunday. Why not encourage people to submit poems to their newspapers? I'll just pass that on to you and let you all know out there that Tom is going to push that at the Cleveland Plain Dealer.

MS. DOVE: Okay. *(Laughs.)*

MR. KLEIN: Can you think of any ways that the mass media could successfully promote poetry? The same type of thing, which is not exactly the question I was going to ask next, but if you have any—

MS. DOVE: Well, since I haven't talked about television that much, maybe I should say something about that. I think—at the moment I've been talking with several television stations from public to cable to prime time. And a few of the ideas that we've been playing with, and some of them are actually going to happen, are public service announcements, which instead of talking and saying, you know, "Read poems, read poems," to actually present a poem.

And there are some public service announcements which are coming on cable which, in fact, present a poem one minute, a 60-second spot with a poem, animation—tasteful animation; not, you know, Rocky the squirrel or anything like that. And it's just a poem; no comments, no hype or anything like that, just a poem with music behind it and an animation that doesn't really explain the action.

And I think that those kinds of things, the little—it's great to have programs and hour specials on poetry, and I've been consulting on a few of those as well, which will probably happen next year, but also just a moment, to have a moment where there's some poetry and you can take it or leave it. You can take from it what you will or leave what you will. It can be very effective. I know that Nickelodeon has been doing for quite a while poetry in motion, little things. And when I asked my daughter about it after I had heard about it, she said, "Oh, yeah, yeah. I know that poem." It sinks in.

MR. KLEIN: This questioner wants to know, have you gotten involved in Washington politics yet? And, of course, what would a poet do in—I mean, think of that. Do you plan to improve the Congressional Record or something? Have you, say, lobbied against curtailment of the hours and budget cuts at the Library of Congress?

MS. DOVE: Well, have I gotten involved? In some ways. I haven't gotten really into the, you know, into the bowels of the Congress and what's going on there. But in October I was asked by the historian of Congress if I wanted to say a few words when the statue of Freedom was raised at the Capitol dome, at the 200th anniversary of the Capitol. And I said sure, not knowing what I was going to say; I said sure.

But as it turned out, I had been working on a poem about the statue of Freedom, which had been sitting, as you know, in the parking lot for a long time as another homeless person, in a sense. And so the poem that I eventually did write kind of collapses those two images. She becomes a homeless person and at the same time she's a representative of freedom. And I did read that poem there because I feel that as a poet, one of the best things that I can do is to keep, like, putting poems out there in situations where people least expect it.

Last week, when the Crow Indian children were here to read their poems, they visited with their representatives and senators. And when they met them, they read a poem. And it was wonderful because I could tell that poems hadn't been read there and that, in fact, it gave room for thought. And it's so interesting to have poetry. When people who haven't heard poetry hear it, there's often a relief, a feeling of "Ah, that wasn't bad at all."

And it is an oral—I mean, poetry does have the—you know, I think it needs that human voice moving through it. You know, it also can be read. And there are poems which only can be read perhaps, but it needs to be read over and over again. But that oral element is very important.

I have also—I have been getting involved, to some extent in politics. The position—I think this position carries with it an enormous, in a way, symbolic value. I become a kind of focal point for concerns about the art. And I would be, I think, very irresponsible if I didn't recognize that and try to do something in that capacity.

I've been working at the National Endowment for the Arts, too, at the literature program, which is still beleaguered. And I think that we have to fight to make sure that that does not happen, and work to say things against censorship. So, I feel that it does—it comes with the territory. My feeling is that every human being, if they really look around at what's happening and are concerned with the world, cannot help but be political in some way.

MR. KLEIN: Is poetry more widely accepted in other countries, and if so, which ones?

MS. DOVE: Yes, it is. And I can't name all of them, but I remember being astounded the first time that I read in Germany, for instance, when I discovered that poets were actually asked often, if there was a—some significant event that happened in the political life of Germany, that on the news, sometimes, poets were asked for their comments—famous poets or famous writers, which would practically never happen—it never happens here, I should say.

I was astounded to discover when I went to Mexico, for instance, that—for an international poetry festival—that for an entire week of readings, which lasted three hours because there were four poets every evening—that this theater of 2,000 people was filled every night, and that people brought their children. And they listened for two hours.

I've been amazed—and it's been often said that in the former Soviet Union, poets filled stadiums, that the arts are subsidized a lot more in other countries, that's there's a famous poetry festival in Macedonia where, you know, it's crowded every night. There are many places where poets are regarded more—with more respect and received, I guess, more eagerly than this country.

MR. KLEIN: We have a number of—well, first of all, we're out of time. But before I ask the last question—and I'm sorry because we have a number of very good questions—here is a National Press Club mug, which every poet needs in those late night hours, when the inspiration, the news is about to hit.

MS. DOVE: Of course.

MR. KLEIN: You have to look through the little owl on that. And there's the lamp of knowledge. Do you see that in there?

MS. DOVE: Good, good. Thank you. *(Laughter.)*

MR. KLEIN: And a certificate of appreciation for being here.

MS. DOVE: Thank you.

MR. KLEIN: Now, we have a number of students here, it looks like, from the NOW Elementary School Junior Beta Club. And so I didn't want to get out of here without asking one of their questions. Did your parents inspire you to become a poem writer or did any poets inspire you? And when did you first decide to be a poet? From Natasha Surless *(sp)*?

MS. DOVE: Miss Surless *(sp)*, I think, yes.

My parents encouraged me to read, and their philosophy was—though they never stated it in so many words—was that I could read anything—we could read anything we wanted. If it was too adult for us, we would soon become bored and not read it. And so I had this feeling of incredible freedom as a child in terms of reading. The library was a place I could go, you know, at any time. And if there was a book I wasn't allowed to take out, my parents would write a note saying let her take it out. So I think that reading was what really was the formative thing for me. They did not encourage me to be a poet. I think that, for them, that was also an idea that they didn't know any poets.

I do know that when I came home from my junior year at college and told my parents that I wanted to be a poet—and up until that point, I was in pre-law, right—that they—my father swallowed, and then he said, "Well, I don't really understand poetry"—again, there it is—"but," he said, "but if that's what you want to do, please don't be upset if I don't read the poems." And I'd thought that this was—to me, this was a real—this was, in fact, an adult kind of agreement. And I took it as encouragement. In a way, it was good that he didn't want to read the poems. But—and he has read the poems.

But my parents have—simply have always, I think, supported me in whatever I wanted to do. I think they were a little bit incredulous that one could, indeed, be a poet and not starve. And they're, of course, reflecting all of the myths about poetry. But poets don't necessarily have to sit in a garret and write all day long. They write poems, but they might be occupied in other things as well. So, I guess I answered that question more or less.

MR. KLEIN: Great.

MS. DOVE: Okay.
Thank you. *(Applause.)*

MR. KLEIN: Thank you very much. That was wonderful. *(Applause.)*

MS. DOVE: Thank you.

NATIONAL PRESS CLUB

LUNCHEON
October 24, 1994

PEAKER

LEON PANETTA
Chief of Staff of the White House

MODERATED BY: Gil Klein

HEAD TABLE GUESTS

BOB RANKIN
Knight-Ridder Newspapers

HOWARD BANKS
Washington Bureau Chief of Forbes

KATHY LEWIS
Dallas Morning News

LEO RENNERT
Washington Bureau Chief for McClatchy Newspapers

MONROE KARMIN
Editor-at-Large for Bloomberg Business News and Vice President of the National Press Club

HELEN THOMAS
Chief White House Correspondent for United Press International

BARRY TOIV
Senior Advisor to Mr. Panetta

JOAN LOWY
*Scripps Howard News Service and the member of the National Press Club Speakers Committee
who arranged today's luncheon*

ANDREW GLASS
Washington Bureau Chief for Cox Newspapers

JACQUELINE THOMAS
Washington Bureau Chief for the Detroit News

GEORGE CONDON
Washington Bureau Chief for Copley News Service

SUSAN GARLAND
Business Week

STEWART POWELL
Hearst News Service

MILES BENSON
Newhouse News Service

GIL KLEIN

MODERATOR

*g*ood afternoon. Welcome to the National Press Club. My name is Gil Klein. I'm the club's president and a national correspondent with Media General Newspapers, writing for the Richmond Times-Dispatch, the Tampa Tribune and the Winston-Salem Journal.

I'd like to welcome my fellow club members in the audience today, as well as those of you who are watching us on C-SPAN or listening to us on National Public Radio or the Internet global computer network.

Today we are pleased to have with us White House Chief of Staff Leon Panetta. When he was a congressman, he said he would find himself envying the enormous power wielded by the White House.

After four rough months negotiating with recalcitrant Republicans and renegade Democrats on Capitol Hill, Mr. Panetta has a new perspective. *(Laughter.)* He recently told the Boston Globe, "Now that I am here, I look up at Capitol Hill and say, 'They sure have a lot of power up there.'"

And it could get worse. Unless all the pundits are wrong, Democrats will be lucky to hang on to control of both the House and Senate in the upcoming elections. The specter of Speaker of the House Newt Gingrich must keep Mr. Panetta up nights. Even if they don't take control of either house, Republicans could wind up with a working majority in both houses, and that spells bad news for the Clinton legislative agenda.

Yet Mr. Panetta comes to the task with good credentials. He is one of the most respected figures in Washington today. David Broder of the Washington Post has called him "intellectually tough, politically savvy, and trusted by politicians of both parties and the press." One writer went so far as to call him "downright cuddly." *(Laughter.)*

Mr. Panetta started out in politics as a moderate Republican—fiscally conservative, but liberal on social issues. He was dismissed from his position enforcing civil rights in the Nixon administration after he persisted in pursuing school desegregation cases.

He went home to California, became a Democrat, and was elected to Congress in 1976. In Congress, Mr. Panetta focused on how to reduce the deficit. He became one of the top budget experts, known for the bulging accordion file he carried under his arm. His appointment by President Clinton to head the Office of Management and Budget was heralded as evidence the new administration was taking the deficit seriously. Two years later, deficit reduction is often cited as the administration's chief accomplishment.

But now that he is chief of staff, his toughest tasks lie ahead: figuring out how to deal with a more Republican Congress, bringing order and discipline to the White House and re-electing a president whose popularity ratings just can't seem to break above 50 percent.

Ladies and gentlemen, please join me in a warm press club welcome for White House Chief of Staff Leon Panetta. *(Applause.)*

LEON PANETTA

Thank you very much. Thanks to all of the members of the press club for inviting me here today.

This is the first time I have spoken here since becoming the president's chief of staff, and it seems like only yesterday that I had the simple life of being the director of the Office of Management and Budget, helping the president to make all of those easy decisions to reduce the deficit—painless spending cuts and tax increases, the personnel cuts, dealing with 13 appropriations bills, some 120 departments and agencies, 26 appropriations chairmen, overseeing 500 OMB employees, helping to reinvent government with two million employees. Now I just work for one person. *(Laughter.)*

Ah, to go back to the easy life again. These are indeed challenging moments for myself and for the country. But the choice I made was to accept this difficult challenge and the honor that goes with it. It is indeed rewarding, as it is demanding.

Today I want to talk about the fundamental choice that faces every American. This election day, I think, will tell us a great deal about the American people, whether we as a people want to work together, accept our responsibility to find solutions, to try to give our children a better life in this country, which is really what the American dream is all about, or whether we will strike out in anger and frustration at our system of government and everyone that's a part of it. It's a pretty basic choice, but it's what this election is really all about.

The conventional wisdom inside the Beltway is that the president and the Congress have in fact accomplished a great deal in the past 21 months, despite the last-minute obstructionism, despite some of the bills that did not make it in the waning hours of this session of the Congress. Conventional wisdom or not, I think it's certainly true that there is a record of accomplishment that was made. But the conventional wisdom is also that it doesn't really matter; that the public is so angry and so cynical about government, about politics, that incumbents, and particularly Democrats, are going into the toughest election in a long time.

But the final result is far from decided. As someone who spent 25 years in and out of this town, including 16 years as a member of Congress, and service in both Republican and Democratic administrations, it's my view that no vote—no vote—should be taken for granted. What is generally the accepted view in Washington is not necessarily the accepted view outside the Beltway. My home is 3,000 miles away in Monterey, California, and the truth is I spent as much time there as a member of Congress as I did here. It's probably the healthiest thing one can do when they're in a government job, is to get the hell out of this town once in a while to really see what people are thinking.

And what I've seen in thinking about political issues and problems is that it is better to stand on the outside looking in, rather than on the inside looking out. Facts do matter to the American people. They really do. The progress we have begun to make does matter. The voters do care about who is seeking to solve the problems of average Americans and who is not. They still have a choice to make. It is a choice between whether they want to accept hope or fear, between solutions to problems or gridlock, between trying to move forward or moving backward, between those who say yes and those who say no.

The American people are deciding their future, and that's as it should be. Whether they want political leadership that confronts the problems, that deals with the challenges that they must face, that works to give them the tools so that they can enhance their prosperity and the quality of their life and that, certainly, of their children, or leadership that says that to some extent the fate of average Americans rests on the success of a very few at the top really is a very fundamental difference here that's involved.

I think most Republicans and Democrats share a belief in freedom. They share a belief in liberty, in our Constitution and in our Constitution's commitment to equal opportunity for all. There's even, I believe, a common concern about the plight of our fellow citizens and the problems that face our economy and our communities. But the difference is whether we have a responsibility as a nation to act on those problems, on those challenges, or to engage in benign neglect; to reach out or to turn our backs on our fellow citizens; to make government try to work to give everyone the opportunity to succeed or to accept the fate of the economy and society and what our families have predestined for us. It's a very fundamental choice and a very fundamental difference in how we approach solutions.

For 12 years I think the key to surviving in political office is basically to complain about the problems, to blame somebody else for the problems, and to vote no. You want to know the formula for surviving in political office? It is basically to complain about the problems and make sure you blame somebody else, and always vote no when you face a solution in the Congress because you then don't have to accept responsibility for anything; you've got the best of all worlds. It's the best Rotary Club speech you can give; it's one that raises the problems, blames others for the problems, but in the end you don't have to come down on a solution because you avoid responsibility for the answers.

For 12 years we have seen that approach to politics and we have reaped the whirlwind. We face a legacy of fundamental problems that have grown over the previous dozen years, and in some cases, over decades. The national debt quadrupled—in 12 years quadrupled—to over $4 trillion, and deficits were projected at $300 billion, rising to $400 billion, to $500 billion, and ultimately to $600 billion each year by the beginning of the next century. We saw an economy that had a pathetic job growth within that economy; it amounted to less than a half a million new jobs over the previous four years; unemployment that was approaching almost 8 percent, little growth in business investment and an inability of Congress and the president to agree or sometimes even work together on needed solutions to long-term issues, not only on the deficit and the economy, but on issues like crime and education and health care, issues like welfare reform, family leave.

In the 1992 election, there was a very clear message that was sent by the American people; it was an election about the people's frustration over the inability, unwillingness, of leaders to address problems. It was about the American people's fear that their children were facing a future of limited opportunity and that, for the first time in 200 years, the dream of my parents and many others that our children could have a better life—that that dream would not be realized. It was about concern about gridlock, about partisanship and about blamesmanship. So the message was very clear from the American people. The message was: "No more excuses. No more complaints. Do something. Do something to deal with the problems that face us."

And that is exactly what the president did on the budget deficit, which is not only a measure of the government's ability to function, but also has a direct impact on people's lives. This is not just about numbers when we talk about the deficit; it is about the impact on people's lives. The deficit was out of control, pushing up interest rates despite the weak economy, crowding out private investment, and standing in the way of improved standards of living for average families now and in the future.

The deficit is not just a statistic. It affects our future and the future of our children. It is the most regressive tax in our country. People talk about tax increases in this country; let me tell you what the most regressive tax is. It is the tax we pass on to our children on interest on the debt. That is the most regressive tax. And what this president and Congress have done is to try to confront the issue of the deficit.

Have we done that? More than any administration in history. The deficit reduction plan we passed last year is reducing the deficit three years in a row, for the first time since Harry Truman was in the White House. And largely because of the president's plan, the deficit will be nearly $700 billion lower—$700 billion lower—over five years. And it's being cut in half as a percentage of the GDP.

Today the president announced the preliminary estimate of the final 1994 deficit. Instead of a deficit that we were projecting at the time we came into office of $305 billion—$305 billion is where it was projected when we came into office—for the 1994 deficit, that number today is $203 billion. It will bring it down here, 2-0-3. (Applause.)

The deficit for '92—just to give you a forum here for what the upper line was—we started at a projected deficit of about $309 billion, we came down to $255 billion in 1993. In '94 we're now at $203 billion. In '95 we were projecting a deficit of $305 billion; again for '95 we will see a deficit that will be at or below $170 billion at that time.

So let us be very clear about the kind of choices that need to be made if you're serious about bringing the deficit down. While part of the reason for lower deficits, without question, is revenue increases due to last year's tax increase, which largely affected the wealthy—and let me just say to those that say, "Oh, my goodness, we shouldn't have raised taxes even on the wealthy in that year," if in a $500-billion deficit reduction plan we are going to ask, as we did, farmers to take their cut, veterans to take their cut, doctors to take their cut, hospitals to take their cut, the elderly to take their share of this responsibility, then surely we could ask the wealthy to share in the responsibility of helping to reduce the deficit as well. And that's what we did. (Applause.)

The primary focus of the plan was on spending cuts. Spending as percentage of GDP is going to be lower in this administration than in the Bush or Reagan administration. Spending—again, you know, sometimes it's tough to believe that Democrats are saying this—spending as a percentage of GDP is going to be lower in this administration than in the Bush and Reagan administration. Domestic discretionary spending in 1998 will be lower as a percent of GDP than in any time in over 30 years. Hundreds of programs have been cut or eliminated entirely. We went after 300 programs that have either been cut—many of them eliminated. And by 1999, the federal work force will be reduced by 272,000. That is smaller than at any time since the Kennedy administration.

For 12 years we heard the Republican administrations talk about the need to cut the deficit and the size of government, but when faced with tough choices, they chose the easy way: to use gimmicks, to use smoke and mirrors, to use false promises. This administration made the tough choices: to cut spending, to cut the size of government and to raise revenues. And very frankly, that is the only way you can reduce the deficit if that's what you are trying to do.

The Contract on America that the Republicans are urging on our society is a return to the riverboat gamble of the 1980s that nearly bankrupted this nation. It's a return to Reaganomics, to trickle-down policies, and the result was exploding deficit and we moved jobs overseas. I will match our record of performance on the deficit against their contract any day of the week. The contract promises, as we heard in the '80s, a balanced budget.

Now, let me just walk through it, because I think everybody needs to understand the elements that are being promised here. The contract says we're for a balanced budget amendment to the Constitution. Fine. To do that in five years requires that you achieve over $700 billion in cuts—in spending savings or revenues. If you are serious about balancing the budget in five years, you've got to come up with $700 billion in either spending savings or tax increases.

Then on top of that, what they pledge is that they would add about $300 billion in tax cuts—largely for the wealthy, but $300 billion in tax cuts, take them as you will. So they've now added, on top of the $700 billion, a revenue loss of $300 billion. You can support or not support the tax cuts—all of us would love to have tax cuts—but let's understand that when you do that you lose revenues, and under the rules of the budget agreement, you've got to pay for that so we don't increase the deficit.

Then on top of that, they say we have to increase defense spending by roughly $61 billion over that period of time. So the end result is that there is $1 trillion worth of promises here, $1 trillion worth of promises, and no one will tell you how that's going to be paid for. That's the problem. The reality is that if you're going to deal with a trillion-plus, in either the need to balance the budget or to cut taxes or to increase defense, then you've got to ask the question, how do you do that, how do you pay for that?

Well, let's look at the arguments that they present. They say, first of all, we certainly are not going to raise taxes, we're going to cut taxes. So taxes are off the table. What about defense spending? They say, no, no, no, defense needs to be increased by $61 billion. So obviously you can't turn to defense for any additional savings. Interest on the debt is off the table because even if they wanted to, they can't take interest off—can't take savings from interest payments on the debt, which is about $220 billion.

What's left? Fifty percent of what's left is in Social Security and Medicare. So let's assume that you keep all of that in spending. To come up with $1 trillion, you need to make about a 20 percent cut across the board on everything. If you want to come up with $1 trillion, 20 percent cut across the board. So the argument is, well, wait a minute, on Social Security, we're going to take that off the table.

All right, take Social Security off the table. Then you're left with a 30 percent cut across the board in Medicare as well as other programs. Let's take Medicare off the table. You take Medicare off the table, you're left with a 50 percent cut—in law enforcement, in the FBI, in drug enforcement, in air safety, in education, in health research.

All we're asking is that somebody tell us how you're going to do it. I'm not saying that, you know, it's something that we ought to not consider, but if it's going to be considered, we have a right to know how it's going to be paid for. When we submit a budget, as we did two years ago, we had to come up with $500 billion in deficit reduction. We had to spell it out, every last line. Last year when we proposed our budget, we had to spell out every bit of savings that was part of that budget, and we will do that again in the next budget. All we ask is that they do the same thing. Tell the American people where $1 trillion in promises is going to be paid for. We're entitled to that as a people. Because otherwise, we are really looking at a repetition of what happened in the '80s, and we then will reap the whirlwind one more time.

Our task is by no means complete. This is obviously the beginning of a good trend in terms of where the deficit is, but we also face the consequence that if we don't deal with additional cost increases, we are going to see the deficit begin to rise again, particularly with regards to health care. We have to keep the deficit headed down. To do that, we must keep working to reform our health care system. If we don't control health care costs, we don't have a prayer of keeping the deficit headed downward. We will pledge to work to ensure that we stay on a path that builds on the progress that we have achieved and that is reflected by this budget and this deficit track today.

A second area the president is working in, as all of you know, is the area of trade. The president completed and got a bipartisan majority in the Congress to approve the NAFTA agreement, which has already begun to increase exports and produce jobs, which is already doing well by this nation. Exports to Mexico are up this year by 19 percent.

After long negotiations, the president has completed the Uruguay Round of the GATT agreement, which is without exaggeration the most significant trade agreement in the history of this country. It will cut foreign tariffs on manufactured products by over one-third, and it will create hundreds of thousands of well-paying jobs in this country. That is, if it is approved by the Congress. There is a strong bipartisan majority in favor of GATT. The only way it will not pass this year is if the Republicans decide to block it. That would be tragic, but stranger things have happened in this session of the Congress.

In addition, the president and Congress have made the tax system fairer, I think, by reducing income taxes for more than 15 million working families. And there have been other important domestic initiatives that have been achieved: the crime bill, the effort to establish strong law enforcement, putting 100,000 cops on the street and banning assault weapons and providing the resources for crime prevention programs. The education and training area has resulted, I think, in the most significant reforms in two decades: the Elementary and Secondary Education Bill; Head Start; Goals 2000; School to Work; the student loan program; the National Service Act, which this year alone is going to put to work some 20,000 young people—more than have ever served at one time in the Peace Corps—tutoring students, immunizing children, reclaiming our parks, patrolling our streets and, in return, receiving education awards that make college or job training more affordable.

The president's initiatives are aimed not just at the short-term, although the economic success they have helped to produce is undeniable. The fundamental goal of this president and this administration is to restore the future for average Americans and for their children, to provide meaningful, well-paying job opportunities and equip them to serve in those jobs. This is the only way we are going to revive the hope of the American dream for hardworking American families.

We're making a start; we have by no means completed this task. We are beginning to turn the country around—4.6 million new jobs, 90 percent in the private sector; unemployment down from 7.7 to 5.9 percent; the pace of business investment has grown and increased sevenfold; and the GDP is up 3.3 percent for the first quarter, 4.1 percent in the second quarter; and at the same time, inflation is under control. We have the core inflation at its lowest level in over 21 years.

Conservative economic authorities, from Alan Greenspan to Paul Volcker, have reaffirmed that this president's economic plan had helped to produce these results. And although this is a beginning, these steps are crucial to the long-term health of this country.

The reason we reduce the deficit is to increase private investment. The reason we expand trade opportunities is to create well-paying jobs now and in the future. The reason we enhance education and training is to improve our workers for tomorrow and the challenges of a world economy. The future is what this is all about—the challenges to produce the kind of solutions, the kind of change that this country has been crying out for. Are there political risks? Yes, there are. Do you pay a price when you make these kinds of tough choices? Yes, you do.

But is it right for this country? You're damned right it's right for this country, because that's what representation is all about. That's why you elect people to office, is to do something about these problems and to take the risks that are associated with them. That's exactly why this is a tough election. People are angry because they want to see results now, not just in the future. There's a lot of frustration and cynicism among the American people about government.

It's the culmination of 25 years of government failures, from Vietnam and Watergate to the promise and ultimate bankruptcy of Reaganomics. As the public's anxieties about the future grew, especially in the 1980s and the early 1990s, they were believing less and less in the ability of government to do anything about any of these problems.

And yet, in 1992, they came to the polls in huge numbers because they wanted somebody to try to solve these problems. The president is trying. The American people, I think, realize that. There have been important short-term results, but the problems that concern the public are long term. This is when the real results of much of the president's agenda will be felt, but the credibility of government has been so eroded in the public's mind that they no longer have the patience to trust or to believe.

Special interests have had their impact, from the NRA, which opposed the Brady Bill and the assault weapon ban, to health insurers who opposed health reform; from the wealthy, who fought the deficit reduction plan, to organized labor, that fought the NAFTA agreement. Millions of dollars have been spent to fight change, to defeat the president, and these attacks, without question, have hurt him politically.

Partisanship has claimed a heavy toll as well. Republicans, particularly over the past several months, generally put partisan advantage ahead of the country's interests, to block, often with great success, the initiatives that would help solve problems in this country. Probably the most cynical of all, I think, was the defeat of the lobbying reform bill. It passed the Senate by a vote of 95 to 2—strong bipartisan support—but it died because Senate Republicans made a cold-blooded partisan decision to kill it.

The administration also bears some of the blame for the public's attitude. We had a crowded agenda. So much has happened that there has been little chance for the public to absorb the successes that have occurred. Our agenda was overloaded, and it overloaded the public circuits. Failures like health care got the bulk of the attention, and the successes that we made were devalued.

The administration, however, has nothing to apologize for in seeking to address the problems that confront this country. There has not been adequate focus; that has hurt us, but we must continue to try to solve the problems that are there.

The issues we are addressing are exactly the ones that the people care about: the economy and education, crime and health care, welfare reform. In foreign affairs, the president has provided, I think, strong and steady leadership in confronting crises from Haiti to the Middle East, from Iraq to Russia, from Ireland to North Korea. Each involved risks, each demanded a careful balance between power and diplomacy. Average Americans know the president and those members of Congress who are fighting for them. There is no question that they want to send a message to Congress, and so what will that message be?

The choice is the same that faced people of this country at crucial times throughout out history. It's the choice that faced immigrants, like my parents, who decided they would leave their despair and their poverty, travel 3,000 miles from Italy to a strange country across the ocean, with no money, with no language ability, with no skills, and take on the risks because they wanted a better life for themselves and for their children.

Today we face the same choice that my parents faced: to move the country forward, to take whatever risks are needed to address the problems of ordinary Americans, or to run and hide, exploit the people's anxieties, tolerate, excuse or blame somebody else for the problems. The voters need to decide what that choice will be. They need to decide whether we vote for the future or whether we return to the past.

To be honest, no one really knows how this election will turn out. It all depends on the decision that each voter makes in his or her heart. And that decision is two weeks away. But if voters decide to vote for their future, to reject the past, then they will make the same choice that my parents made when they came here, and the nation will be stronger for it.

Regardless of the results, those who are elected on election day must accept the responsibility that comes with the election, responsibility to help lead this country. Regardless of the results, this president will work closely with the Congress to continue the fight on behalf of ordinary Americans. And regardless of the results on election day, our future and our children's future is at stake, and there can be no turning back.

Thank you very much. *(Applause.)*

Patrick Hayes, Felisa Kazen and Leon Panetta. March 26, 1993.

MR. KLEIN: Thank you very much, Mr. Panetta. There are many, many questions and never enough time. Many of them concern the hot news of the day, which of course is Alice Rivlin's memo to the president that was leaked somehow, that included, among other things, calling for reducing the Social Security spending and Medicare spending as a way to continue with deficit reduction, and the Republicans, of course, have picked up on that. That being said for everybody who didn't know about that. *(Laughter.)*

Now, the first question is: Given your own past statements about the fiscal problems of entitlement spending and given the preliminary findings of the presidential commission on entitlements, and now the Rivlin memo, is it appropriate to rule out Social Security and Medicare cuts? Isn't this just another example of politics as the enemy of the honest public policy debate?

MR. PANETTA: Well the president, when we did the plan, the economic plan for $500 billion in deficit reduction, the president made very clear his position—and it continues to be his position—that there ought not to be any cuts in Social Security benefits as part of that plan. That continues to be his position.

With regards to Medicare and savings in Medicare, it is not that we have taken Medicare off the table in terms of looking at savings. Clearly, we will look at savings in Medicare, but to get savings in Medicare, it ought to be part of the context of developing health care reform in this country. As we presented in our health care reform bill, yes, you get savings out of Medicare, but in return for that, you're not only providing benefits, expanded benefits, but you're also providing the kind of cost controls that have to be part of any health care reform proposal.

We are not walking away from that responsibility. As I pointed out, if we don't deal with health care costs, then the deficit is going to continue to rise in the out years. We're looking in the next five years at 50 percent of the increase in spending being in health care. So we have to confront the need to control health care costs, but it can only be done in the context of developing health care reform for this country.

So the point is this: We do need to look at the recommendations that are going to be presented by the Kerrey Commission. We do need to look at other recommendations as we develop our budget proposal. And we will do that, and we will be straight and we will be honest with the American people about what ought to be in that package because we've done that when we first came into office, we did it last year, and we will do it this year again.

All I ask is for the Republicans to provide us with the same honesty. If they're promising $1 trillion in additional tax cuts, in wanting to balance the budget, additional defense spending, just tell us how that's going to be paid for. They owe the public the same thing we owe the public, which is being honest with them about what the price is for making those kinds of promises. That's what I'm asking for, and I think, you know, very frankly, I have still not heard an answer to that question.

MR. KLEIN: Also in that memo was a proposal to eliminate the second home mortgage interest deduction. Is this a realistic proposal?

MR. PANETTA: I have never found that to be a realistic proposal. And all of the—let's understand that the memo was a summary of all of the ideas that have been proposed when it comes to trying to develop any kind of deficit reduction package. CBO, the Congressional Budget Office, has been doing this for years; proposing a number of proposals that are on the table for consideration when you're trying to develop either savings or revenues to try to deal with the deficit. And that's exactly what the Rivlin memo was, essentially that kind of summary of those kinds of ideas, and they range, as you can see, from tax proposals to other proposals across the board.

Again, none of them are necessarily ones that make themselves into a final package for a lot of reasons. And it is ultimately—I think you have to test every budget proposal by what is ultimately put down in writing as a part of a budget because that's ultimately what members have to vote on. I think part of the problem, you see, is that when it comes to answering that question, "How do you in fact balance the budget?" it is much easier to take the position that we ought to pass a constitutional amendment to balance the budget. Or we ought to do some kind of cap on entitlements. Or we ought to pass something similar to a Gramm-Rudman proposal. Because then you don't have to answer the next question, which is, "How do you do that?" I mean if we passed a constitutional amendment to balance the budget today, tomorrow we would be faced with the question, "What entitlements are we going to look at, what discretionary spending are we going to look at, what taxes are we going to look at?"

And so what we're saying to the Republicans, and what we're saying to the American people is, let's be honest about that part of the debate. Because it's easy to cast votes for gimmicks. It is tough to cast votes for real solutions to problems.

MR. KLEIN: This questioner would like to know—as do many others—who is the, quote, "Public-spirited senior administration official," closed quote, who leaked the memo; and how much will it hurt the president?

MR. PANETTA: Those would not be the words I would use to describe that individual, and that's probably enough said. *(Laughter, applause.)*

MR. KLEIN: Do you think the Republicans are going to use this as a—they're saying, they're going to say now that, "Look, they want to cut Social Security just like us."

MR. PANETTA: I think it's a dangerous tack for the Republicans to use, and I'll tell you why. Because they may draw attention to the memo and the elements of the memo, but in return they also draw attention to their failure to answer the question how are they going to pay for $1 trillion in their contract. I mean, this is a memo, an internal memo, that suggests a number of ideas, as other memos ought to suggest. But nobody signed a contract on this memo. Three hundred and fifty of their members signed a contract in the front of the United States Capitol that said they will commit to adopting a program that balances the budget, increases defense spending, and provides for the tax cuts. But nowhere in that contract did they say how they would pay for it. I think—I relish the debate with the Republicans on this issue, because ultimately they've got to provide the answer.

MR. KLEIN: What do you see as the initiative, if any, on health care reform coming from the administration next year? And are you looking at a more bipartisan approach?

MR. PANETTA: I would assume that on election day that we will, as a first priority, need to reach out on a bipartisan basis to the members of Congress to try to develop an answer with regards to health care reform. That is going to be absolutely essential. I think the president wanted to do that this time around. For whatever reason, it became very partisan in the end. And that's unfortunate, because whether you're Republican or Democrat, you've got this problem to deal with. You can't just walk away from it. The reality is, if you don't confront the health care issue in this country, we are headed towards bankruptcy because of the costs involved with health care, both in the private as well as the public sector. So ultimately it is a responsibility that we have to deal with.

Obviously, it is going to be a task in which both sides are going to have to sit down and try to develop what are the steps that can be taken to meet the needs in this area. We've learned some lessons, obviously, from the debate in this last Congress. The first and most important is that we need to sit down and work with key members of the Congress from both sides of the aisle to develop an approach on health care reform. We will do that: the president's committed to that. But my hope is—and again it's a two-way street, the president will reach out. We need Republicans to work with us to develop the kind of answer that will serve the American people.

MR. KLEIN: Will the president outline a specific legislative agenda in the final two weeks before the election, and what will that agenda include?

MR. PANETTA: The president has, obviously, from the very beginning, had a set of initiatives that he feels are important for this country, obviously beginning with the economy and the need for the kind of deficit reduction that we put in place, but also in terms of education and crime, in health care as well as with regards to welfare reform and trade and the continuing effort to reinvent government and reduce the size of government. All of those are kind of priority areas that the president has tried to target at. We've been successful in many of these areas, and in many we failed, particularly as I said, in the last weeks of Congress.

I think if you were to look at the priorities for this next Congress, it would be, obviously, to continue to try to implement the deficit path that we're on, which means that we've got to look at a tough budget that will be presented to the Congress and the country.

Secondly, to look at health care reform and try to develop an approach that can move us in an incremental way towards the kind of health care reform that this country needs.

Thirdly, to work on welfare reform. We have—the president, and I think this country, recognizes that it is very important for us not to have a welfare system in this country that makes people dependent, but try to develop a system that makes them independent, puts people back to work. And that is something I think again, that on a bipartisan basis hopefully both parties share.

And lastly, to implement campaign and lobbying reform in the Congress. This was probably our greatest disappointment, because it relates to a lot of the other issues you confront. When you take on these issues, one of the things you constantly run into are the interests that are out there that will stop you at every turn. It is extremely important that we implement lobbying reform in this next Congress as a major part of our agenda, and in doing that I think we will give people a greater say in what happens here in Washington, rather than the interests that we had to confront in the remaining months of this last session.

MR. KLEIN: This questioner says that, despite the fact that President Clinton promised to be a leader on environmental issues, every major legislative initiative failed. Will the administration have any environmental priorities in the 104th Congress?

MR. PANETTA: Well, there's a lot of leftover work, obviously.

Number one is the Superfund bill. We thought we had developed a very strong and balanced proposal in the Superfund area. It was supported by the chemical companies. It was supported by labor. It was supported by the Sierra Club. It was supported by a broad coalition of interests that usually are at each other's throats when it comes to environmental issues. Unfortunately, again we ran into a block on the Senate side with regards to the Superfund bill. We have to go back at that bill. That'll be a major priority in this next Congress.

Safe drinking water—again, the need to basically provide safe drinking water in this country has been an important initiative. It, too, got blocked in the waning weeks of this last session of the Congress.

We did achieve some successes, particularly the success on the California Desert bill. We achieved some successes with regards to targeting greater funds within the appropriations bills at environmental areas, particularly the need to clean up our parks and do some of the investments that have to be done in existing parks.

But frankly, the president was very disappointed at losing those other major initiatives. We will continue to work at those, make no mistake about it. We intend to ensure that those environmental issues are adopted in this next session of the Congress.

MR. KLEIN: A question on the organization of the White House now. How many persons, and who, have direct access to the president? Have you reduced or expanded this number? *(Laughter.)*

MR. PANETTA: The challenge in dealing with the White House is that there were really three goals that I thought had to be implemented as chief of staff.

One was to provide greater discipline in terms of the operation of the White House, that there was not sufficient discipline with regards to people having access, as well as the briefings and the memos, and those who would not go through a process to reach the president of the United States. And so for that reason, I thought it was very important to centralize the authority in the chief of staff so that there would be a one-stop approach to that. It may be the Italian in me, but I thought it was important to centralize authority in the chief of staff's office. *(Laughter.)*

The second area was lines of organization, organizational authority, knowing who you responded to. We had, at the time, individuals that were—we used to use the term "floaters" as opposed to having a line responsibility in which they would report to someone who would then have some kind of accountability in terms of their role. The reorganization itself basically provided for that. I established a deputy's position that was responsible for overall operations of the White House, and reporting to that deputy are key areas like scheduling, advance, the Oval Office operation, as well as again controlling access to the Oval Office, became a responsibility of that deputy. The other deputy is responsible for political and policy affairs, and there we have a group that reports to that deputy. So that now there is an organizational line of authority that basically says, if you're in this position, you report to this individual, and that individual reports to the chief of staff, and ultimately to the president.

The last area was to create better focus. Again, with the large number of issues that we were dealing with, the large agenda we were dealing with, unfortunately on a day-to-day basis it became clouded as to the message we were trying to deliver to the American people. What we try to do at a 7:30 staff meeting is basically provide better focus: What is the issue we want to focus on that day? What do we want the president to speak to in terms of the country? And try to create a better focal point for the country as well as for the White House.

So those are the areas that I've tried to implement. Obviously, it's an ongoing task. It is by no means complete. You just continue to work at it. I think the operation is much better. I think we've got very talented and capable people who are part of the White House, but obviously it has to work as a team in order to make it work for the president.

MR. KLEIN: Do you expect any changes in the press office?

MR. PANETTA: We have reorganized the press office. At the time that I came in, there was both a director of communications as well as a press secretary, and the problem is you never knew who had what responsibility. You basically had a director of communications who was doing the same kind of work covering the press, as the press secretary, and the press secretary was not part of the key meetings that the press secretary needed to be a part of if, in fact, they're going to report to the press. And so for that reason we have reorganized it, centralizing authority again in the press secretary's job, and we are, you know, very satisfied that we have now provided the kind of reorganization that ought to make that operation work better.

What we did with the communications director, which makes sense, because that's really what a communications director is all about, is to put that individual in charge of strategic planning for the future. The purpose of the communications director is to look at the long term, to look at what needs to be the long-term message. Where do we want to be? How do we get that message out? And so strategic planning is really where that needed to be placed, and that's why we put Mark Gearan in that position. But I think that approach works much better if you really want to get a clear message out to the public.

MR. KLEIN: We are, unfortunately, about out of time, though we have many, many, many more questions, and maybe you'd like to stick around afterwards. I'm sure you would—

MR. PANETTA: No.

MR. KLEIN: No? *(Laughter.)* Before asking the last question, let me present you with a certificate of appreciation for appearing here—

MR. PANETTA: Thank you.

MR. KLEIN: —and, of course, the ever popular National Press Club mug, which you have many now, and I think you might almost have a complete set. And we've also decided to give out now "Eye on Washington"—pictures taken by former New York Times photographer George Thames, many of which are on the back of our wall here.

MR. PANETTA: That's great.

MR. KLEIN: And we thank you very much for being here.

MR. PANETTA: Thank you very much. It could have been "The Agenda."

MR. KLEIN: Yeah, well—*(laughter)*—that's a good idea. *(Laughter.)*

Last question for us is: Did you go to Hillary's birthday sock hop, and what did you wear? *(Laughter.)*

MR. PANETTA: No. I went to California and saw my wife, and I thought that was number one as far as I was concerned. That's a hell of a lot better than a sock hop, let me tell you. Thank you. Thank you very much. *(Applause.)*

NATIONAL PRESS CLUB

LUNCHEON
June 28, 1994

PEAKER

JEAN-BERTRAND ARISTIDE
President of the Republic of Haiti

MODERATED BY: Gil Klein

Head Table Guests

❦

Steven Greenhouse
State Department Correspondent for the New York Times

Bethany Steuart
State Department Producer for NBC News

Ken Dalecki
Editor of Kiplinger's Florida Business Letter

Marcia Stepanek
Correspondent for Hearst Newspapers

Andy Mosher
Assistant Foreign Editor of the Washington Post

Herve Denis
Minister of Information for the Republic of Haiti

Mary Crowley
*Executive Editor of Business Publishers, Inc. and Vice Chairwoman of the
National Press Club Speakers Committee*

Ambassador Jean Casimir
Ambassador of the Republic of Haiti

David Anderson
*U.S. Department of Housing and Urban Development and the member of the
National Press Club Speakers Committee who organized today's luncheon*

Patrick McGrath
Capitol Hill Correspondent for Fox Television

Larry Lipman
Correspondent for the Palm Beach Post

Chris Marquis
Diplomatic Correspondent for the Miami Herald

Todd Lassa
Assistant Managing Editor of the Economic Opportunity Report

GIL KLEIN

g ood afternoon. Welcome to the National Press Club. My name is Gil Klein. I'm the club's president and a national correspondent with Media General Newspapers, writing for the Richmond Times-Dispatch, the Tampa Tribune and the Winston-Salem Journal. I'd like to welcome my fellow club members in the audience today, as well as those of you who are watching us on C-SPAN or listening to us on National Public Radio or the Internet global computer network.

Now, two years and three months ago, our speaker, President Jean-Bertrand Aristide of Haiti, spoke at our podium about the possibilities for his imminent return to power. Yet here he is, standing before us, still as the exiled leader, the first popularly elected president of Haiti. And his return still appears to be imminent—or maybe not.

The story is as fresh as this morning's paper. The Washington Post reported that the Coast Guard is surprised by the huge number of Haitians who are again gambling their lives on rickety boats to seek a chance to plead for political asylum in the United States. I don't know why the Coast Guard is surprised. Every indication pointed to such a development once President Clinton changed U.S. policy to allow refugees entry. Critics of the Clinton administration charge that the president is leading the nation toward an inevitable armed intervention in Haiti to restore Aristide to power, and there isn't a lot of popular support for that.

What has changed in the past two years is that our speaker has become the focal point of the debate. Even though he was elected in certifiably fair and free elections with 67 percent of the vote, there are those in the United States who contend that he is not personally committed to democracy. Former President Bush, who had supported Aristide during his administration, made a rare public announcement recently that he no longer thought returning Aristide to power should be the central part of American policy toward Haiti.

President Aristide has been criticized for not being willing to compromise to broaden his base of support within Haiti to allow for a peaceful return. Mr. Aristide was a radical priest who risked his life to denounce Haiti's corrupt regime from the pulpit of the Cathedral of Port-au-Prince. He drew his power from the masses of poverty stricken Haitians angered at the wealth and power of the elite. He contends that he has been the target of character assassination.

The Clinton administration has renewed its support for Aristide, changed its policy towards Haitian refugees and tightened the economic embargo on the country. With refugees again streaming out of Haiti, some kind of showdown is inevitable.

Here to give us his perspective of what is happening, please join me in a warm press club welcome for President Jean-Bertrand Aristide. *(Applause.)*

JEAN-BERTRAND ARISTIDE

SPEAKER

r. President, distinguished members of the National Press Club, distinguished guests, your friends, it is a pleasure for me to be here with you. And on behalf of the Haitian people, I thank you for giving me this opportunity to be here again with you.

Twenty-two thousand three hundred miles above the Earth's equator a communication satellite orbits the globe. This satellite follows the Earth's rotation on its axis, circling the planet over a 24-hour period. To any observer it is immobile, as it provides worldwide link-up of radio and television transmissions from locations across the globe.

The launching of the first satellite in 1957 contributed in transforming this century into the century of global communication. With these invisible eyes in space—the satellites—and the visible eyes of the media on Earth—your cameras, pens, and computers—the world is moving towards greater knowledge of itself. Information has become the fundamental element of modern life.

Journalists are like satellites. You receive information, then convert it into words or images for broadcasting. Images of Rwanda, Somalia, and Bosnia fill the television screens and let us know of the horrors occurring across the world. Since the coup d'etat of September, 1991, but more particularly for the past three months, Haiti has been the subject of many of those transmissions.

In April, over 151 articles on Haiti appeared in major American newspapers. In May, the number surpassed 340. And for the month of June, it has already reached 195. Some journalists are not visible, as for instance, your colleagues in Haiti. They operate underground, and from there, risk their lives to report on the nation's heroic resistance to 33 months of repression and violence. We should take this moment to salute them and all journalists who work with them in this important endeavor. The media, the press, and you the journalist, can play an historic role in helping Haiti raise the collective consciousness of the world on the challenges that we face; the struggle for dignity, for peace, for justice. In fact, Haiti has a long history of raising the collective consciousness of the international community.

In 1779, over a thousand Haitian soldiers sailed from Haiti to fight with Americans against British forces in the Battle of Savannah. How peculiar, 18th Century Haitians, themselves enslaved, fighting for the independence of the United States, blacks fighting side by side with whites. The national struggle to liberate Haiti directly benefited the United States and other countries in the Western Hemisphere.

In 1801, Bonaparte set out to conquer Haiti, France's wealthiest colony. Instead, Haiti defeated Napoleon's best troops. History recalls that in response to this defeat, Napoleon promptly sold his largest remaining colony in the New World to President Thomas Jefferson in what is known as the Louisiana Purchase.

And finally, winning its independence in 1804, Haiti made sure that its liberty profited the struggle of General Bolivar in freeing North and South America.

This historic evidence of Haiti's contribution to raising the collective consciousness of the international community was recognized in 1949, when American President Harry Truman delivered a message to Haiti on the occasion of the bicentennial of our capital city,

Port-au-Prince. He praised Haiti for steadfastly supporting the democracies during two World Wars and for speaking on behalf of peace and concord among nations.

Today, the struggle for justice, dignity and peace by the people of Haiti again raises the collective consciousness of the international community. Our struggle in Haiti and the victory of our sisters and brothers in South Africa bring the world one step further in what Hegel calls, "The progress of the consciousness of freedom." South Africa proves to others that events do shift with dramatic impact. Changes occur which, the moment before they happen, seem impossible. Who among us will believe that we would live to see an inter-racial democracy in South Africa? How could we imagine that the man imprisoned for 27 years could rise to be that nation's president? World events do move from the seemingly impossible to the possible. So, too, can they move in Haiti.

In the 1930s and '40s, the problems of the Jewish refugees too seemed like an impossible situation to resolve. Their experience is not unlike our Haitian refugee experience. In May, 1939, nine hundred Jews traveled on the St. Louis from one country to the next in search of refuge. At each port, they were turned away and never allowed to disembark. After some time, the boat was forced to return to their repressive regime from which it was fleeing. Let's say, in Hebrew. *(Speaks Hebrew.)*

Haitians, too, continue to meet this fate. Just last Monday, 29 refugees were returned to Haiti. They included two pregnant women and a baby. After their return to Haiti, most were detained by Haiti's military. Three are still in detention. On Thursday, another 61 were repatriated. Indeed, since May 8th, when it was announced that there would be a change in the policy towards our refugees, 1,957 people have been summarily returned to Haiti.

What do the refugees face when they return to Haiti? Escalating violence and political oppression, the U.N. civilian mission continues to report, adding to the already five thousand murders since the September 1991 coup.

In our move towards the restoration of democracy in Haiti, we must recognize that the refugee crisis will not end until democracy is restored to Haiti. Given the escalating violence and repression, it would be immoral to ask people whose very lives are at risk to stay in Haiti, a Haiti which I am compelled to describe as a house on fire.

Democracy must be restored to Haiti. After the restoration of democracy there will be reconciliation. Peace will lead us to the political stability that we established during our first seven months in office. It will allow us to build a state of love, to build a nation where there is peace for all, respect for every single citizen, unity and justice among all of us, a Haiti that will embrace its refugees and end the massive migration of its citizens to the coast of Florida as we had done for seven months. This is reconciliation.

This climate of respect and peace will lead to the political stability needed for the nation to progress. This is the new Haiti that we envision. This is the new Haiti that you and our brave journalists in Haiti, will soon write of. This is the new Haiti that will be heir to democracy restored.

Today we stand on the eve of the one year anniversary of the Governors Island agreement. At issue is not whether this agreement can fulfill its mandate to restore democracy in Haiti. The issue is how long will it take, despite this long one year interlude that has claimed many lives, including that of our Minister of Justice. We are certain that with the political will of the international community, it can. Democracy must be restored not through military intervention, but through the implementation of the Governors Island agreement.

This is not based on an illusion, nor is it based on fiction. In the past six weeks new dynamics in Haiti—the enforcement of the embargo at the Dominican border, the suspension of financial transactions, the ban on commercial flights by some nations, but not all, the freeze of the assets of those determined to be supporters of the coup—make the seemingly impossible look possible. But how much longer will this added suffering last? Months? No. Weeks? No.

Robert F. Kennedy once said "Justice delayed is democracy denied." Let us hope that the political will of the international community will force implementation of the Governors Island agreement so that the end to this horrible crisis in Haiti can come quickly. That means clearly first the departure of the coup leaders. Second, deployment of the United Nations technical assistance mission in Haiti. Third, my prompt return to Haiti. And fourth, implementation of a program of reform contemplated by the agreement.

Now let's move step by step through this program. First, military reform. Please don't try to understand the Haitian army in the light of your army. It consumes 40 percent of the national budget. From the year of our independence, 1804, to the year of 1957 when Francoise Duvalier took office, among 36 Haitian heads of state, 24 were overturned by a coup. So this army involved in a tradition of coup is today involved in drug trafficking. Every year it's a question of 46 to 48 tons of cocaine passing through Haiti to come here, and that brings $1.2 billion of dollars to them. This army has to be professionalized.

Second, judicial reform. Our program for judicial reform will be financed by the $65 million allocated for institutional reform in Haiti. A reformed judiciary will ensure justice, instill confidence in the integrity of government, and offer a constitutional avenue for recourse to equity. As we said, we repeated today, and will continue saying the same, no to vengeance, no to retaliation, no to impunity; yes to justice, yes to reconciliation.

Third, the economic stability. We must respond to Haiti's ravaged economy by adopting a macroeconomic policy to immediately curb inflation, balance the budget and control government spending. The international community has committed $228 million to assist us in these areas. The gross national product declined by 10.8 percent during the 1991–92 fiscal year, and by another 4 percent in 1992–93. We must regain the confidence of the World Bank, which in 1991 commended our government for "providing a window of opportunity for the country to finally move toward sustained social and economic progress."

This can be achieved through proper management of government resources, including improved public administration of ministries and diligent enforcement of the tax code. The budget must be restructured. A nation devoting 40 percent of its budget to the military cannot prosper and will not grow. In 1991, we succeeded in balancing the budget, and for the first time in many years created a surplus. We saw an increase by 41 million goods, approximately $5.8 million in the government's monthly revenues. This again must be our goal.

Fourth, health care for all. I will not tell you that in Haiti, although on one side we have one soldier for each 1,000 Haitians, unfortunately, for each 10,000 Haitians we still have 1.8 doctors, in a country where we say we have 56 hospitals. But unfortunately, we have just 1.5 hospital beds for each 1,000 Haitians. It's not fair. We have to have health care for all.

Fifth, education for all. Also, I will tell you that only 10 percent of our schools are public. It's not fair, in a country where we still have 85 percent illiteracy rate, to continue maintaining the status quo without reducing this too high level of illiteracy rate. Eighty-five percent is too much. One school ought to be built in each of our 565 districts.

Sixth, reverse environmental deterioration. Haiti is moving dangerously close to an irreversible ecological disaster. Deforestation has accelerated, and soil erosion has grown worse. Since the onset of the political crisis, charcoal production has increased by 40 percent, which means that an additional 7,500 trees are cut down each month. In 1978, forests accounted for 7 percent of the land's surface. By 1989, that number was reduced to 1.3 percent. A simple campaign to plant fruit trees, starting first with the near 200,000 acres of state-owned land, then extending to other lands, can alter this dangerous course.

Seven, revitalize the agricultural sector. Due to severe deforestation and erosion, 20 percent of our topsoil has already washed away to the sea. Every year we lose another 1 percent.

Eight, revamp our communications system to bring Haiti into the century of global communication. Those of you who have traveled to Haiti as journalists know how bad our communications system is. We will have to change it.

Nine, institutional reform. We will reform and strengthen the nation's institutions, especially our Parliament, and provide its members with the opportunity to work with the nation. As during our seven months, members of Parliament will work in safety. They will not be ruled by the guns, as they are now. They will not be forced to live in hiding, as they are today. And they will not be threatened, harassed or killed, as they have been since the 1991 coup.

And finally, encourage growth and development of an open market system. As we have done since the beginning of our term in office, we will promote goals in the private sector. We recognize the pressing need to revitalize the industrial sector and attract jobs to replace those lost as a result of the coup. The 75 percent unemployment rate cannot stand. The industrial sector, which is generally limited to Port-au-Prince, employs approximately 5.7 percent of the population, yet accounts for 15 percent of the GNP. New businesses and present businesses will be supported by major improvements in the country's infrastructure.

This is what the nation can look forward to after the restoration of democracy. The restoration of democracy will bring peace for all, reconciliation among all, and for all a climate in which to prosper. As during the first seven months of my mandate, we will continue moving from misery to poverty with dignity. And I would like to repeat, because it's very important for all of us as a people: We will continue to move from misery to poverty with dignity.

An old proverb reads, "Give light, and the people will find their own way." Haiti needs the light of a free press, the light of our brave journalists and those who work with them. We must change the conditions where for every 1,000 citizens only 46 have radios, only seven have access to daily newspapers, and only five have access to televisions. We need a satellite hovering outside of Haiti ready to spread the story of our struggle, to raise the collective consciousness of the world on the challenges that we face and ready to report on our success in restoring justice, peace and reconciliation.

Dear friends, with great joy the world assembled in South Africa on May 10th to celebrate democracy. So, too, will this happen in Haiti. We invite you there one day soon to witness this new beginning. Thank you. *(Applause.)*

MR. KLEIN: Thank you very much, Mr. President. We have a lot of questions here, of course, and many of them are like the first one here. So I will ask that one first. You have said that you would not oppose a military strike to oust the coup leaders. Yet on Saturday you said you would never, never, never support a U.S. invasion. Please explain.

PRESIDENT ARISTIDE: Thank you for your question. On February 7, 1986, Jean-Claude Duvalier left Haiti without a military intervention. Years later, General Namphy left Haiti almost the same way. And after him, General Avril left Haiti almost the same way. We do believe that, as I said, we can restore democracy not through military intervention but through the implementation of the Governors Island agreement, which means clearly pressure, keeping pressure on the coup leaders in order to have them stepping aside. Jean-Claude Duvalier left. They also can leave.

MR. KLEIN: But if the Coast Guard is soon to be overwhelmed with a new flood of refugees, how long do you think the Clinton administration can put off not having some kind of resolution to the problem in Haiti?

PRESIDENT ARISTIDE: It's a real drama. It's a real tragedy. It's a real genocide. The more we wait before the restoration of democracy, unfortunately, the more we may see refugees leaving Haiti, fleeing political repression. You do believe that the Haitians love Haiti. They want to stay home. For instance, when I was in Haiti during seven months, the Haitians were staying in Haiti.

As I said, and allow me to say it again, we were moving from misery to poverty with dignity and they were staying home. The international community understood what we were doing. That's why they said they would be giving $511 million to us. Before receiving this money, the Haitians were staying home. So that's why I think, and I say it again, let's speed this process of restoring democracy, because that's the only way we will solve this crisis.

It will be good for Haiti as it will be good for the United States. It's not good for the president of United States to see many refugees coming to the United States. It's not good for the president of Haiti to see the Haitians fleeing Haiti. Once we start democracy, President Clinton and I, the American people and the Haitian people together, we will celebrate because we will have the solution.

MR. KLEIN: This questioner says the New York Times reports today that an aide to Lieutenant General Cedras says Cedras plans to retire in October. Do you lend any credence to such a report?

PRESIDENT ARISTIDE: Yes, I do. It's an important question because General Cedras said at Governors Island, when we signed this agreement on July 12th, he would step aside to allow our return to Haiti on October 30th. And he didn't. So he lies. He doesn't care when he has to lie. In the face of the world he did that. Again, he is trying to do the same because that means for themselves one more day for the coup leaders and one less for us. It's a dilatory maneuver to waste time when we have so many refugees coming to us. Today we read it in the press. The New York Times said clearly from Friday to today, 1,800 Haitians were intercepted. And for some people, more were trying to flee. How long do we have to wait before stopping this fleeing from repression? It is a house on fire. How could they stay in that house on fire? It's a big question. Fortunately, we have the solution, which is the restoration of democracy soon.

MR. KLEIN: Is there any chance that General Cedras and his colleagues can be paid to give up power and leave Haiti in exchange for amnesty?

Haitian President-in-exile Jean-Bertrand Aristide is greeted by Gil Klein, NPC governor. March 19, 1992.

PRESIDENT ARISTIDE: I'm glad to have the wonderful opportunity to renew my commitment not only to Haiti but to the entire world. I say no to vengeance, no to retaliation, no to impunity; yes to justice, yes to reconciliation. That's why I already gave political amnesty to the coup leaders because to save lives I want them to be out.

If some people want to pay them, that's their business. I want them to be out because that's the way we can save Haiti. That's the way we can have reconciliation for all of us—respect, justice, unity, among all of us. So if there are some people in Haiti or here in the United States and in the international community who would like to help us in speeding this process, they may do it the way they think they should be doing this. And regarding myself, I already gave political amnesty to them according to the Article 147 of our constitution. I will be back to feed reconciliation among all of us in my country.

MR. KLEIN: One of the charges against you is that while you were president, you were beginning to incite the lower classes against the ruling elite. What assures the ruling elite in Haiti that if you return, they will not be the target of violent reprisals?

PRESIDENT ARISTIDE: That's an important question. It's a charge. And when you are a president, you have to be ready to listen to people criticizing you. Sometimes there is basis for those critics and some of the time no; for instance, for this one, no. We need a political stability in Haiti. Without this political stability, there is no way to create a climate in which we can prosper.

In Haiti, although our army of 7,000 officials and soldiers control 40 percent of the national budget and moving from one coup to another one—let's say it again; we are the first black independent country in the world. We got our independence in 1804. And from that year to 1957, we had 36 Haitian head of states and 24 were overturned by a coup. That means in this country, where less than 1 percent can have more than 45 percent of the national revenue, you have a situation of using this army to keep the status quo moving from one coup to another one.

How did I do? How do I want to do it again? On February 7, 1991, the day of my inauguration, I said, "No more blood, not even one drop of blood in our country." We celebrated a marriage between the Haitian army and the Haitian people because we wanted to move with this climate of unity. We had that seven months of political stability, which is indispensable for the elite to go up with business. And we were creating this climate of political stability to have the elite investing, because we want them and they have the right to stay home, to work, to invest.

And as the president of every single citizen, I have to protect the rights of the elite as I have the obligation to protect the rights of the employees. Those who will be investing, the elite, and you businesses, you will be welcome. Those who will find jobs, also they will find the same climate of security, of political stability. I can promise again the elite will find their president working with them to create jobs for those who need jobs, and the president will be respecting again their rights and the rights of every single citizen.

MR. KLEIN: This questioner asks: Tomorrow, if General Cedras agreed to step down only if simultaneously you too, would also step down in order to put in place a coalition temporary government which would lead to a presidential election in the fall of '94, would you mutually agree to step aside in order to end the embargo and suffering of your people and restore order in the economy and avoid invasion?

PRESIDENT ARISTIDE: I distinguish two aspects in this question. The first one; maybe many people don't know what did I do in terms of building unity in the country. In our first government, we had people from the bourgeoisie. To have the second one, I was the one deciding to choose one of the wealthiest families in Haiti to become our prime minister. I wanted to do that, and I did.

I had to face opposition because many people did not want me to bring someone who looked like a white person from the wealthy family to become the prime minister. They did not want it. But I did, because I wanted to create a bridge, a social bridge, between rich and poor in the country. And I did. That's the way we have to do it to save the nation, rich and poor working together. In the same government, they already resigned, the prime minister and the other ministers. But in this same government we have other ministers from the bourgeoisie; for instance, the minister of finance. She's from the bourgeoisie. Our former minister of commerce is from the bourgeoisie. And I could move on.

Two other ministers are from the army. The minister of defense is a general; the minister of interior is a colonel. Four other ministers are from four political parties; all that to not talk about unity without giving the proof, without proving that we can do it, and we did. Again, we will continue moving this same way to build unity, reconciliation, reforming our judicial system, to save the nation.

Second aspect: Someone in Haiti said in a public meeting, or quite a public meeting, "I am giving jobs to hundreds of Haitians. They went to vote on December 16, 1990. I also went to vote. How could you imagine that I would accept that their votes can be equal to my vote?" he says. And I said to him, "Well, it's an apartheid reality if you talk that way." And he answered, "Of course. That's the reality."

We had our first free and fair democratic election on December 16, 1990, where 67 percent of the population voted for me. Thirty-three months later, they still continue fighting peacefully to have me back. That means after testing democracy during seven months, they know what they did by choosing their president. They know why they can continue to suffer under the weight of this embargo, because they want to have democracy back in the country.

Now, it's not only those 67 percent who voted for me, it's more than that. I would say clearly close or more to 90 percent of the population are waiting for my return. That's why, if I respect the results of those elections, if I respect my people, I have to continue saying yes to the mandate of five years. So it's not a question of doing what I want, it's a question of doing what they want me to do due to our first fair and free elections.

MR. KLEIN: How do you explain former President Bush's change of position on your return to Haiti?

PRESIDENT ARISTIDE: I respect former President Bush. I have to respect every single citizen in the world, that's my way to be. As the president, I have to listen to people. When I realize they are right, I have to thank them because they can help me changing my position when they are right. But also, when I realize they are wrong, I have to be honest, to say, "No, it's not fair. It's wrong."

If you want to hide your body, you cannot use one finger to hide that. With something which is not true, you cannot hide a policy which is false regarding our refugees. So I think the best way to continue moving is to listen to people who may disagree. This is democracy. In that case, I disagree and I continue showing respect for former President Bush and with every single citizen in the entire world.

MR. KLEIN: There are several questions along this line: The State Department has asked you for some time to give an accounting for the finances of your government. So far, you have not complied. When will you give this accounting, and how do you explain the millions of dollars paid for public relations and lobbyists, and what about the $2.5 million in checks you have received from the ambassador from Taiwan?

PRESIDENT ARISTIDE: I was talking about criticism having basis or not. For those there is no basis.

Our lawyers—I have the pleasure to see some of them here—are working to prepare a clear answer for those who want to know about why we are spending money here for lobbyists and what.

In Haiti, we have a situation where folks, after killing over 5,000 people, continue to spend money, money—sometimes they just plunder the national treasury to get that, sometimes they just take it from the drug trafficking, which brings $1.2 billion to them every year. And part of this money, they spend it here in Washington through allies or lobbyists in order to keep the status quo in Haiti, so they are using this money against the nation.

As the duly elected president of the nation, I have the obligation to spend some money to have lawyers defending the nation, because they have lobbyists lying for them to defend their coup. So it's an obligation.

When the day will come, as usual, we will use transparency—and we have to—to explain to the nation why and what: Why we spent money, what did we spend?

MR. KLEIN: What is your message to the refugees fleeing Haiti today? Should they stay or leave?

PRESIDENT ARISTIDE: I just had a wonderful meeting with Reverend Bill Gray. Together, we'll work, and I'm very glad to work with him, I think President Clinton did a good move by choosing him, and with him, we'll continue working in a very good relationship to restore the democracy.

With him, we are working with a program to put back to Haiti. That may start soon.

Obviously, because everybody can recognize that Haiti looks like a house on fire, we cannot ask people to stay in this house on fire. Do we have to ask them to leave? No. Because when they leave, they may die. That's why, if I cannot ask them to stay in this house on fire, if